Communications in Computer and Information Science 829

More information about this series at http://www.springer.com/series/7899

Eric Ras · Ana Elena Guerrero Roldán (Eds.)

Technology Enhanced Assessment

20th International Conference, TEA 2017
Barcelona, Spain, October 5–6, 2017
Revised Selected Papers

Springer

Editors
Eric Ras
Luxembourg Institute of Science and Technology
Esch-sur-Alzette
Luxembourg

Ana Elena Guerrero Roldán
Faculty of Computer Science, Multimedia and Telecommunications
Universitat Oberta de Catalunya
Barcelona
Barcelona
Spain

ISSN 1865-0929 ISSN 1865-0937 (electronic)
Communications in Computer and Information Science
ISBN 978-3-319-97806-2 ISBN 978-3-319-97807-9 (eBook)
https://doi.org/10.1007/978-3-319-97807-9

Library of Congress Control Number: 2018950660

This Springer imprint is published by the registered company Springer Nature Switzerland AG
The registered company address is: Gewerbestrasse 11, 6330 Cham, Switzerland

Preface

The objective of the International Technology-Enhanced Assessment Conference (TEA) is to bring together researchers and practitioners with innovative ideas and research on this important topic. This volume of conference proceedings provides an opportunity for readers to engage with refereed research papers that were presented during the 20th edition of this conference, which took place in Barcelona, Spain, at Casa Macaya. Each paper has been reviewed by at least three experts and the authors revised their papers based on these comments and discussions during the conference.

In total, 17 submissions from 59 authors were selected to be published in this volume. These publications show interesting examples of current developments in technology-enhanced assessment research. Technology is gaining more and more importance in all phases of assessment as well as in the many difference assessment domains (i.e., school education, higher education, and performance measurement at the workplace).

We see a progression in research and technologies that automatize phases in assessment: Several contributions focused on using natural language processing techniques to automatically analyze written essays or open text answers; presentations were given to show how reports could be automatically generated from scoring data; and last but not least, approaches were explained of how to automatically generate feedback in the context of formative assessment. Complementary to the automatizing approaches, means were elaborated to raise the engagement of students in assessment as well as approaches for online proctoring. Like last year's conference, several submissions dealt with the topic of higher-order skills, such as collaborative problem solving or presentation skills, but also with the development of tools for assessors. Since last year, assessment in MOOC has been included and during this year's conference we learned how to use our own device for assessment purposes (i.e., BYOD) to handle huge numbers of students in the same course.

The papers will be of interest for educational scientists and practitioners who want to be informed about recent innovations and obtain insights into technology-enhanced assessment. We thank all reviewers, contributing authors, keynote speakers, and the sponsoring institutions for their support.

April 2018

Eric Ras
Ana Elena Guerrero Roldán

Organization

The International Technology-Enhanced Assessment Conference 2017 was organized by Universitat Oberta de Catalunya and the Embedded Assessment Research Group of LIST, the Luxembourg Institute of Science and Technology.

Executive Committee

Conference Chairs

Eric Ras	Luxembourg Institute of Science and Technology, Luxembourg
Ana Elena Guerrero Roldán	Universitat Oberta de Catalunya, Spain

Local Organizing Committee

Eric Ras	Luxembourg Institute of Science and Technology, Luxembourg
Ana Elena Guerrero Roldán	Universitat Oberta de Catalunya, Spain
Hélène Mayer	Luxembourg Institute of Science and Technology, Luxembourg
Nuria Hierro Maldonado	Universitat Oberta de Catalunya, Spain
Marc Vila Bosch	Universitat Oberta de Catalunya, Spain
Cristina Ruiz Cespedosa	Universitat Oberta de Catalunya, Spain

Program Committee

Santi Caballe	Universitat Oberta de Catalunya, Spain
Geoffrey Crisp	University of New South Wales, Australia
Jeroen Donkers	University of Maastricht, The Netherlands
Silvester Draaijer	Vrije Universiteit Amsterdam, The Netherlands
Teresa Guasch	Universitat Oberta de Catalunya, Spain
Ana Elena Guerrero Roldán	Universitat Oberta de Catalunya, Spain
David Griffiths	University of Bolton, UK
José Jansen	Open University, The Netherlands
Eka Jeladze	Tallinn University, Estonia
Desirée Joosten-ten Brinke	Welten Institute, Open University, The Netherlands
Marco Kalz	Welten Institute, Open University, The Netherlands
Ivana Marenzi	Leibniz Universität Hannover, Germany
Hélène Mayer	Luxembourg Institute of Science and Technology, Luxembourg
Rob Nadolski	Open University, The Netherlands
Ingrid Noguera	Universitat Oberta de Catalunya, Spain
Hans Põldoja	Tallinn University, Estonia

Luis P. Prieto	Tallinn University, Estonia
James Sunney Quaicoe	Tallinn University, Estonia
Eric Ras	Luxembourg Institute of Science and Technology, Luxembourg
M. Elena Rodriguez	Universitat Oberta de Catalunya, Spain
María Jesús Rodríguez-Triana	Tallinn University, Estonia
Peter Van Rosmalen	Open University, The Netherlands
Ellen Rusman	Welten Institute, Open University, The Netherlands
Christian Saul	Fraunhofer IDMT, Germany
Marieke van der Schaaf	University of Utrecht, The Netherlands
Sonia Sousa	Tallinn University, Estonia
Slavi Stoyanov	Open University, The Netherlands
Esther Tan	Open University, The Netherlands
William Warburton	Southampton University, UK
Denise Whitelock	Open University, UK

Sponsoring Institutions

Universitat Oberta de Catalunya, Barcelona, Spain
Luxembourg Institute of Science and Technology, Esch-sur-Alzette, Luxembourg
H2020 Project TESLA http://tesla-project.eu/, TeSLA is coordinated by Universitat Oberta de Catalunya (UOC) and funded by the European Commission's Horizon 2020 ICT Programme

Contents

What Does a 'Good' Essay Look Like? Rainbow Diagrams Representing Essay Quality

Denise Whitelock[1(✉)], Alison Twiner[1], John T. E. Richardson[1], Debora Field[2], and Stephen Pulman[2]

[1] Institute of Educational Technology, The Open University, Walton Hall, Milton Keynes MK7 6AA, UK
Denise.Whitelock@open.ac.uk
[2] Department of Computer Science, University of Oxford, Parks Road, Oxford OX1 3QD, UK

Abstract. This paper reports on an essay-writing study using a technical system that has been developed to generate automated feedback on academic essays. The system operates through the combination of a linguistic analysis engine, which processes the text in the essay, and a web application that uses the output of the linguistic analysis engine to generate the feedback. In this paper we focus on one particular visual representation produced by the system, namely "rainbow diagrams". Using the concept of a reverse rainbow, diagrams are produced which visually represent how concepts are interlinked between the essay introduction (violet nodes) and conclusion (red nodes), and how concepts are linked and developed across the whole essay – thus a measure of how cohesive the essay is as a whole. Using a bank of rainbow diagrams produced from real essays, we rated the diagrams as belonging to high-, medium- or low-scoring essays according to their structure, and compared this rating to the actual marks awarded for the essays. On the basis of this we can conclude that a significant relationship exists between an essay's rainbow diagram structure and the mark awarded. This finding has vast implications, as it is relatively easy to show users what the diagram for a "good" essay looks like. Users can then compare this to their own work before submission so that they can make necessary changes and so improve their essay's structure, without concerns over plagiarism. Thus the system is a valuable tool that can be utilised across academic disciplines.

Keywords: Academic essay writing · Automated feedback
Rainbow diagrams · Visual representation

1 Introduction

1.1 Literature Review

This paper reports on an essay-writing study using a computer system to generate automated, visual feedback on academic essays. Students upload their essay draft to the system. The system has then been designed to offer automated feedback in a number of

E. Ras and A. E. Guerrero Roldán (Eds.): TEA 2017, CCIS 829, pp. 1–12, 2018.
https://doi.org/10.1007/978-3-319-97807-9_1

forms: highlighting elements of essay structure (in line with assessed elements identified in Appendix 1), key concepts, dispersion of key words and sentences throughout the essays, and summarising the essay back to the student for their own reflection. This is achieved through linguistic analysis of the essay text, using key phrase extraction and extractive summarisation, which is then fed through a web application to display the feedback. Thus the system can offer feedback based on single essays, and does not require a 'bank' of essays. We should emphasise at the outset that the purpose of our project was to demonstrate proof-of-concept rather than to produce a final system ready for commercial exploitation. Nevertheless, our findings demonstrate the potential value of automated feedback in students' essay writing.

Within this paper we focus specifically on one of the visual representations: rainbow diagrams. Based on the concept of a reverse rainbow, "nodes" within the essay are identified from the sentences, with the nodes from the introduction being coloured violet, and the nodes from the conclusion being red. This produces a linked representation of how the argument presented in the essay develops and builds the key points (related to key elements of "good" quality and structure of an academic essay – see Appendices 1 and 2): outlining the route the essay will take in the introduction, defining key terms and identifying the key points to be raised; backing this up with evidence in the main body of the essay; and finishing with a discussion to bring the argument together. The resulting diagrammatic representation for a "good" essay should therefore have red and violet nodes closely linked at the core of the diagram, with other coloured nodes tightly clustered around and with many links to other nodes.

It has been well documented in the literature that visual representations can be powerful as a form of feedback to support meaningful, self-reflective discourse (Ifenthaler 2011), and also that rainbow diagrams produced from "good", "medium" and prize-winning essays can be correctly identified as such (Whitelock et al. 2015). This paper goes one step further: to link the rainbow diagram structure to the actual marks awarded. Thus, the rainbow diagrams incorporate a "learning to learn" function, designed to guide users to reflect on what a "good" essay might look like, and how their own work may meet such requirements or need further attention.

From our analysis of rainbow diagrams and the marks awarded to essays, we will conclude that, to a certain degree, the quality of an academic essay can be ascertained from this visual representation. This is immensely significant, as rainbow diagrams could be used as one tool to offer students at-a-glance and detailed feedback on where the structure of their essay may need further work, without the concern of plagiarism of showing students "model essays". This could equally support teachers in enabling them to improve their students' academic writing. We begin by outlining the key principles of feedback practice, as highlighted in the research literature, before moving on to consider automated feedback as particularly relevant to the current study.

Feedback. The system developed for this study is designed to offer formative feedback during the drafting phase of essay writing, which is different to the common practice of only receiving feedback on submitted work. Despite this unique feature of the system, it is important to review the purpose of feedback in general which underpins the technical system. Chickering and Gamson (1987) listed "gives prompt feedback" as the fourth of seven principles of good practice for undergraduate education. In addition, the third principle identified is "encourages active learning". Therefore from this perspective, facilitating students to take ownership of and reflect on their work, through provision of feedback at the point when they are engaging with the topic and task, could have significant positive impact on students' final submissions and understanding of topics.

Butler and Winne (1995) defined feedback as "information with which a learner can confirm, add to, overwrite, tune, or restructure information in memory, whether that information is domain knowledge, metacognitive knowledge, beliefs about self and tasks, or cognitive tactics and strategies (Alexander et al. 1991)" (p. 275). Thus the nature of feedback can be very diverse, but must have the purpose and perception of enabling learners to learn from the task they have just done (or are doing), and implemented in the task that follows. From this Butler and Winne concluded that students who are better able to make use of feedback can more easily bridge the gap between expectations, or goals, and performance.

Evans (2013) built on this notion of the student actively interpreting and implementing suggestions of feedback, in stating:

> Considerable emphasis is placed on the value of a social-constructivist assessment process model, focusing on the student as an active agent in the feedback process, working to acquire knowledge of standards, being able to compare those standards to one's own work, and taking action to close the gap between the two (Sadler 1989). (p. 102)

Also raising the importance of students as active agents in their interpretation of feedback, Hattie and Timperley (2007) concluded that "feedback is conceptualized as information provided by an agent (e.g., teacher, peer, book, parent, self, experience) regarding aspects of one's performance or understanding" (p. 81). This therefore relates to what feedback is, but Hattie and Timperley went on to explain what it must do in order to be useful:

> Effective feedback must answer three major questions asked by a teacher and/or by a student: Where am I going? (What are the goals?), How am I going? (What progress is being made toward the goal?), and Where to next? (What activities need to be undertaken to make better progress?) These questions correspond to notions of feed up, feed back, and feed forward. (p. 86)

Thus we can see from this that feedback must look at what has been done, but use this to provide guidance on what should be done next – feed forward – on how to improve current work and so reduce the gap between desired and actual performance. Any feedback that can support a student in understanding what needs to be done and how to do it, and motivating them that this is worthwhile, would be very powerful indeed.

Working along similar lines, Price et al. (2011) commented that, unlike a traditional understanding of feedback, feed forward has potential significance beyond the immediate learning context. For this significance to be realised however, a student must engage with and integrate the feedback within their ongoing learning processes. This often involves iterative cycles of writing, feedback, and more writing.

Gibbs and Simpson (2004) also commented that feedback must be offered in a timely fashion, so that "it is received by the students while it still matters to them and in time for them to pay attention to further learning or receive further assistance" (p. 18).

The features of the technical system being developed in the current study, including the rainbow diagrams, would fit this requirement, since it is an automated, content-free system available to students at the time that they choose to engage with the essay-writing task. Thus, the onus is again on students to prepare work for review, and then to seek feedback on that work, and to implement their interpretations of that feedback.

Price et al. (2011) raised the dilemma, often felt by tutors, of the appropriate level of feedback to offer students:

> "Doing students' work" will ultimately never help the student develop self-evaluative skills, but staff comments on a draft outline may develop the student's appreciation of what the assessment criteria really mean, and what "quality" looks like. What staff feel "allowed" to do *behaviourally* depends on what they believe they are helping their students to achieve *conceptually*. (p. 891, emphasis in original)

The rainbow diagrams offered in the current study provide a means to highlight key points of structure and progression of argument within students' essays – identifying "what 'quality' looks like" in Price et al.'s terms – without having to pinpoint exactly how students should word their essays. This visual representation serves to show quickly where essay structure may need tightening, as well as where it is good – the underlying concept of what makes a good essay, as well as identifying how concepts are evidenced and developed in the essay – without spoon-feeding content or fears of plagiarism.

Having addressed the research on feedback, it is now appropriate to turn more directly to the literature on automated feedback.

Automated Feedback. There has been widespread enthusiasm for the use of technologies in education, and the role of these in supporting students to take ownership of their learning. Steffens (2006), for instance, stated that "the extent to which learners are capable of regulating their own learning greatly enhances their learning outcomes" (p. 353). He also concluded that "In parallel to the rising interest in self-regulation and self-regulated learning, the rapid development of the Information and Communication Technologies (ICT) has made it possible to develop highly sophisticated Technology-Enhanced Learning Environments (TELEs)" (p. 353).

Greene and Azevedo (2010) were similarly enthusiastic about the potential of computer-based learning environments (CBLEs) to support students' learning, but wary that they also place a high skill demand on users:

> CBLEs are a boon to those who are able to self-regulate their learning, but for learners who lack these skills, CBLEs can present an overwhelming array of information representations and navigational choices that can deplete working memory, negatively influence motivation, and lead to negative emotions, all of which can hinder learning (D'Mello et al. 2007; Moos and Azevedo 2006). (p. 208)

This cautionary note reminds us of the potential of such technologies, but as with the need to offer instruction/guidance before feedback, students need to be given the necessary opportunities to realise how any tool – technological or otherwise – can be used to support and stretch their learning potential. Otherwise it is likely to be at best ignored, and at worst reduce performance and waste time through overload and misunderstanding.

Banyard et al. (2006) highlight another potential pitfall of using technologies to support learning, in that "enhanced technologies provided enhanced opportunities for plagiarism" (p. 484). This is particularly the case where use of technology provides access to a wealth of existing literature on the topic of study, but for students to make their own meaningful and cohesive argument around an issue they must understand the issue, rather than merely copying someone else's argument. This reinforces the reasoning behind not offering model essays whilst students work on their assignments, which was one of the concerns as we were devising our technical system, but giving students feedback on their essay structure and development of argument without the temptation of material to be simply copied and pasted.

The opposite and hopeful outcome of giving students the opportunity to explore and realise for themselves what they can do with technologies can be summed up in Crabtree and Roberts' (2003) concept of "wow moments". As Banyard et al. (2006) explained, "Wow moments come from what can be achieved through the technology rather than a sense of wonder at the technology itself" (p. 487). Therefore any technology must be supportive and intuitive regarding how to do tasks, but transparent enough to allow user-driven engagement with and realisation of task activity, demonstrating and facilitating access to resources as required.

Also on the subject of what support automated systems can offer to students, Alden Rivers et al. (2014) produced a review covering some of the existing technical systems that provide automated feedback on essays for summative assessment, including E-rater, Intellimetric, and Pearson's KAT (see also Ifenthaler and Pirnay-Dummer 2014). As Alden Rivers et al. identified, however, systems such as these focus on assessment rather than on formative feedback, which is where the system described in the current study presents something unique.

The system that is the subject of this paper aims to assist higher education students to understand where there might be weaknesses in their draft essays, before they submit their work, by exploiting automatic natural-language-processing analysis techniques. A particular challenge has been to design the system to give meaningful, informative, and helpful advice for action. The rainbow diagrams are based on the use of graph theory, to identify key sentences within the draft essay. A substantial amount of work has therefore been invested to make the diagrams transparent in terms of how the represented details depict qualities of a good essay – through the use of different colours, and how interlinked or dispersed the nodes are. Understanding these patterns has the potential to assist students to improve their essays across subject domains.

Taking all of these points forward, we consider the benefits of offering students a content-free visual representation of the structure and integration of their essays. We take seriously concerns over practices that involve peer review and offering model essays: that some students may hold points back from initial drafts in fear that others might copy them, and that other students may do better in revised versions by borrowing points from the work they review. On this basis, in working toward implementing the technical system under development, we have deliberately avoided the use of model essays. This also has the advantage that the system could be used regardless of the essay topic.

2 Research Questions and Hypothesis

Our study addressed the following research questions. First, can the structure of an essay (i.e., introduction, conclusion) and its quality (i.e., coherence, flow of argument) be represented visually in a way that can identify areas of improvement? Second, can such representations be indicative of marks awarded? This leads to the following hypothesis:

1. A rainbow diagram representation of a written essay can be used to predict whether the essay would achieve a high, medium or low mark. The predicted marks will be positively correlated with those awarded against a formal marking scheme.

3 Method

3.1 Participants

Fifty participants were recruited from a subject panel maintained by colleagues in the Department of Psychology consisting of people who were interested in participating in online psychology experiments. Some were current or former students of the Open University, but others were just members of the public with an interest in psychological research. The participants consisted of eight men and 42 women who were aged between 18 and 80 with a mean age of 43.1 years (SD = 12.1 years).

3.2 Procedure

Each participant was asked to write two essays, and in each case they were allowed two weeks for the task. The first task was: "Write an essay on human perception of risk". The second task was: "Write an essay on memory problems in old age". Participants who produced both essays were rewarded with an honorarium of £40 in Amazon vouchers. In the event, all 50 participants produced Essay 1, but only 45 participants produced Essay 2.

Two of the authors who were academic staff with considerable experience in teaching and assessment marked the submitted essays using an agreed marking scheme. The marking scheme is shown in Appendix 1. If the difference between the total marks awarded was 20% points or less, the essays were assigned the average of the two markers' marks. Discrepancies of more than 20% points were resolved by discussion between the markers.

Rainbow Diagrams. Rainbow diagrams follow the conventions of graph theory, which has been used in a variety of disciplinary contexts (see Newman 2008). A graph consists of a set of nodes or vertices and a set of links or "edges" connecting them. Formally, a graph can be represented by an adjacency matrix in which the cells represent the connections between all pairs of nodes.

Our linguistic analysis engine removes from an essay any titles, tables of contents, headings, captions, abstracts, appendices and references – this is not done manually. Each of the remaining sentences is then compared with every other sentence to derive the cosine similarity for all pairs of sentences. A multidimensional vector is constructed to show the number of times each word appears in each sentence, and the similarity between the two sentences is defined as the cosine of the angle between their two vectors.

The sentences are then represented as nodes in a graph, and values of cosine similarity greater than zero are used to label the corresponding edges in the graph. A web application uses the output of this linguistic analysis to generate various visual representations, including rainbow diagrams. Nodes from the introduction are coloured violet, and nodes from the conclusion are coloured red. As mentioned earlier, the resulting representation for a "good" essay should have red and violet nodes closely linked at the core of the diagram, with other coloured nodes tightly clustered around and with many links to other nodes.

We used our system to generate a rainbow diagram for each of the 95 essays produced by the participants. Without reference to the marks awarded, the rainbow diagrams were then rated as high-, medium- or low-scoring by two of the authors, according to how central the red nodes were (conclusion), how close they were to violet nodes (introduction), and how tightly clustered and interlinked the nodes were. Any differences between raters were resolved through discussion. (For detailed criteria, see Appendix 2, and for examples of high-ranking and low-ranking rainbow diagrams, see Fig. 1).

Fig. 1. Examples of a high-ranking rainbow diagram (left-hand panel) and a low-ranking rainbow diagram (right-hand panel) (Color figure online)

4 Results

The marks awarded for the 50 examples of Essay 1 varied between 27.0 and 87.5 with an overall mean of 56.84 (SD = 15.03). Of the rainbow diagrams for the 50 essays, 6 were rated as high, 17 as medium and 27 as low. The mean marks that were awarded to these three groups of essays were 67.25 (SD = 24.20), 56.29 (SD = 12.54) and 54.87 (SD = 13.67), respectively. The marks awarded for the 45 examples of Essay 2 varied between 28.5 and 83.0 with an overall mean of 54.50 (SD = 15.93). Of the rainbow diagrams for the 45 essays, 7 were rated as high, 10 as medium and 28 as low. The mean marks that were awarded to these three groups of essays were 65.36 (SD = 13.77), 54.70 (SD = 14.07) and 51.71 (SD = 16.34), respectively.

A multivariate analysis of covariance was carried out on the marks awarded to the 45 students who had submitted both essays. This used the marks awarded to Essay 1 and Essay 2 as dependent variables and the ratings given to the rainbow diagrams for Essay 1 and Essay 2 as a varying covariate. The covariate showed a highly significant linear relationship with the marks, $F(1, 43) = 8.55$, $p = .005$, partial $\eta^2 = .166$. In other words, the rainbow diagram ratings explained 16.6% of the between-subjects variation in marks, which would be regarded as a large effect (i.e., an effect of theoretical and practical importance) on the basis of Cohen's (1988, pp. 280–287) benchmarks of effect size. This confirms our Hypothesis.

An anonymous reviewer pointed out that the difference between the marks awarded to essays rated as high and medium appeared to be larger than the difference between the marks awarded to essays rated as medium and low. To check this, a second multivariate analysis of covariance was carried out that included both the linear and the quadratic components of the relationship between the ratings and the marks. As before, the linear relationship between the ratings and the marks was large and highly significant, $F(1, 42) = 8.44$, $p = .006$, partial $\eta^2 = .167$. In contrast, the quadratic relationship between the ratings and the marks was small and nonsignificant, $F(1, 42) = 0.41$, $p = .53$, partial $\eta^2 = .010$.

In other words, the association between the ratings of the rainbow diagrams and the marks awarded against a formal marking scheme was essentially linear, despite appearances to the contrary. The unstandardised regression coefficient between the ratings and the marks (which is based on the full range of marks and not simply on the mean marks from the three categories of rainbow diagrams) was 9.15. From this we can conclude that essays with rainbow diagrams that were rated as high would be expected to receive 9.15% points more than essays with rainbow diagrams rated as medium and 18.30 (i.e., 9.15×2)% points more than essays with rainbow diagrams rated as low.

5 Discussion

This paper has described a study exploring the value of providing visual, computer-generated representations of students' essays. The visual representations were in the form of "rainbow diagrams", offering an overview of the development and also the integration of the essay argument. We used essays that had been marked according to set criteria, and generated rainbow diagrams of each essay to depict visually how closely related points raised in the introduction and conclusion were, and how inter-linked other points were that were raised during the course of the essay.

Essay diagrams were rated as high-, medium- and low-scoring, and these ratings were analysed against the actual marks essays were awarded. From this we found a significant relationship between essay diagrams rated as high, medium and low, and the actual marks that essays were awarded. We can therefore conclude that rainbow diagrams can illustrate the quality and integrity of an academic essay, offering students an immediate level of feedback on where the structure of their essay and flow of their argument is effective and where it might need further work.

The most obvious limitation of this study is that it was carried out using a modest sample of just 50 participants recruited from a subject panel. They were asked to carry out an artificial task rather than genuine assignments for academic credit. Even so, they exhibited motivation and engagement with their tasks, and their marks demonstrated a wide range of ability. Moreover, because the relationship between the marks that were awarded for their essays and the ratings that were assigned to the rainbow diagrams constituted a large effect, the research design had sufficient power to detect that effect even with a modest sample.

It could be argued that a further limitation of the current study is that it suggests potential of the rainbow diagrams and automated feedback system to support students in writing their essays, and also offers an additional tool to teachers in supporting their students' academic writing – it has not however tested whether this potential could be achieved in practice. For this a further study would be needed, to address the effect of rainbow diagram feedback/forward on academic essay writing and performance. For this to be implemented, providing guidance to students and teachers on how to interpret the rainbow diagrams would also be essential.

6 Conclusions and Implications

These results hold great significance as a means of automatically representing students' essays back to them, to indicate how well their essay is structured and how integrated and progressive their argument is. We conclude that having an accessible, always-ready online system offering students feedback on their work in progress, at a time when students are ready to engage with the task, is an invaluable resource for students and teachers. As the system is content-free, it could be made easily available for students studying a wide range of subjects and topics, with the potential to benefit students and teachers across institutions and subjects.

Feedback is considered a central part of academic courses, and has an important role to play in raising students' expectations of their own capabilities. To achieve this, however, it has been widely reported that feedback must be prompt and encourage active learning (Butler and Winne 1995; Chickering and Gamson 1987; Evans 2013). Through the feedback process, therefore, students must be enabled to see what they have done well, where there is room for improvement, and importantly how they can work to improve their performance in the future (Hattie and Timperley 2007). This latter issue has brought the concept of "feed forward" (Hattie and Timperley 2007; Price et al. 2011), in addition to feedback, into the debate. Thus students need to be given guidance on task requirements before they commence assignments, but they also need ongoing guidance on how they can improve their work – which rainbow diagrams could offer.

There exists great potential for educational technologies to be used to support a large variety of tasks, including the writing of essays. One such technology is of course the system developed for the current study. As the literature relates however, it is critical that any resource, technological or otherwise, be transparent and intuitive of its purpose, so that students can concentrate on the learning task and not on how to use the technology (Greene and Azevedo 2010). This is when "wow moments" (Crabtree and Roberts 2003) can be facilitated: when students find the learning task much easier, more efficient, or better in some other way, due to how they can do the task using the technology – what they can do *with* the technology, rather than just what the technology can do (Banyard et al. 2006).

The rainbow diagram feature of the current system therefore offers a potential way of both feeding back and feeding forward, in a way that is easily understood from the visual representation. Students would need some guidance on how to interpret the diagrams, and to understand the significance of the colouring and structure, but with a little input this form of essay representation could be widely applied to academic writing on any topic. We have shown that the structure of rainbow diagrams can be used to predict the level of mark awarded for an essay, which could be a very significant tool for students as they draft and revise their essays. By being content-free the provision of rainbow diagrams is also free of concerns about plagiarism, a critical issue in modern academic practice with widespread access to existing material.

7 Compliance with Ethical Standards

This project was approved by The Open University's Human Research Ethics Committee. Participants who completed both essay-writing tasks were rewarded with a £40 Amazon voucher, of which they were informed before agreeing to take part in the study.

Acknowledgements. This work is supported by the Engineering and Physical Sciences Research Council (EPSRC, grant numbers EP/J005959/1 & EP/J005231/1).

Appendix 1

Marking Criteria for Essays

Criterion	Definition	Maximum marks
1. Introduction	Introductory paragraph sets out argument	10
2. Conclusion	Concluding paragraph rounds off discussion	10
3. Argument	Argument is clear and well followed through	10
4. Evidence	Evidence for argument in main body of text	20
5. Paragraphs	All paragraphs seven sentences long or less	5
6. Within word count	Word count between 500 and 1000 words	5
7. References	Two or three references	5
	Four or more references	10

(*continued*)

(*continued*)

Criterion	Definition	Maximum marks
8. Definition	Provides a clear and explicit definition of risk or memory	10
9. Written presentation	Extensive vocabulary, accurate grammar and spelling	10
10. Practical implications	Understanding of practical issues, innovative proposals	10
Maximum total marks		100

Appendix 2

Rating Criteria for Rainbow Diagrams

Low-scoring diagrams	Medium-scoring diagrams	High-scoring diagram
Not densely connected	Densely connected area but some outlying nodes	Densely connected
Red nodes (conclusion) not central	Red (conclusion) and violet (introduction) not so closely connected	Red nodes (conclusion) central
Few links between violet (introduction) and red (conclusion) nodes		Close links between violet (introduction) and red (conclusion) nodes

References

Alden Rivers, B., Whitelock, D., Richardson, J.T.E., Field, D., Pulman, S.: Functional, frustrating and full of potential: learners' experiences of a prototype for automated essay feedback. In: Kalz, M., Ras, E. (eds.) CAA 2014. CCIS, vol. 439, pp. 40–52. Springer, Cham (2014). https://doi.org/10.1007/978-3-319-08657-6_4

Alexander, P.A., Schallert, D.L., Hare, V.C.: Coming to terms: how researchers in learning and literacy talk about knowledge. Rev. Educ. Res. **61**, 315–343 (1991). https://doi.org/10.2307/1170635

Banyard, P., Underwood, J., Twiner, A.: Do enhanced communication technologies inhibit or facilitate self-regulated learning? Eur. J. Ed. **41**, 473–489 (2006). https://doi.org/10.1111/j.1465-3435.2006.00277.x

Butler, D.L., Winne, P.H.: Feedback and self-regulated learning: a theoretical synthesis. Rev. Educ. Res. **65**, 245–281 (1995). https://doi.org/10.3102/00346543065003245

Chickering, A.W., Gamson, Z.F.: Seven principles for good practice in undergraduate education. Am. Assoc. High. Educ. Bull. **39**(7), 3–7 (1987). http://www.aahea.org/aahea/articles/sevenprinciples1987.htm. Accessed 23 Jun 2015

Cohen, J.: Statistical Power Analysis for the Behavioral Sciences, 2nd edn. Academic Press, New York (1988). https://doi.org/10.1016/B978-0-12-179060-8.50001-3

Crabtree, J., Roberts, S.: Fat Pipes, Connected People: Rethinking Broadband Britain. The Work Foundation, London (2003). http://www.theworkfoundation.com/DownloadPublication/Report/121_121_fat_pipes.pdf. Accessed 23 Jun 2015

D'Mello, S.K., Picard, R., Graesser, A.C.: Toward an affect-sensitive AutoTutor. IEEE Intell. Syst. **22**(4), 53–61 (2007). https://doi.org/10.1109/MIS.2007.79

Evans, C.: Making sense of assessment feedback in higher education. Rev. Educ. Res. **83**, 70–120 (2013). https://doi.org/10.3102/0034654312474350

Gibbs, G., Simpson, C.: Conditions under which assessment supports students' learning. Learn. Teach. High. Educ. **1**, 1–31 (2004). http://insight.glos.ac.uk/tli/resources/lathe/documents/issue%201/articles/simpson.pdf. Accessed 23 Jun 2015

Greene, J.A., Azevedo, R.: The measurement of learners' self-regulated cognitive and metacognitive processes while using computer-based learning environments. Educ. Psychol. **45**, 203–209 (2010). https://doi.org/10.1080/00461520.2010.515935

Hattie, J., Timperley, H.: The power of feedback. Rev. Educ. Res. **77**, 81–112 (2007). https://doi.org/10.3102/003465430298487

Ifenthaler, D.: Intelligent model-based feedback: helping students to monitor their individual learning progress. In: Graf, S., Lin, F., Kinshuk, McGreal, R. (eds.) Intelligent and Adaptive Learning Systems: Technology Enhanced Support for Learners and Teachers, pp. 88–100. IGI Global, Hershey (2011)

Ifenthaler, D., Pirnay-Dummer, P.: Model-based tools for knowledge assessment. In: Spector, J. M., Merrill, M.D., Elen, J., Bishop, M.J. (eds.) Handbook of Research on Educational Communications and Technology, 4th edn, pp. 289–301. Springer, New York (2014). https://doi.org/10.1007/978-1-4614-3185-5_23

Moos, D.C., Azevedo, R.: The role of goal structure in undergraduates' use of self-regulatory variables in two hypermedia learning tasks. J. Educ. Multimed. Hypermed. **15**, 49–86 (2006)

Newman, M.E.J.: Mathematics of networks. In: Durlauf, S.N., Blume, L.W. (eds.) The New Palgrave Dictionary of Economics, vol. 5, 2nd edn, pp. 465–470. Palgrave Macmillan, Houndmills (2008)

Price, M., Handley, K., Millar, J.: Feedback: focusing attention on engagement. Stud. High. Educ. **36**, 879–896 (2011). https://doi.org/10.1080/03075079.2010.483513

Sadler, D.R.: Formative assessment and the design of instructional systems. Instr. Sci. **18**, 119–144 (1989). https://doi.org/10.1007/BF00117714

Steffens, K.: Self-regulated learning in technology-enhanced learning environments: lessons from a European review. Eur. J. Ed. **41**, 353–380 (2006). https://doi.org/10.1111/j.1465-3435.2006.00271.x

Whitelock, D., Twiner, A., Richardson, J.T.E., Field, D., Pulman, S.: OpenEssayist: a supply and demand learning analytics tool for drafting academic essays. In: Proceedings of the Fifth International Conference on Learning Analytics and Knowledge, pp. 208–212. ACM (2015)

How to Obtain Efficient High Reliabilities in Assessing Texts: Rubrics vs Comparative Judgement

Maarten Goossens(✉) and Sven De Maeyer

University of Antwerp, Antwerp, Belgium
{Maarten.goossens, sven.demaeyer}@uantwerpen.be

Abstract. It is very difficult and time consuming to assess texts. Even after great effort there is a small chance independent raters would agree on their mutual ratings which undermines the reliability of the rating. Several assessment methods and their merits are described in literature, among them the use of rubrics and the use of comparative judgement (CJ). In this study we investigate which of the two methods is more efficient in obtaining reliable outcomes when used for assessing texts. The same 12 texts are assessed in both a rubric and CJ condition by the same 6 raters. Results show an inter-rater reliability of .30 for the rubric condition and an inter-rater reliability of .84 in the CJ condition after the same amount of time invested in the respective methods. Therefore we conclude that CJ is far more efficient in obtaining high reliabilities when used to asses texts. Also suggestions for further research are made.

Keywords: Reliability · Rubrics · Comparative judgement · Efficiency

1 Introduction

To assess a text on its quality is a demanding task. And even after great efforts like providing training, there is a small chance independent raters would agree on their mutual ratings which undermines the reliability of the rating [1–3]. To try to bring judgments of raters closer together, the use of rubrics is suggested [4]. It is assumed that these rubrics make raters look at the same way to all the texts and assess each text on the same predefined criteria. Nevertheless, the use of a rubric is not a guarantee for reliable judgements [2, 5]. Even training the raters in the use of the rubric, will not eliminate all differences between raters [6]. Another way to increase the reliability is to request two raters to rate all the texts instead of distributing the texts over the raters [7]. Together with the time investment to construct the rubric, the use of rubrics to generate reliable judgements would cost a lot of effort.

An alternative and promising assessment method can be found in comparative judgement (CJ) [8]. This method works holistic and comparative [9] instead of analytic and absolute like rubrics. In CJ, raters are presented with a random pair of, for instance texts and they only have to choose the better one in light of a certain competence. As a result of the assessment process, a rank order is created from the text with the lowest quality to the text with the highest quality [10] and the quality of the texts are quantified

E. Ras and A. E. Guerrero Roldán (Eds.): TEA 2017, CCIS 829, pp. 13–25, 2018.
https://doi.org/10.1007/978-3-319-97807-9_2

using the Bradley-Terry-Luce model and the resulting parameters. This rank order is and the quantified scores are based upon a shared consensus among the raters [10, 11] and have been shown to obtain high reliabilities in educational settings [12, 13]. Several raters take part in the assessment and all have to make several comparisons. Although texts only have to be compared to a fraction of the other texts, research shows that a minimum of 9 up to a maximum of 20 comparisons is necessary to reach high reliabilities [14].

Nevertheless the positive features and the strengths of this method, questions can be asked about the effectiveness of this method. So more information is needed about how reliability relates to time investment using rubrics or CJ. Therefore we compare the evolution over time of the inter-rater reliabilities for the use of rubrics versus the use of CJ in the assessment of writing tasks.

In what follows, we first describe the theoretical framework which leads to the research questions. Secondly we point out the methodology of the study. We describe the results as third after which a conclusion is drawn. At last we discuss the limitations of the study and make recommendations for further research.

2 Theoretical Framework

Although comparative judgement is considered a reliable assessment method in educational settings [12], its efficiency remains unclear. In what follows we describe the meaning of reliability concerning comparative judgement and secondly, we describe the research on the efficiency of comparative judgement. This leads us at last to the research questions of the present study.

2.1 Reliability

The question of the replicability of the results of an evaluation is a question of the reliability of that evaluation [1]. In this study we focus on inter-rater reliability. This refers to the extent to which different raters agree on the scores of students' work. A low inter-rater reliability means that the result of the evaluation depends on the person who judged [15].

Absolute judgements, whereby every text is judged on its own using a description of the competence or a criteria list, are difficult [16–18]. And, we don't want subjective raters to determine the score of a text because we know raters differ in severity and interpretation [5]. Therefore, it is proposed to include multiple raters in the context of rubrics [18]. However, they all make different absolute ratings [19]. As a consequence research about the reliability of rubrics shows it is very difficult to come to consensus among raters [2, 19].

This consensus, or the match between raters' scores, is needed to speak of reliability in the use of rubrics. There are many reliability measures, but when more than 2 raters are involved, the ICC is a good measure [20]. The ICC is calculated by mean squares (i.e., estimates of the population variances based on the variability among a given set of measures) obtained through analysis of variance. A high ICC means the variation in scores linked to the texts is bigger than the variation by error, which include the raters [20]. Correspondingly a low ICC is an indication of low inter-rater reliability. Like studies of Lumley and McNamara [21] and Bloxham [5]. Bloxham, den-Outer, Hudson and Price [19] suggest, raters have a great impact on the final judgements even when they use a rubric.

In the case of CJ, multiple raters are involved and they all make comparisons [9]. As Thurstone [22] states in his law of comparative judgment, people are better and far more reliable in comparing two stimuli then to score one stimulus absolutely. The reliability in CJ is quantified by a scale separation reliability [SSR; 14]. A statistic derived in the same way as the person separation reliability index in Rasch and Item Response Theory analyses [14]. The SSR can be interpreted as the proportion of 'true' variance in the estimated scale values [14], expressing the stability over raters. Therefore the SSR can be interpreted as the inter-rater reliability [23]. Research on CJ shows high inter-rater-reliabilities [9, 12, 24].

Thus, although the ICC and the SSR are calculated differently, they both can be interpreted as inter-rater reliabilities.

2.2 Relationship Between Reliability and Time Investment

Only one study takes the effort to compare the reliability of rubrics and CJ in relation to the time invested in the method during the assessment. Coertjens, Lesterhuis, Van Gasse, Verhavert and De Maeyer (in progress) investigated differences in the stability of the rank orders of texts assessed with a rubric on one hand and CJ on the other hand. 35 texts of 16–17 year old pupils were judged by 40 raters in the CJ condition and 18 raters in the rubric condition. As a result all 35 texts were at least 5 times judged with a rubric and 27 times compared to other texts in the CJ condition. The ICC of 2 rubrics was .67 and increased till .85 by 5 judgements per text. In comparison, the SSR in the CJ condition was .70 by 12 comparisons per text (same time investment as 2 rubrics per text) and .88 by 27 comparisons per text (same time investment as 5 rubrics per text). Comparing, however, the stability of the rank order over time for both conditions, this study concludes that it was more difficult to obtain a stable rank order in the rubric condition. In contrast, in the CJ condition the rank order stabilized over time. Therefore, it can be assumed that CJ is a faster and more accurate method to gain insight in the quality of the texts.

Other studies like Pollitt [17] and McMahon and Jones [25] also mentioned the comparison on time investment in working with rubrics and working with CJ. However, in both studies no insight is given in the reliability of scoring with rubrics. Hence, more research is needed in the efficiency – reliability trade off, when using other raters and tasks.

2.3 Research Questions

As the use of multiple raters can increase the reliability as suggested by Bouwer and Koster [18] it is necessary to gain insight in how the judgements of the different raters relate to each other. This leads to the first two research questions:

(1) To what extent can we speak of a consensus in the awarded scores in the rubric condition?
(2) To what extent can we speak of consensus amongst the raters in the CJ condition?

Even more important, we want to compare the reliabilities of both assessment methods (rubrics and CJ) in relation to the time invested in the respective assessment method. However, before comparing both methods, we aim to understand whether both methods measure a similar construct. Therefore the third research question is:

(3) To what extent do we measure the same construct with rubrics and CJ?

Only after we can decide whether both methods measure a similar construct, we can directly compare the time investment necessary to obtain reliable scores. Resulting in the fourth research question:

(4) Which method gains the most reliable results with equal time investments?

3 Method

3.1 Texts

12 students of the fifth grade general education (16–17 year) in Flanders wrote a review about a song of choice in light of a writing course in mother tongue. In advance lessons were spend on, for instance, relevant aspects of songs and poetic value of a song. All reviews had to be between 250 and 300 words and were anonymously submitted.

3.2 Creation of the Rubric

The transparency of criteria is one of the key elements to support the use of rubrics for formative purposes [26]. Arter and McTighe [27] state that involving students in the creation of rubrics can have a positive effect on interpretation of the criteria, motivation and performance. As drawing on mentioned research Fraile, Panadero and Pardo [28] highly recommend the co-creating rubrics through the collaboration of the teacher and the students. In this study we co-created the rubric as followed.

The rubric was created by dividing the 12 students, who also wrote the reviews, into three groups. Each group got 4 reviews, none of which was one of the group members. Then each group had to choose the best out of the 4 reviews and discussed the aspects that made these review better than the others. In a plenary discussion, the students came to one list with determining aspects of review quality. Two teachers in training and the tutor of the course, translated this list in a final rubric. The main part of the rubric honored the content of the task. Also the use of language (spelling and grammar), syntax and structure were honored. And, extra points were given for sticking to the word count and for originality.

3.3 Raters and Procedure

6 teachers in training (master students) participated in the judgment procedure. All 6 teachers in training judged all 12 reviews independently using the rubric. The scores on the sub criteria were added to a final score per review resulting in 72 scores for 12 reviews (see Table 1). One of the raters recorded the time spend on judging with the rubric. From the judgement of 7 reviews data was gathered on the time that was spent to fill in the rubric.

3 weeks later the same 6 teachers in training were invited to take part in a CJ session using the D-PAC software (digital platform for the assessment of competences). This software is developed by a research team of the University of Antwerp, University Ghent and imec, especially to investigate the merits and drawbacks of CJ in educational settings [see: 8]. In the CJ session in D-PAC, randomly selected pairs were selected out of the 12 reviews and were presented to the raters (see Fig. 1). The raters had to choose which one of the two presented reviews was the best. After declaring which was the better, the raters were asked to give feedback on the reviews by describing what the strengths and weakness of the reviews were and why (see Fig. 2). After completing the feedback a new pair was automatically generated and presented to the raters. Each rater made 20 comparisons resulting in 120 comparisons in total. So, every review was compared 20 times to another review. By using the D-PAC software it was possible to record time data for every step in the judgment process.

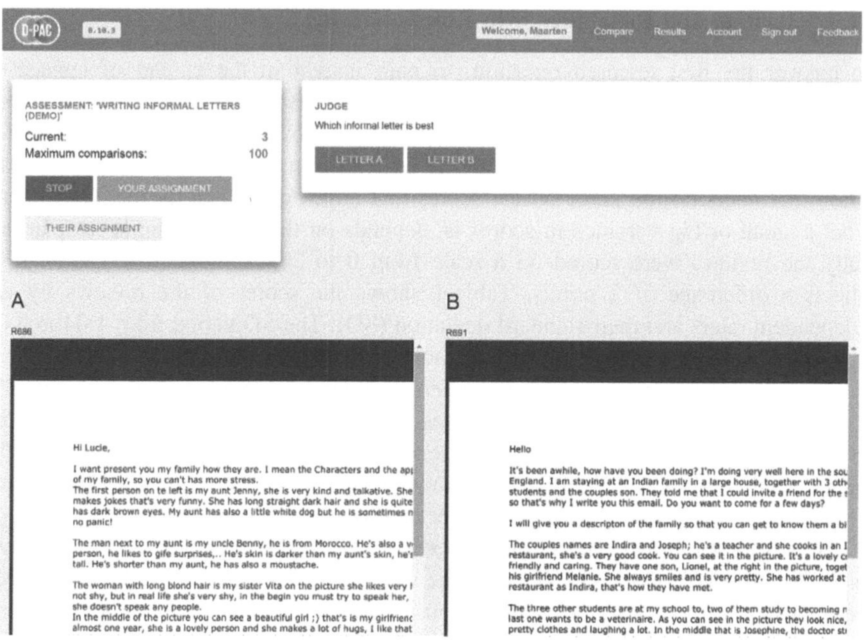

Fig. 1. Presentation of a random selected pair.

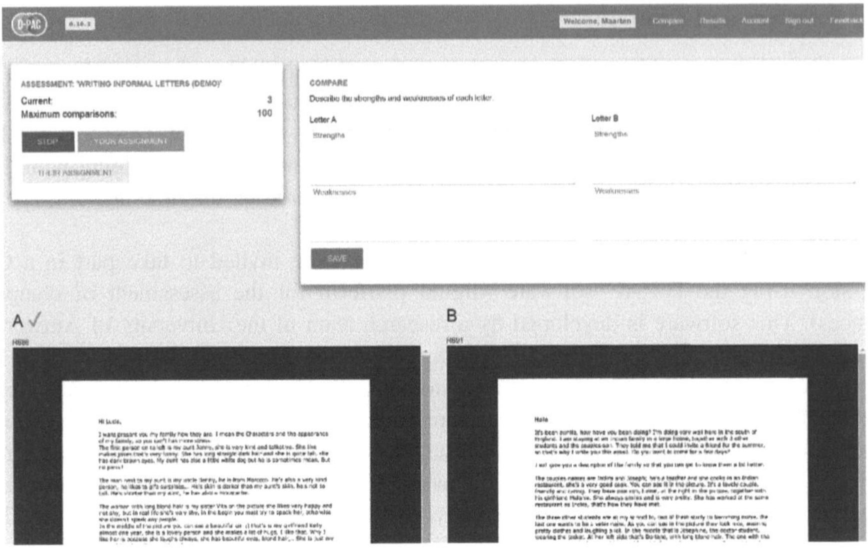

Fig. 2. Feedback possibility

4 Analysis and Results

4.1 Variation and Reliability with Rubric Scoring

To answer the first research question, to gain insight in the extend of consensus between scores of raters when they use a rubric to assess reviews, we first calculated the variance between the scores given for each review by the raters. A small variance indicates consensus among raters about the scores given. A large variance is an indication that raters do not agree on the scores that have been given by the other raters. What a small or big variance in scores is, depends on the scale of the scores. In this study the reviews were scored on a scale from 0 to 20. A standard deviation of 1 reflects a difference of 2 points. Table 1 shows the scores of the reviews by the independent raters and their standard deviation (SD). The SD varied from 1.04 to 3.01 or in other words a variation of 10% to more than 30% in the scores.

A certain variance in scores over raters could be an indication of difference in severity as can be seen in the mean scores of the raters. So is 11.9 the mean of the scores from rater 1 and 16.3 the mean of the scores of rater 4. This severity effect is also found in other research [29, 30]. This, however, does not have to mean these raters differ in which reviews they find of higher quality.

To be sure the variance is not due to severity, we created rank orders of the reviews for each individual rater and calculated the spearman rank order correlations between these ranks. Table 2 shows no unambiguously correlation between the individual rank orders of the raters. 60% of the correlations are positive and 40% of the correlations are negative. Correlations go from −.50 for to .42.

Table 1. Individual scores per review and the SD

Review	Rater 1	Rater 2	Rater 3	Rater 4	Rater 5	Rater 6	SD
Review 1	8	14.5	14	16	11	15	3.01
Review 2	13.5	14.5	11.5	16	13	14	1.51
Review 3	15.5	17	17.5	17	15	15.5	1.04
Review 4	10	14	16.5	16.5	15	15	2.41
Review 5	10.5	15	14	16	12	15	2.1
Review 6	11	16	14	18	13	16	2.5
Review 7	14.5	14	17	15	13	14.5	1.33
Review 8	10	14	16	16	15	15.5	2.29
Review 9	10.5	16.5	13	16.5	16	16	2.46
Review 10	14.5	12	11	16	13.5	14	1.79
Review 11	12	14.5	14.5	16.5	17	16	1.82
Review 12	12.5	17.5	19	16.5	16	17.5	2.21
Mean	11.9	15.0	14.8	16.3	14.1	14.2	2.24

Table 2. Spearman rank correlations of the reviews per rater

	Rater 1	Rater 2	Rater 3	Rater 4	Rater 5	Rater 6
Rater 1	1.00000					
Rater 2	−0.5034	1.00000				
Rater 3	−0.0559	0.30769	1.00000			
Rater 4	0.23776	−0.1328	0.42657	1.00000		
Rater 5	0.30769	−0.2027	0.04895	−0.2937	1.00000	
Rater 6	0.05594	0.13986	−0.0489	0.13286	0.37062	1.00000

The inter-rater reliability refers to the extent to which different raters agree on the scores of students' work. A low inter-rater reliability means that the result of the evaluation depends on the person who judged [15]. In this study we used the ICC, a good measure for inter-rater reliability [31]. The ICC was calculated in R using the package 'psych'. Because every rater judges every review we need the two-way random measure or ICC2. Looking at this fixed sample of raters the ICC2 is .18 ($p > 0.01$). But it is common practice when more raters are involved to take the average of their scores (Coertjens et al. 2017). Therefore we have to calculate the two-way random average or ICC2k which in this case is .57 ($p > 0.01$) (Table 3).

Table 3. Intraclass correlation coefficients

	Type	ICC	F	df1	df2	p	Lower bound	Upper bound
Single_random_raters	ICC2	0.18	2.9	11	55	0.0046	0.125	0.28
Average_random_raters	ICC2k	0.57	2.9	11	55	0.0046	0.461	0.70

4.2 Variation and Reliability with CJ Scoring

CJ data give us the opportunity to gain insight in the quality of the assessment [17]. We used these quality measures to answer the second research question. First, the chi-squared (χ^2) goodness of fit statistic make it possible to quantify how far judgements deviate from what the model predicts [8]. When aggregated, this provides an estimation of how much raters differ from the group consensus or how equivocal a representation, in this case a review, is [8]. There are two fit statistics, the *infit* and the *outfit*. Because research from Linacre and Wright [32] state that the infit is less subject to occasional mistakes, we prefer the infit statistic.

Pollitt [9] states that a large infit for raters suggests that they consistently judge away from the group consensus. Those raters are called misfits. As can be seen in Fig. 3 no rater misfits in this assessment. Representations with a large infit are representations which lead to more inconsistent judgments [33]. Figure 4 show there are no misfit-representations in this particular assessment under research.

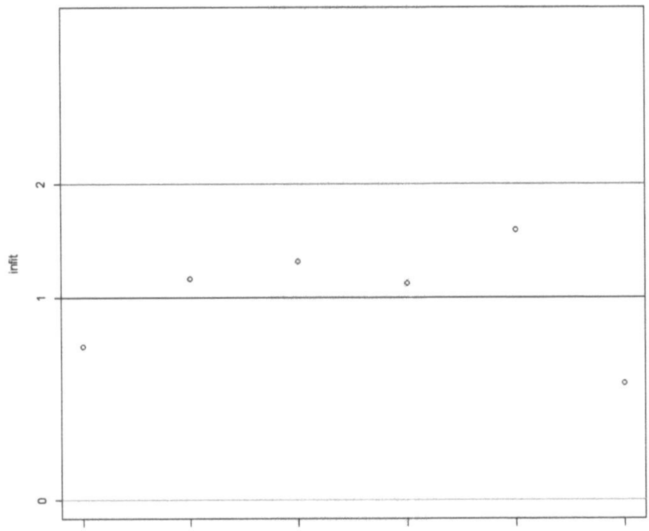

Fig. 3. Infit of the raters

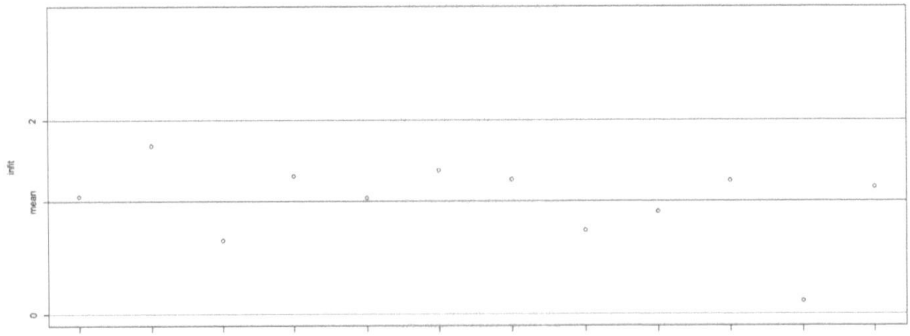

Fig. 4. Infit of the representations

Second, we calculated the reliability of the rank order of the reviews as a result of CJ. Seeing the Rasch model can be used to analyze CJ data [29], one can calculate the Rasch separation reliability. This reliability measure is also known as the Scale Separation Reliability [SSR; 14], which in turn is a measure of inter-rater reliability [23]. The SSR of the rank of the reviews was calculated in R (package BradleyTerry2) and is .84 for 20 comparisons per text, which can be considered as high [14].

4.3 Do Rubrics and CJ Measure a Similar Construct

In order to compare the reliabilities and efficiency, we firstly determine whether or not both methods measure a similar construct (third research question). By comparing the mean scores of the rubric with the final scores of the CJ condition using the spearman rank order correlation, we gain insight in what extent both methods result in similar rank orders of the reviews.

The spearman rank order is .78 ($p > 0.01$). So we conclude both methods measure a similar construct.

4.4 Reliability and Time Investment

For the fourth research question we had to make an estimation of the time spend in each judgment condition in relation to the reliability at that moment. First we calculated the average time spend on a rubric, this was 891 s. per review. By multiplying this with 12, the amount of reviews, we know what it takes for one rater to rate all 12 reviews using the rubric. On average a rater needed 10 692 s. (one time lap) to complete all 12 rubrics. With a similar time investment (10 440 s.) each review was compared 10 times in the CJ conditions over all raters. To judge each review 6 times in the rubric condition took 64 152 s. in total. The CJ assessment stopped after 20 rounds which took 20 880 s. in total.

The ICC calculated for the rubric condition is the ICC of the 6 raters. Using the Spearman-Brown formula we can calculate the reliability for 2 up to 5 raters [18]. The Spearman-Brown formula makes it also possible to forecast the SSR in the CJ condition. As the CJ condition stopped at 20 rounds (20 880 s.) we wanted to forecast the SSR when more time should be spend on this judgement method. Table 4 and Fig. 5 show the evolution of the reliabilities of the judgment methods in relation to the time spend in each judgement method. As can be seen, the reliability of the CJ assessment is always higher than the reliability of the use of rubrics in comparison to an equal time investment in the judgment methods. When looking at the time the CJ assessment stopped, 20 880 s., the reliability in the CJ condition (.84) was almost tipple the reliability in the rubric condition (.30).

Table 4. Reliability evolution over time spend in the assessment method

	Rubric condition		CJ condition	
Time lap	Time spend	Reliability	Time spend	Reliability
1	10 692	NA	10 440	.71
2	21 384	.30	20 880	.84
3	32 076	.39	31 320	.89
4	42 768	.46	41 760	.91
5	53 460	.52	52 200	.93
6	64 152	.57	62 640	.94

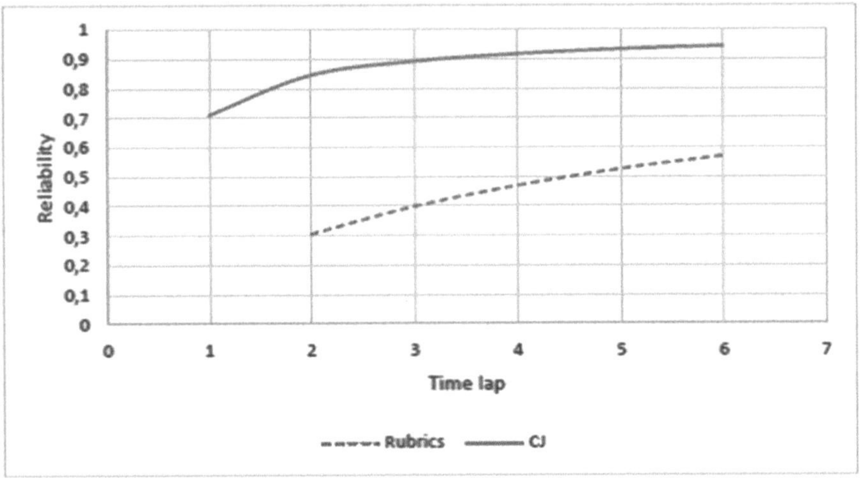

Fig. 5. Reliability evolution in time of rubric and CJ condition

5 Conclusion

As for the use of rubrics we can conclude there is no consensus among the raters about the scores they awarded the reviews with. The variation in SD of the scores of the rubrics runs up to 3.01 and shows there is no consensus at all among raters about the quality of the reviews. This is confirmed by the analysis of the individual rank orders of the reviews based on the rubric scores. No straightforward correlation could be found between the these rank orders. The highest positive correlation was .42. Even 40% of the correlations was negative, showing inversely proportional accreditation of reviews' quality. When looking at the inter-rater reliability, the same conclusion can be drawn. The absolute inter-rater reliability (ICC2) was only .18 indicating 82% of the variance in the scores is due to error which include the raters. Whereas the average reliability (ICC2k) was .57 indicating still 43% of the variance in scores is caused by error which includes the raters.

On the other hand using CJ to evaluate reviews shows a great consensus between the raters. According to the infit statistics, no misfit-judges or misfit-representations are reported. For the infit of the judges this means that the differences between the raters in the judgements stay between specific boundaries (2 SD) and all raters judge the reviews more or less in the same way. Confirmation can be found in the infit of the representations as finding no misfit-representation indicates all raters addresses an equal quality to the individual reviews. When we take the SSR of .84 of the CJ rank order of the reviews into account, we can conclude there is a high degree of agreement among raters showing a high consensus in the ratings given by judges.

Similar constructs are measured in both conditions as the spearman rank order of the mean scores of the rubrics and the final scores of the CJ condition is .78. When we compare the obtained reliabilities of the two judgement methods, rubrics vs CJ and considering the time invested in both methods, we can state that CJ is far more efficient and reliable than the use of rubrics by rating reviews. Therefore substantial gains in reliability of the ratings and substantial time savings, can be accomplished by using CJ for the evaluation of texts.

6 Discussion

Despite the strong conclusion, this study has its limitations. First, unless the careful creation of the rubric, it isn't a validated instrument. Nevertheless it is common practice in educational settings to create a rubric yourself and use this as an instrument to actually rate students work. Since we want to investigate the common practice, this was more an advantage than a disadvantage. Second, only the time investment of seven rubrics was captured. But when looking at the time investments chronologically, we can distinguish a trend in working faster and faster. This trend was also found in another research study running at the moment by Coertjens and colleagues and convinced us the average time spend of the seven rubrics was the best estimation possible.

Last, in this study the validity of the judgement process wasn't incorporated in the research. Supplementary research on this topic is necessary to make a founded choice for one of this two methods to evaluate reviews. Nevertheless, research on the validity of CJ is promising as the research of van Daal, Lesterhuis, Coertjens, Donche and De Maeyer [13] suggest the final decision about the quality of an essay reflects the divers visions on text quality as every text is evaluated several times by divers raters.

Acknowledgements. Jan 'T Sas, Elies Ghysebrechts, Jolien Polus & Tine Van Reeth.

References

1. Bevan, R.M., Daugherty, R., Dudley, P., Gardner, J., Harlen, W., Stobart, G.: A systematic review of the evidence of reliability and validity of assessment by teachers used for summative purposes (2004)
2. Jonsson, A., Svingby, G.: The use of scoring rubrics: reliability, validity and educational consequences. Educ. Res. Rev. **2**(2), 130–144 (2007)

3. Tisi, J., Whitehouse, G., Maughan, S., Burdett, N.: A review of literature on marking reliability research (2011)
4. Hamp-Lyons, L.: The scope of writing assessment. Assess. Writ. **8**(1), 5–16 (2002)
5. Bloxham, S.: Marking and moderation in the UK: false assumptions and wasted resources. Assess. Eval. High. Educ. **34**(2), 209–220 (2009)
6. Stuhlmann, J., Daniel, C., Dellinger, A., Kenton, R., Powers, T.: A generalizability study of the effects of training on teachers' abilities to rate children's writing using a rubric. Read. Psychol. **20**(2), 107–127 (1999)
7. Marzano, R.J.: A comparison of selected methods of scoring classroom assessments. Appl. Meas. Educ. **15**(3), 249–268 (2002)
8. Lesterhuis, M., Verhavert, S., Coertjens, L., Donche, V., De Maeyer, S.: Comparative judgement as a promising alternative to score competences. In: Innovative Practices for Higher Education Assessment and Measurement, p. 119 (2016)
9. Pollitt, A.: Comparative judgement for assessment. Int. J. Technol. Des. Educ. **22**(2), 157–170 (2012)
10. Jones, I., Alcock, L.: Peer assessment without assessment criteria. Stud. High. Educ. **39**(10), 1774–1787 (2014)
11. Whitehouse, C., Pollitt, A.: Using adaptive comparative judgement to obtain a highly reliable rank order in summative assessment (2012)
12. Heldsinger, S., Humphry, S.: Using the method of pairwise comparison to obtain reliable teacher assessments. Aust. Educ. Res. **37**(2), 1–19 (2010)
13. van Daal, T., Lesterhuis, M., Coertjens, L., Donche, V., De Maeyer, S.: Validity of comparative judgement to assess academic writing: examining implications of its holistic character and building on a shared consensus. Assess. Educ.: Princ. Policy Pract. 1–16 (2016)
14. Bramley, T.: Investigating the reliability of adaptive comparative judgment. Cambridge Assessment Research Report. Cambridge Assessment, Cambridge (2015). http://www.cambridgeassessment.org.uk/Images/232694-investigating-the-reliability-ofadaptive-comparative-judgment.pdf
15. Jones, I., Inglis, M.: The problem of assessing problem solving: can comparative judgement help?'. Educ. Stud. Math. **89**, 337–355 (2015)
16. Yeates, P., O'neill, P., Mann, K., Eva, K.: 'You're certainly relatively competent': assessor bias due to recent experiences. Med. Educ. **47**(9), 910–922 (2013)
17. Pollitt, A.: The method of adaptive comparative judgement. Assess. Educ.: Princ. Policy Pract. **19**(3), 281–300 (2012)
18. Bouwer, R., Koster, M.: Bringing writing research into the classroom: the effectiveness of Tekster, a newly developed writing program for elementary students, Utrecht (2016)
19. Bloxham, S., den-Outer, B., Hudson, J., Price, M.: Let's stop the pretence of consistent marking exploring the multiple limitations of assessment criteria. Assess. Eval. High. Educ. **41**(3), 466–481 (2016)
20. Gwet, K.L.: Handbook of Inter-Rater Reliability: The Definitive Guide to Measuring the Extent of Agreement Among Raters. Advanced Analytics, LLC, Gaithersburg (2014)
21. Lumley, T., McNamara, T.F.: Rater characteristics and rater bias: implications for training. Lang. Test. **12**(1), 54–71 (1995)
22. Thurstone, L.L.: Psychophysical analysis. Am. J. Psychol. **38**(3), 368–389 (1927)
23. Webb, N.M., Shavelson, R.J., Haertel, E.H.: 4 reliability coefficients and generalizability theory. Handb. stat. **26**, 81–124 (2006)
24. Jones, I., Swan, M., Pollitt, A.: Assessing mathematical problem solving using comparative judgement. Int. J. Sci. Math. Educ. **13**(1), 151–177 (2015)

25. McMahon, S., Jones, I.: A comparative judgement approach to teacher assessment. Assess. Educ.: Princ. Policy Pract. **22**, 1–22 (2014). (ahead-of-print)
26. Panadero, E., Jonsson, A.: The use of scoring rubrics for formative assessment purposes revisited: a review. Educ. Res. Rev. **9**, 129–144 (2013)
27. Arter, J., McTighe, J.: Scoring Rubrics in the Classroom: Using Performance Criteria for Assessing and Improving Student Performance. Corwin Press, Thousand Oaks (2000)
28. Fraile, J., Panadero, E., Pardo, R.: Co-creating rubrics: the effects on self-regulated learning, self-efficacy and performance of establishing assessment criteria with students. Stud. Educ. Eval. **53**, 69–76 (2017)
29. Andrich, D.: Relationships between the Thurstone and Rasch approaches to item scaling. Appl. Psychol. Meas. **2**(3), 451–462 (1978)
30. Bloxham, S., Price, M.: External examining: fit for purpose? Stud. High. Educ. **40**(2), 195–211 (2015)
31. Shrout, P.E., Fleiss, J.L.: Intraclass correlations: uses in assessing rater reliability. Psychol. Bull. **86**(2), 420 (1979)
32. Linacre, J., Wright, B.: Chi-square fit statistics. Rasch Meas. Trans. **8**(2), 350 (1994)
33. Pollitt, A.: Let's stop marking exams (2004)

Semi-automatic Generation of Competency Self-assessments for Performance Appraisal

Alexandre Baudet(✉), Eric Ras, and Thibaud Latour

IT for Innovative Services, Luxembourg Institute of Science and Technology, 5, Avenue des Hauts-Fourneaux, 4362 Esch-sur-Alzette, Luxembourg
{alexandre.baudet, eric.ras, thibaud.latour}@list.lu

Abstract. Competency self-assessment for Performance Appraisal is receiving increasing attention from both researchers and practitioners. Nevertheless, the accuracy and supposed legitimacy of this type of assessment is still an issue. In the context of an industrial use case, we aim to develop and validate a computer-based competency self-assessment technology able to import any type of competency document (for performance appraisal, training need identification, career guidance) and generate semi-automatically self-assessment items. Following the model of Appraisal Effectiveness designed by Levy and Williams, our goal was to build an effective tool meaning that several perspectives must be taken into account: psychometric, cognitive, psychological, political and the reaction's perspective. In this paper, we will only focus on one specific psychometric property (interrater reliability between an employee and its supervisor). According to a specific rating process and format, our Cross Skill™ technology showed promising results related to interrater reliability in a use case with bank officers and their supervisor.

Keywords: Competency Assessment · Interrater-reliability · Rating scale Cross Skill™

1 Introduction

To win the talent war, organizations have to master performance management (PM), including Competency Management (CM) and especially Competency Assessment (CA). Organizations have "to enhance their own competencies" and therefore to effectively assess them [1].

Competency modelling and assessment is a challenging "art" [2] that can lead to inconsistencies among model and assessment content [3]. As highlighted by Campion et al. [4], many challenges are proposed to academics and practitioners from which we will address the following ones:

- CA has to combine a great degree of *usability* without compromising the *psychometric validity* (e.g. accuracy, reliability, etc.).
- Competency models should be presented "in a manner that facilitates *ease of use*" with an organization-specific language.

E. Ras and A. E. Guerrero Roldán (Eds.): TEA 2017, CCIS 829, pp. 26–39, 2018.
https://doi.org/10.1007/978-3-319-97807-9_3

- As the amount of effort to define and update competencies can be an obstacle, a *cost-effective and meaningful* solution must be available for Human Resources (HR) services and job's incumbents.
- *Information Technology* has to enhance the effectiveness of competency modelling and assessments and not limit them.

Today, PM is a "continuous process of identifying, measuring, and developing the performance of individuals and teams and aligning performance with the strategic goals of the organization" [1]. PM entails six steps, including performance assessment and performance review [1]. As a growing trend [5], CA is now an essential sub-dimension of the performance assessment and review steps. Therefore, research and practice still face several challenges that led us to the design of a computer-based CA tool called Cross Skill™.

Our overall research aim was to build a usable, meaningful, cost-effective and accurate CA tool for every actor related to PA[1]. The research goal is refined into two main objectives:

1. Develop a CA generator in order to obtain a sound accuracy (including interrater reliability, which is the main focus of this article).
2. Develop item templates in order to increase the meaningfulness and cost-effectiveness of the competency modelling and assessment processes.

Section 2 will sum up the state of the art and practice about competency modelling, rating scales effectiveness and the related challenges and drawbacks of current solutions in which Cross Skill™ emerged. Section 3 elaborates on our solution which tackles the previously mentioned challenges. Section 4 describes a use case in finance where our technology has been tested. Section 5 discusses the data analysis and Sect. 6 reflects about our results and provides future avenues of research.

2 State of the Art and Practice

We will first explore the state of the art and state of the practice of competency modelling and then we will focus on the different rating scales and their effectiveness. Each subsection will highlight challenges to tackle.

2.1 Competency Modelling

If competency models (also called profiles) are a mandatory input to enhance CM and broadly every HR Management processes [5], their frame and content are very diverse and could illustrate many differences about competency modelling theories and practices. If PM consider performance - the *what* of a job - you cannot neglect competency - the *how* of a job, one of the main input needed to perform. One of the first challenge you face in the design of a CA solution, is the selection of a competency definition and

[1] Employees, supervisors and HR department in charge of building and updating Competency model and deploying related HR processes.

model. Depending on the country (USA, UK, Germany, France, etc.) or domain (Education, Management, Industrial and Organizational Psychology, etc.), hundreds of definitions are available but the definition to choose has to be theoretically relevant and usable in practice.

As a prerequisite with the definition of the assessment's purpose, organizations must choose between three competency modelling options: 1. purchasing a generic commercial Competency Dictionary (also called Library), 2. building their own Competency Dictionary from scratch or 3. considering a mixed option, meaning to build a tailor-made model with a generic Dictionary input. If a tailor-made Competency Dictionary may better reflect key competencies for an organization, it may also better express culture, values, vision of a unique organization [4].

If the "from scratch option" is risky because of the cost and the potential poor quality of the generated outcome, using a generic Competency Dictionary is also not the best practice. It may seem efficient [4] but we consider it efficient only at a short term. The costs of development of unique organization-language competencies you might save at a first glance, will negatively impact the meaningfulness and quality of the CA. The mixed option combines the advantages of the two others options, but even if the cost is lower compared to building a model from scratch, it remains still high. For each competency, it takes time and money to purchase a Competency Dictionary. Moreover, the tailoring phase to the particular needs of an organization requires relevant expertise to keep the tailored dictionary and assessments up-to-date. Although job's competencies needed to perform are constantly evolving (even minor changes can have big impact on performance) [6], this update task is unfortunately neglected.

In addition to a sound theoretical and practically usable definition, the competency model and its modelling option have to be cost-effective and able to produce meaningful content (competency labels and assessments). When a competency model is stable, then you can deploy several processes (e.g. objectives definition, monitoring and assessment). We will now detail the existing rating scales and their pros and cons.

2.2 Rating Scales Effectiveness

Several rating methods exist for Performance Appraisal (checklist, essay, comparison, rating scales, etc.) but we will only focus on rating scales because they are the most common. Following the model of Appraisal Effectiveness designed by Levy and Williams [7] for Performance, we consider that it can be extended to CA because Performance and Competence share common properties (for example accuracy, satisfaction, etc.) as suggested by Saint-Onge et al. [8].

Because rating scales effectiveness is a research topic in assessment since long, several perspectives exist. As our goal for Cross Skill™ is to build an effective CA tool, several perspectives have therefore been taken into account: psychometric, cognitive, psychological or political for example. For this paper, we are going to focus on one specific psychometric property, i.e., interrater reliability. Other psychometric properties and other effectiveness perspectives of CA will be addressed in future publications.

From a psychometric perspective, maximizing CA's accuracy is the goal of every rater.

Mainly based on psychometric objectives, researchers built different rating scales with their own advantages and weaknesses. Nevertheless, till today, none of the existing scales has evolved to become the most effective. The Graphic Rating Scale (GRS) is the most common scale, it is very cheap to develop but it has limitations regarding accuracy and lack specificity. The Behaviorally Anchored Rating Scale (BARS) and the Computerized Adaptive Rating Scale (CARS) both contain "specific performance-relevant behaviors of varying levels of effectiveness" [9] and both seem to be more valid and reliable. But contrary to GRS, BARS and CARS have very high development costs.

If the time and effort required to design and update rating scales can be a cue for the cost effectiveness of CA, interrater reliability could be an indicator of a valid and reliable rating scale. Indeed, Conway and Huffcutt [10] considered "important to examine correlations between pairs of rating sources in order to determine whether these sources contribute unique perspectives on performance[2]." Researchers highlighted that the discrepancies between two sources are high, especially between the self-assessment of a subordinate and the assessment of the same subordinate by its supervisor ($r = 0.19$ for [10]; $r = -0.09$ for [11]). This specific subordinate-supervisor dyad is the most important one in performance and competency management and that's why we choose to focus on it in this article.

As a pragmatic objective for an HR CA tool, accuracy and cost effective deployment and management are essential. Without accuracy, rating may lead to inappropriate assessment and unfair and inefficient human resource management. Without cost-effectiveness, the "best" accurate tool may be ignored because cost, accessibility, and face validity are the first criteria when selecting an assessment tool [12].

To sum up, we identified in the previous parts the following issues:

- Competency models have to meet two conflicting objectives: 1. allow a reasonable development and update cost of the modelling but also, 2. provide a meaningful competence model for end-users. HR departments should not use a sterile and alien language of researchers and they also have to avoid simplistic and parsimonious models [4].
- Rating scales are diverse but cannot yet combine cost-effectiveness and accuracy. As GRS are cost-effective but inaccurate, others like BARS or CARS are the other side of the coin: potentially accurate but not cost-effective, i.e., each competency needs an expensive process of modelling with specific criteria in order to guarantee the use of an organizational-language competency set.

As a consequence of these drawbacks, it's logic that PA and CA often leads to dissatisfaction. The following section will present our solution to tackle these issues.

[2] We extended this consideration to competency.

3 Our Solution to Tackle the Challenges: Cross Skill™

We developed a semi-automatic generator of CA and tested it in real life settings for a Performance Appraisal purpose [13]. The tool has also been tested for other purposes (training plan identification, career guidance) but this is out of scope of this paper.

Our first choice, in order to ease the management of the different competency processes was to select the Knowledge, Skills and Attitudes taxonomy (KSA). If several weaknesses are known, the KSA taxonomy has the advantage to be well-known and easily understandable by proficient and "naïve" potential end-users of our solution. "Influential" in the training and HR world, two of our targets, KSA is "fairly universal" and "clearly consistent with the French approach (savoir, savoir-faire, savoir-être)" [14], one of the border countries which influence Luxembourgish CA practices. A competency is therefore broken down into three subdimensions or resources.

As KSA is chosen and explained as the assessment's object, we will now elaborate our decision to use a specific type of rating method, implemented by item templates [15]. We will first explain the different phases of the test generation process before we detail the item templates, the item sequencing and finally the item responses used.

3.1 Cross Skill™ Test Generation Process

The Cross Skill™ process consists of four phases. The first two phases are dedicated to modelling competencies, whereas the third phase uses the model to generate a random and adaptive test. The last phase generates a results report based on the scores of the test (Fig. 1).

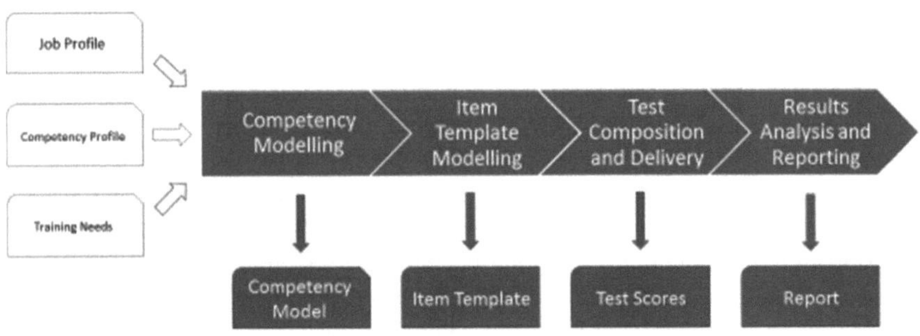

Fig. 1. Cross Skill™ test generation process

By using a competency model and generic item templates, Cross Skill™ allows institutions to keep their specific competency vocabulary ("organizational language") which is not the case when an off the shelf commercial Competency Dictionary is used.

Typically, in order to define a KSA-based competence model from scratch, we use job profiles if they exist. Additionally, specific competency profiles from the institution might exist or even PA reports. Another source of information are training needs reports which might be available from previous PA. The influence of a KSA element on the final proficiency level can be defined by specifying weights in the model.

During the second phase, the test designer prepares the item templates, which defines the structure of the stem as well as the placeholders to retrieve the KSA elements of the competence model. An example of an item template is provided in the Sect. 3.3.

During the third phase, Cross Skill™ generates test items which are then composed to form a test for CA. Item templates, item responses and item sequencing (i.e., random and adaptive) will be detailed in Sect. 3.3.

After taking the test, Cross Skill™ immediately generates a report based on the test scores and weightings in the competency model. Till today, the results report is a common report as you can find them in other commercial solutions.

The following subsections elaborate in detail the item templates and options which allow Cross Skill™ to (semi)automatically generate an adaptive and random CA.

3.2 Item Templates

Following a similar approach as presented by Ras et al. [3], Cross Skill™ items - illustrating competencies - are generated from so-called item templates. Item templates for Automatic Item Generation (AIG) have been deeply studied by cognitive, educational and psychometrics researchers; we applied the AIG process partly to meet the HR objective of our tool. Because "classical" AIG process [15] may lead to higher validity but it is expensive and hardly understandable for the HR community[3], we simplified[4] the process (avoiding the cognitive modelling phase for example) and built three item templates for the three types of resources of the KSA taxonomy: knowledge, skills and attitudes.

Attitudes are handled by a classical frequency scale (Behaviorally Observation Scale) where the rater has to precise the frequency of a behavior. Knowledge and skill have similar item templates with hardcoded competency proficiency criteria (knowledge transfer, vocabulary mastery, autonomy, situation complexity[5], etc.).

With current tools and practices, for every new competency or competency updates, organizations have to organize Subject Matter Expert meetings to build every component (label, definition, proficiency indicators, etc.).

The three Cross Skill™ item templates free HR officers of creating specific competency proficiency criteria, and like Graphic Rating Scale (GRS), the CA update process is straight forward.

The following snapshot illustrates the Cross Skill™ module of item templates, with a focus on the Skill (named Know-How in the tool) item template.

XXXPlaceholderXXX (element) is automatically filled (in the stem/prompt level 1..4) with the upload of a competency document, called Skill-cards in the Fig. 2.

If the typographic syntax rules in the item template are well respected in a competency profile (mandatory input), no extra-manual work is needed when a profile is

[3] The privileged criteria by end-users when choosing assessment tool are cost, practicality, legality and not always validity. See [12].

[4] Comment about the potential consequences are in Sect. 6.2.

[5] The detailed list is under patent filing. https://www.google.com/patents/EP3188103A1?cl=en.

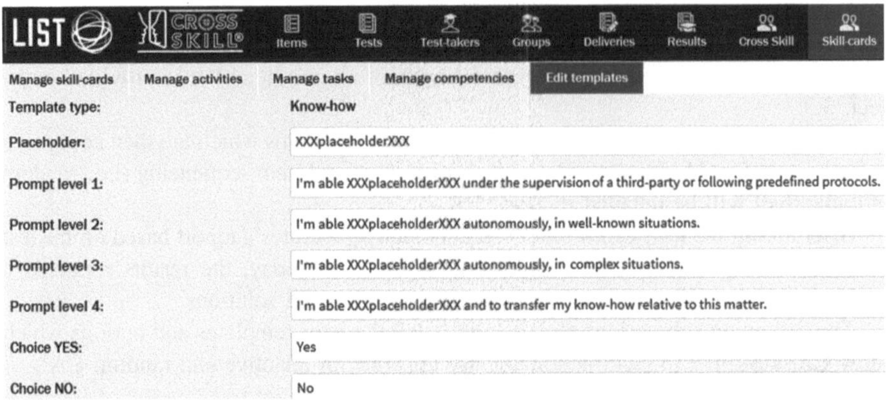

Fig. 2. Screenshot of the Cross Skill™ module with a focus on the skill item template.

uploaded to *automatically* generate CA. With a few clicks the test (items and sequencing) is generated. Manual editing (meaning a *semi-automatic* generation) is most of the time related to definite articles with specific languages (English, French, German and Luxemburgish are available), to the singular/plural form of objects, punctuation, uppercase, etc.

After presenting the first element of an item template (i.e. stem), we will now focus on the item sequencing and response options.

3.3 Item Sequencing and Item Response Options

Random and adaptive strategies have been chosen to reduce the appraisal duration (and therefore fatigue) as a cost-effectiveness objective but also to guarantee a reasonable accuracy.

The rating scale and response for Attitudes have been chosen to allow easy automatic generation (i.e., to address cost-effectiveness objective) and also to fit with current practices. The item response options for Knowledge and Skill (i.e. Yes/No response option) were selected to obtain a reasonable accuracy. Despite the weaknesses of the dichotomous response format, we still choose it because potential advantages might overcome the existing weaknesses of other formats. It will be presented in the last part of Sect. 3.3.

Item Sequencing: Random and Adaptive Features

For each knowledge and each skill, the test-taker has to answer between two to three questions (out of a 4-level scale). In order to have similar appraisal duration for experts and beginners, the test designer can influence the generation process by specifying the first and second proficiency level displayed to the test-taker (called CSI first and first level alternative in the Fig. 3 below). The designer can choose any level (out of 4) as first question.

Fig. 3. Snapshot of the test generator with the randomization and first question selection (choice between 4 proficiency levels)

If the test displays as a first question the 1st level (beginner), a beginner has only one question to answer but an expert would have three or four. And vice-versa.

As the test displays the X + 1 question according to the response to X question, in order to save time, the test can be called "adaptive" (but without link to IRT). The test is delivered using the TAO™ platform.

In addition to be adaptive, we have also decided to randomize items in order to reduce the motivation to bias and also the possibility to bias the rating (see the model of faking of Goffin and Boyd [16]). By making the items random, we aim to reduce the "fakeability" of our test, considering that transparent "items" and understandable scales increase desirable response (e.g. according to humble or very confident personality tendencies) [16–19].

Contrary to existing "transparent" scales (BOS, BARS, but also our scale for Attitudes), our scales for knowledge and skills are not "transparently" displayed to the test-taker, he will not see the four proficiency levels of a skill item for example.

In other words, a set of four questions to assess a skill can be scattered by Cross Skill™ during generation process and randomized with every other KSA type. As shown in the Fig. 4 below, Cross Skill™ may deliver as a first question, a knowledge item (K2: 2nd proficiency level), then alternatively display an attitude item (upper part of the figure) or if you follow the lower part of the tree, a skill item (S1: 1st proficiency level). The test-taker will then answer to another knowledge item (K3: 3rd level) or another knowledge item (4th level), etc. Maybe 10 or 20 questions later, the same first knowledge item (K2) might be again assessed with the X + 1 or X − 1 level, according to the test taker's previous answer. Finally, after completing each path (finding the final rating of each KSA), Cross Skill™ will display the report.

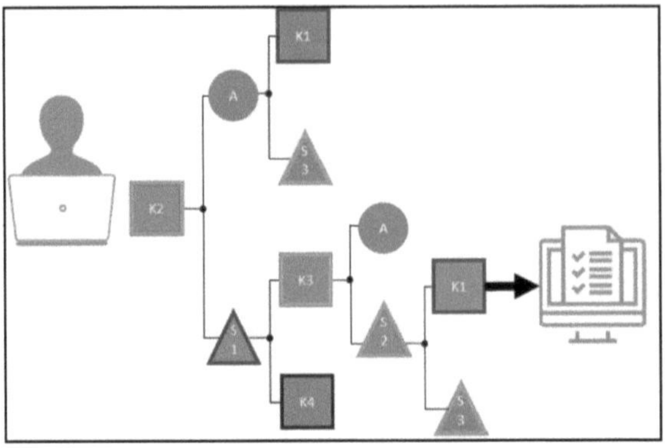

Fig. 4. Example of an adaptive test

Yes/No Response Option for Knowledge and Skill Items

For knowledge and skill items, Cross Skill™ rating format displays a kind of a forced-choice method with only one statement where the test taker has to answer *Yes* or *No* according to the proficiency level of the rater.

As mentioned in Sect. 2, if several rating formats exist, none have reached a perfect consensus in terms of superior accuracy compared to others. We dig out this "old" question by trying a new option inspired by literature related to the transparency of a construct [19] and the desire to overestimate or underestimate a construct [16].

For Cross Skill™, we selected the closed-ended responses option and especially dichotomous yes/no response. For knowledge and skill elements, it has the advantage to be quick to administer and easy to score. Close-ended responses have less depth and richness than open questions but analyzing the responses is straightforward [20]. Dichotomous response may reduce the "flexibility to show gradation" in an opinion (as in a CA) and test-taker may become frustrated but this "transparent" gradation in continuum for example (e.g. from 1 to 5 or to 10) are, to our opinion, one of the reason of low validity and weak interrater reliability.

4 Use Case: "Luxbank"

4.1 Design

"Luxbank" is a Luxembourgish bank who tested the Cross Skill™ tool in order to facilitate its annual performance appraisal for their subordinates (self-assessment) and their supervisors (assessment of their subordinates). The test took place from January to April 2016 and no administrative decision has been formally made with Cross Skill™ results (as a request from the management). This condition may help to have good interrater reliability compared to formal higher stake assessment (salary, bonuses, etc.). Nevertheless, we still think that this assessment has been perceived as a high stake assessment, at least by subordinates, because the subordinates were the ones may suffer the strongest consequences on their careers.

The sample of this study was composed of 59 employees (38 male; 21 female) who share a similar set of competencies from two jobs profiles (30% of account manager and 29% of sales officers).

Employees self-assessed their competencies ("I'm able to") with Cross Skill™. 59 assessments of the subordinates have been made by their supervisors ("My subordinate is able to") with Cross Skill™.

Tests were available in French and Luxemburgish in order to allow taking the test in their native language. As a first level (Fig. 3) to display to the test-taker, we choose the 2nd proficiency level and the 3rd as an alternative level, because as previously mentioned it generates homogeneous test durations for "junior" and "senior".

Post-CA satisfaction has been measured for subordinates and supervisors with structured interviews and a usability questionnaire. Even if we are aware that satisfaction is critical for an assessment tool, we will not detail this part and only focus on psychometric criteria of the effectiveness. Nevertheless, both interviews and questionnaires highlighted very positive opinions.

4.2 Results

Cronbach's alpha for the shared set of competencies (the overall composite score) used for further interrater analyses are 0.90 for the self-assessment and 0.81 for supervisor assessment, which indicates a high level of internal consistency for the Cross Skill™ CA.

For an average of 29 competencies per competency profile, the average duration of a self-assessment or supervisor's assessment was 12 min. On average, each competency profile was composed of one Knowledge, eight Skills and 20 Attitudes resources. Every resource has the same weight in the competency profile.

The statistical analysis was made with SPSS 18. Our data are normally distributed.

On average, subordinates have a global score of 79.7/100 (SD = 9.14) for the Cross Skill™ competency self-assessment, 76.8/100 for supervisors (SD = 13.0). The global score is the addition of every resource's score (K+S+A) and as in PA, we assume that this global score is composed of items (K+S+A) that assess the same construct, for example a "Job's overall Competency".

On average, for the *Knowledge* resource (i.e., one item), subordinates have a score of 89.8/100 (SD = 22.3) for the self-assessment, 86/100 for supervisors (SD = 24.7). On average, for the *Skill* resource (eight items), subordinates have a score of 89.8/100 (SD = 22.3) for the self-assessment, 86/100 for supervisors (SD = 24.7). On average, for the *Attitude* resource (20 items), subordinates have a score of 76.3/100 (SD = 9.8) for the self-assessment, 73.3/100 for supervisors (SD = 12.3).

The interrater reliability (Pearson correlation for continuous variables) between the global scores of the subordinate and supervisor CA revealed to be significant with r (59) = .26, $p < .048$. Our main focus is on the global score as it is the case in many organizations: Sometimes the global score of a CA is used as a cut-off score to give bonus, promotion, etc. Note that contrary to the global score, the three resources (K, S, A) do not reveal any significant interrater correlations.

Age, gender, experience or other variables have normal distributions and no impact on inferential statistics.

5 Discussion

Consistent with the PA literature [10], our sample revealed higher self-assessment scores compared to supervisor's assessments. Without objective measure, no one can say if subordinates are overconfident, supervisors severe or both.

The sample also showed that low correlations between self-ratings and ratings from the supervisors. For the global CA's score, our sample gave slightly better correlations (r = .26 compared to .19 for Conway et al. [10]) but these are still low correlations and subdimensions (K, S, A) were not significantly correlated. If it is "unreasonable to expect interrater reliabilities of job performance ratings for single raters to exceed .60" [21] and by extension for our competency ratings, there is still room for improvement for the global scores and the subscores. As we will detail it in the limitations of this article, for the present study, we conclude that our low correlations can be explained by our relatively small sample size. Note that our future publication with bigger samples and different jobs (e.g. 357 mechanics and their supervisors) revealed a much higher correlation (r = .59) for the global score but also high and significant correlations for the subscores.

Our data analysis showed few "extreme" discrepancies between self and supervisor overall ratings. For example, one supervisor gave very low ratings (more than 25% lower as the subordinates) in comparison with high self-ratings. These three dyads' ratings negatively impacted the magnitude of the sample's interrater correlation. By removing these three outliers we reach $r(56) = .41$, $p < .012$ for the global score. If a correlation of .26 is a correct result according to literature, .41 is a much more encouraging sign to pursue our research.

As we did with several supervisors and subordinates after the assessment period, we also conducted an interview between the "severe" supervisor and one of the subordinates in order to discuss results and the satisfaction of the process. Nothing relevant came out from the subordinates' interview. Nevertheless, the supervisor told us that during the test, when he[6] had doubts about the rating, he always chose the lowest level. He also confided that he considers himself as a severe supervisor in terms or ratings, and that our tool confirmed logically his tendency. He also thinks that this formal comparison done with Cross Skill™ may help him to revise his judgements (meaning give higher and more fair ratings). Whatever he did it later or not, for this specific supervisor, our tool (partly) failed to mitigate bias, in this case, to reduce severity. On the contrary, if he will really give higher ratings in the future, this is also positive because the given ratings will reflect more the "truth".

According to the internal consistency analysis, the Cronbach's alpha (both superior to .80) is satisfying. This is a good result showing that despite the random feature of the Cross Skill™, reliability is still satisfactory. This positive result confirms also other future publications (work in progress) which can be compared to test-retest reliability analyses made with two other samples (T2 ran between 2 and 8 weeks after T1): both analyses obtained good (superior to .80) results for self-assessment and for supervisor assessment.

---

6 The masculine is used in this publication without prejudice for the sake of conciseness.

6 Conclusion and Future Work

In this paper we demonstrated the implementation and preliminary validation of a Competency Assessment technology for Performance Appraisal, following the application of the model of Appraisal Effectiveness [7]. This model illustrates the research-practice gap in appraisal and our article is one of the needed operationalization academics and practitioners have to investigate to decrease the end-users' disappointment.

Focusing in this article on a psychometrics' effectiveness point of view, we managed to obtain an interesting result for the overall CA's interrater reliability (r = .26) but no significant correlations for subdimensions. If interrater correlations higher than .60 are utopic, researchers and practitioners must act to reduce "abnormal" discrepancies between raters (e.g., due to bad tools, non-trained raters) because it can lead to career failure. A disagreement between two raters can highlight different but "true" opinions about the assessed construct. But other disagreement can be explained by weaknesses (personality biases, tool's, etc.) which Cross Skill™ may at least reduce.

6.1 How Drawbacks Have Been Addressed

In Sect. 2 we identified two issues:

- the competency model development and update's effectiveness (meaningfulness for every actor and cost-effectiveness)
- the lack of interrater reliability for CA.

Using the KSA taxonomy to ease the understanding and using by end-users, we developed item templates in order to provide a cost-effective CA generator. Instead of running subject-matter expert groups to define or update competency documents, our generator can, almost instantly, create new competencies and assessment statements.

In addition to cost-effectiveness, our generic item templates are also useful to allow organizations to keep their organization-language competencies [4].

Although several of our design choices[7] may have had negative consequences on interrater correlation, our use case highlighted interesting interrater correlation results.

We assume that the ability to allow the use of organization-language in competency profiles, our specific "hidden" rating format and random sequencing could be explanations of our results. Even when high discrepancies were found between three dyads, our tool might be helpful to generate constructive discussion during a PA as mentioned during the "severe" supervisor's interview.

From a theoretical perspective, to the best of our knowledge, this use case represents the first time that the Performance Appraisal Effectiveness literature is used for a Competency Appraisal Effectiveness use case. According to our use case, research related to bias in Performance Appraisal and their consequences on interrater reliability seem to be also applicable to Competency Assessment. Although it is suggested in

[7] KSA taxonomy, generic proficiency criteria in our item templates instead of specific criteria- for each competency, random sequencing, adaptive test, etc.

some Canadian studies [22], to the best of our knowledge, no applied research has been conducted until now.

Despite positive results about the challenges addressed, our research shows some limits we have to mention.

6.2 Limitations and Future Work

On the one hand, our design choices (KSA, rating format and response options) can be criticized but on the other hand, they might be the reasons of our preliminary positive results. In line with the comment of an anonymous reviewer, the dichotomous responses are cost-effective but may lead to problematic inaccuracies (validity mainly). Nevertheless, following the results of a parallel project, we showed that despite the dichotomous response of our competency self-assessment, we reached a significant and positive convergence with an objective multiple choice questionnaire (assessing the same competencies): $r(326) = .55$, $p < .01$.

As our results are only slightly better as those demonstrated by Conway et al. [10] for example, and only significant for the overall score, work is still needed to increase the interrater reliability correlations and increase the generalizability of our results with bigger samples (the main limit of our use case), with managerial positions (known to be harder in terms of interrater reliability) and with a variety of blue and white-collar jobs.

If we consider that interrater correlation is an important issue, we still have to admit that we only addressed a limited portion of the psychometrics' effectiveness of our CA tool. Moreover, as mentioned in Sect. 2.2, psychometrics' effectiveness is important for CA's overall effectiveness, but many other perspectives (related to personality, fairness, reactions, cognitive, etc.) have to be assessed to obtain an overall effective tool [7]. A hard challenge will also be to distinguish the contribution (positive or negative) of several variables to the validity and reliability of the CA (Cross Skill™ rating scales, random sequencing, specificity of use case, etc.). The main challenge will be to find the right balance between psychometrics "guarantees" (ignoring the cognitive modelling phase is a risk that we took consciously) and the usability for HR Department and CA's end-users (not always interested in psychometrics issues).

In terms of Cross Skill™'s effectiveness, two main future activities are planned: (1) increase the level of automation of the item generation process so as to limit the effort of adapting competency statements from competency profile into Cross Skill™ compliant competency statements and (2) increase the variety of assessments statements (isomorphic statements for the same proficiency level) generated in order to reduce fatigue effect and increase the accuracy by limiting the transparency of the scale.

References

1. Aguinis, H.: Performance Management. Pearson Prentice Hall, Upper Saddle River (2013)
2. Lucia, A.D., Lepsinger, R.: The Art and Science of Competency Models: Pinpointing Critical Success Factors in Organizations. Jossey-Bass, San Francisco (1999)
3. Ras, E., Baudet, A., Foulonneau, M.: A hybrid engineering process for semi-automatic item generation. In: Joosten-ten Brinke, D., Laanpere, M. (eds.) TEA 2016. CCIS, vol. 653, pp. 105–116. Springer, Cham (2017). https://doi.org/10.1007/978-3-319-57744-9_10

4. Campion, M.A., Fink, A.A., Ruggeberg, B.J., Carr, L., Phillips, G.M., Odman, R.B.: Doing competencies well: best practices in competency modeling. Pers. Psychol. **64**, 225–262 (2011)
5. Spencer, L.M., Spencer, S.M.: Competence at Work. Models for Superior Performance. Wiley, New York (1993)
6. Vincent, C., Rainey, R., Faulkner, D., Mascio, C., Zinda, M.: How often should job descriptions be updated? Annual Graduate Conference in Industrial-Organizational Psychology and Organizational Behavior, Indianapolis, IN (2007)
7. Levy, P.E., Williams, J.R.: The social context of performance appraisal: a review and framework for the future. J. Manag. **30**, 881–905 (2004)
8. Saint-Onge, S., Morin, D., Bellehumeur, M., Dupuis, F.: Manager's motivation to evaluate subordinate performance. Qual. Res. Organ. Manag.: Int. J. **4**, 272–293 (2009)
9. Darr, W., Borman, W., St-Pierre, L., Kubisiak, C., Grossman, M.: An applied examination of the computerized adaptive rating scale for assessing performance. Int. J. Sel. Assess. **25**, 149–153 (2017)
10. Conway, J.M., Huffcutt, A.I.: Psychometric properties of multi-source performance ratings: a meta-analysis of subordinate, supervisor, peer, and self-ratings. Hum. Perform. **10**, 331–360 (1997)
11. Atwater, L.E., Yammarino, F.J.: Does self-other agreement on leadership perceptions moderate the validity of leadership and performance predictions? Pers. Psychol. **45**, 141–164 (1992)
12. Furnham, A.: HR professionals' beliefs about, and knowledge of, assessment techniques and psychometric tests. Int. J. Sel. Assess. **16**, 300–305 (2008)
13. Baudet, A., Gronier, G., Latour, T., Martin, R.: L'auto-évaluation des compétences assistée par ordinateur: validation d'un outil de gestion des carrières. In: Bobillier Chaumon, M.E., Dubois, M., Vacherand-Revel, J., Sarnin, P., Kouabenan, R. (eds.) La question de la gestion des parcours professionnels en psychologie du travail. L'Harmattan, Paris (2013)
14. Winterton, J., Delamare Le Deist, F., Stringfellow, E.: Typology of Knowledge, Skills and Competences: Clarification of the Concept and Prototype. Cedefop Reference Series, vol. 64. Office for Official Publications of the European Communities, Luxembourg (2006)
15. Luecht, R.M.: An introduction to assessment engineering for automatic item generation. In: Gierl, M.J., Haladyna, T.M. (eds.) Automatic Item Generation. Routledge, New York (2013)
16. Goffin, R.D., Boyd, A.C.: Faking and personality assessment in personnel selection: advancing models of faking. Can. Psychol. **50**, 151–160 (2009)
17. Alliger, G., Lilienfeld, S., Mitchell, K.: The susceptibility of overt and covert integrity tests to coaching and faking. Psychol. Sci. **7**, 32–39 (1996)
18. Furnahm, A.: Response bias, social desirability and dissimulation. Pers. Individ. Differ. **7**, 385–406 (1986)
19. Tett, R.P., Christiansen, N.D.: Personality tests at the crossroads: a response to Morgeson, Campion, Dipboye, Hollenbeck, Murphy, and Schmitt. Pers. Psychol. **60**, 967–993 (2007)
20. Kline, T.: Psychological testing: a practical approach to design and evaluation. Sage Publications, Thousand Oaks (2005)
21. Viswesvaran, C., Ones, D.S., Schmidt, F., Le, H., Oh, I.-S.: Measurement error obfuscates scientific knowledge: path to cumulative knowledge requires corrections for unreliability and psychometric meta-analyses. Ind. Organ. Psychol. **7**, 505–518 (2014)
22. Foucher, R., Morin, D., Saint-Onge, S.: Mesurer les compétences déployées en cours d'emploi: un cadre de référence. In: Foucher, R. (ed.) Gérer les talents et les compétences, Tome 2, pp. 151–222. Editions Nouvelles, Montréal (2011)

Case Study Analysis on Blended and Online Institutions by Using a Trustworthy System

M. Elena Rodríguez[1], David Baneres[1(✉)], Malinka Ivanova[2], and Mariana Durcheva[2]

[1] Open University of Catalonia, Rambla del Poblenou, 156, Barcelona, Spain
{mrodriguezgo,dbaneres}@uoc.edu
[2] Technical University of Sofia, Kl. Ohridski 8, Sofia, Bulgaria
{m_ivanova,m_durcheva}@tu-sofia.bg

Abstract. For online and blended education institutions, there is a severe handicap when they need to justify how the authentication and authorship of their students are guaranteed during the whole instructional process. Different approaches have been proposed in the past but most of them only depend on specific technological solutions. These solutions in order to be successfully accepted in educational settings have to be transparently integrated with the educational process according to pedagogical criteria. This paper analyses the results of the first pilot based on the TeSLA trustworthy system for a blended and a fully online institutions focused on engineering academic programs.

Keywords: Trustworthy system · Authentication · Authorship
Blended learning · Fully online learning

1 Introduction

Assessment of students in online and blended education is one of the most important ongoing challenges [1–3]. Educational institutions are, in general, resistant to wager for an online education and, at the end, keep relying on traditional assessment systems such as final on-site exams, face-to-face meetings, etc. Unfortunately, this attitude is shared by accrediting quality agencies and society at large, being reluctant to give the social recognition or credibility that online alternative may deserve [4]. This causes obstacles in the acceptance of online and blended education as an alternative to the traditional model. However, many citizens simply cannot continuously attend an on-site institution, especially in regards to higher and lifelong learning education and new approaches are needed to fulfil the requirements of these students [5–7].

The TeSLA project [8] has appeared to give an answer to this challenge. The overall objective of the project is to define and develop an e-assessment system, which provides an unambiguous proof of students' academic progression during the whole learning process to educational institutions, accrediting quality agencies and society, while avoiding the time and physical space limitations imposed by face-to-face examination. The TeSLA project aims to support any e-assessment model (formative, summative and continuous) covering the teaching-learning process as well as ethical, legal and technological aspects. In order to do so, the project will provide an

E. Ras and A. E. Guerrero Roldán (Eds.): TEA 2017, CCIS 829, pp. 40–53, 2018.
https://doi.org/10.1007/978-3-319-97807-9_4

e-assessment system where multiple instruments and pedagogical resources will be available. The instruments may be deployed in the assessment activities to capture students' data to ensure their authentication and authorship. Such instruments need to be integrated into the assessment activities as transparent as possible and according to pedagogical criteria to avoid interfering in the learning process of the students.

The TeSLA project is funded by the European Commission's Horizon 2020 ICT program. In order to provide an achievable and realistic solution the consortium is composed of multiple Higher Education institutions (including online and blended universities), technological companies (specialised in security, cryptography and online recognition techniques) as well as accrediting quality agencies.

To test the e-assessment system the project plans to conduct three pilots from 500 students in the first to 20,000 in the third. This paper focuses on the first pilot of the project. Specifically, the paper aims to analyse and compare the challenges and findings of the preparation, execution and evaluation of the pilot in a blended institution and a fully online institution focused on academic engineering programs. This will help to identify the strengths and weaknesses to ensure a better design of the upcoming pilots.

The paper is structured as follows. Section 2 introduces the objectives of the first pilot, while Sect. 3 describes the used technological infrastructure. Next, the preparation and execution, and the evaluation are explained in Sects. 4 and 5, respectively. Finally, the conclusions and future work are detailed in Sect. 6.

2 Objectives of the First Pilot

The first pilot had several objectives. The most relevant one was related to the identification of the key phases (and the tasks included in each phase) of the pilot agreed for all the universities involved in the pilot. At this stage, the development of the TeSLA system was ongoing. Thus, the second objective was to use the instruments to ensure authentication and authorship of the assessment activities for validating how student's data should be collected, and for further testing of the instruments when the initial version of the system was ready. Also, the pilot aimed to identify legal/ethical issues at the institutional level, to identify the requirements of students with special educational needs and disabilities (SEND students), to envisage the critical risks at institutional level, and to study the opinions and attitudes of the participants (mainly students and teachers) towards the use of authentication and authorship instruments in assessment.

The expected number of participants for the first pilot was 500 students, homogeneously distributed among the 7 universities involved in the pilot (i.e. approximately 75 students per each university).

The instruments to be tested were face recognition, voice recognition, keystroke dynamics, forensic analysis and plagiarism. Face recognition uses web camera and generates a video file with the student's face. Voice recognition aims to record student's voice by creating a set of audio files. Keystroke dynamics is based on student's typing on the computer keyboard and recognises two key features: the time for key pressing and the time between pressing two different keys. The forensic analysis compares the writing style of different text typed by the same student and verifies that he/she is their author. Plagiarism checks whether the submitted documents by a student are his/her original work and they are not copy-pasted from other works. On the one hand, face recognition, voice recognition and keystroke dynamics allow students' authentication based on the analysis of captured images, audio and typing while the students perform an assessment activity. In the case of face and voice recognition, authentication can also be checked over assessment activities submitted by the students (for example, video/audio recordings). On the other hand, forensic analysis checks authentication and authorship based on the analysis of text documents provided by the same student, while plagiarism detects similarities among text documents delivered by different students ensuring thus authorship. The authentication instruments require learning a model for the user (i.e. a biometric profile of the student needs to be built). This model is used as a reference for subsequent checking.

The identified key stages of the pilot include three main phases: (1) preparation (2) execution and (3) reporting. At the preparation phase, each university designed its strategy and criteria for selecting the courses and for motivating the students' participation in the first pilot. Similarly, each university planned and designed the most appropriate assessment activities (and the instruments to be used in them for authentication and authorship purposes) to be carried out by the students participating in the pilot.

At the execution phase, the technological infrastructure provided for the execution of the first pilot was a Moodle instance for each university which constituted an early development of the TeSLA system. The execution phase is described next:

1. Sign consent: Students signed a consent to participate in the pilot due to the collection of personal data (i.e. biometric data) for authentication and authorship purposes.
2. Pre-questionnaire: Students and teachers gave their opinion about online learning and assessment and project expectations.
3. Enrollment activities: These special and non-assessment activities were designed to gather the required data to generate a biometric profile for each student.
4. Assessment (or follow-up) activities: Students solved and submitted some assessment activities using the Moodle instance.
5. Post-questionnaire: Students and teachers gave their opinion about the pilot experience.

At the reporting phase, all the collected information was analysed to obtain the findings related to the pilot preparation and execution.

3 Technological Infrastructure

Aforementioned, one of the objectives of the first pilot was to test how to collect data from participants. The TeSLA system was not ready at the beginning of the pilot. Therefore, another technological solution was required in order to conduct the pilot. Figure 1 illustrates the relationships between the stages of the pilot execution and the technological solutions used in the pilot that are almost similar for both universities – The Technical University of Sofia (TUS) that is a blended institution and the Open University of Catalonia (UOC) that is a fully online institution.

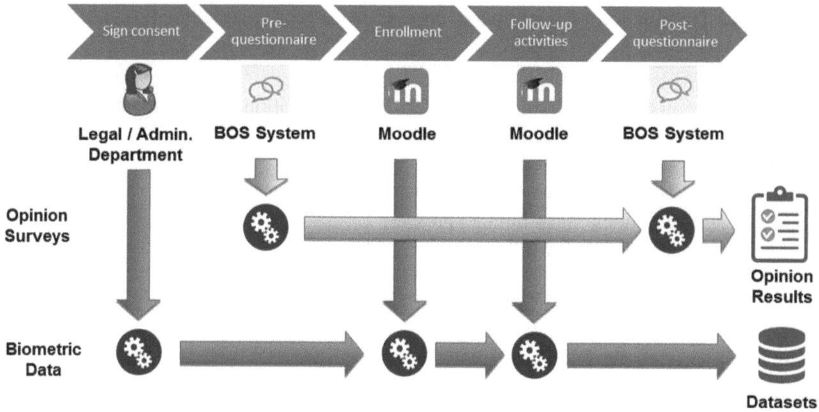

Fig. 1. Technological infrastructure and outputs produced in the pilot

In the beginning, the signature of a consent form was required to participate in the pilot. This step was critical because impersonation should be avoided. On the one hand, TUS decided that the process should be performed manually by signing a physical document. The students' registration was provided by university e-mail system. Administrative personal was responsible for processing and validation all the documents, and for validation the learners to the Moodle instance as students. On the other hand, at UOC, the signature of the consent form was managed by the legal department. The consent form was shared in the classrooms of the UOC virtual learning environment (VLE) in the course selected for the pilot. Students willing to participate sent an email (using their UOC credentials) which included personal information to the legal department who validated the petitions. Based on that, students were granted to access to the Moodle instance.

Questionnaires were handled by another tool, the BOS online survey tool [9]. It was used due to its flexibility to create personalised surveys and export the data for further analysis. Both TUS and UOC followed the same strategy. The links to the pre and post questionnaires for students were posted in the Moodle instance, while the links to the pre and post questionnaires for teachers were sent via email.

Finally, the instructional process concerning the pilot was performed on a standard instance of Moodle because it met all the requirements to carry out the pilot. Moodle [10] is capable of providing support during the teaching-learning process by accepting different learning resources (e.g. videos, wikis, electronics books, open source solutions, etc.), communication tools (e.g. forums, videoconferencing) and different assessment activities (e.g. documents submission, automated questionnaires, essays, question with open answer, third-party plugins etc.). The Moodle instances were standard ones without any adaptation. Only a third-party plugin was used to record online videos and audios from students and to capture their keystroke rhythms and texts for forensic analysis and plagiarism checking. For both universities the access to Moodle was using an LTI connection available in the classrooms. Note that, the collection process of all students' data was a post-process at the end of the pilot by

Table 1. Distribution of instruments on assessment activities and courses at TUS

Course	Assessment activity	Exercise	Face recognition	Keystroke dynamics	Forensic analysis
Internet Technologies	Continuous assessment Activity 1	Multiple-choice quiz combined with open answers	√	√	
	Continuous assessment Activity 2	Individual project work	√	√	
Computer Networks	Continuous assessment Activity 1	5 multiple choice quizzes	√	√	
	Continuous assessment Activity 2	2 practical tests	√	√	
Higher mathematics	Formative/summative assess. Activity 1	2 quizzes combined with open answers	√	√	
Course project on Information technologies in public administration	Continuous assessment Activity 1	Project analysis and investigation	√		√
	Summative assessment Activity 2	Project presentation	√		√

accessing to the Moodle database and extracting all data referred to the enrolment and follow-up activities. This information was stored as datasets for testing the real instruments for the second pilot.

4 Preparation and Execution at Institutional Level

This section discusses the preparation and execution phases of the first pilot of the TeSLA project in both institutions.

4.1 Blended Learning Institution

The Technical University of Sofia [11] is the largest educational institution in Bulgaria preparing professionals in the field of technical and applied science. The educational process occurs in contemporary lecture halls, seminar rooms and specialised laboratories following the principles of close connection with high-tech industrial companies, increased students' mobility and international scientific partnership. It is supported by the university VLE facilitating the access to educational content, important information and collected knowledge. Typically, the exams are organised in written form in face-to-face mode, but also assessment process is facilitated through quizzes, engineering tasks and projects organised in online form. The e-assessment is not well developed in TUS, because it is a blended-learning institution where the offline practical sessions play an important impact on the future engineers. Thus, the TeSLA project gives a new opportunity to enhance the assessment process by implementing new methodologies for improving students' knowledge and skills evaluation.

In the first pilot, several courses were involved: "Internet Technologies" and "Computer Networks" that belong to the College of Energy and Electronics and "Information Technologies", "Higher Mathematics" and "Project of IT in Public Administration" that are part of the curriculum of Faculty of Management. They were selected, because it was considered that different assessment models should be covered during the pilot: continuous, summative, formative and their combination, as well as to evaluate projects activities. Table 1 summarises the applied assessment models and used instruments. Face recognition, keystroke dynamics, and forensic analysis was tested. The same instruments were utilised during enrolment and all assessment activities planned for a given course. TUS team discussed whether to include the instrument for voice recognition and decided not to test it. The main reason is that this instrument does not match to the pedagogy of involved courses. For the included courses the most suitable instruments were face recognition and keystroke dynamics, and the instrument for forensic analysis in the course "Course project on IT in public administration". The TeSLA assessment activities were combined with standard face-to-face examination and thus TUS realised a blended assessment model.

A big part of students participated in the first pilot successfully accomplished the assessment tasks and their final grades were higher than the grades of the rest students. For instance, for the course "Higher mathematics", results of the exam of the students, who participated in TeSLA, are on average 10–15% higher than those of the other students. This phenomenon is explained for two different reasons: On the one hand, mainly motivated students, who have a deeper interest in science, participated in the pilot. On the other hand, the fact monitoring during the assessment also led the students who were less ambitious to take more care and effort. The teacher who tested a combination of the instruments face recognition and forensic analysis reported that most of the students in her course suggested innovative decisions in their course projects.

Participation in the pilot worked on a voluntary basis and the initial canvas was set to 240 students from the different faculties and departments. The involved students had to perform almost the same assessment activities than the rest of students who were not part of the pilot. The main reason for differences was the presumption for decreasing the number of assessment activities performed with instruments to 2 or 3 in comparison to the number of the assessment activities that were planned for the standard courses. This stems from the decision of the consortium the instruments to be tested in 1 enrollment activity and 1 or 2 follow-up activities. Also, there were differences in the form how these assessment activities were done. The students who were involved in the pilot had to perform their assessment activities in Moodle using the planned for testing instruments, while the other students performed their activities in a paper-based format, in other learning management system (LMS) or/and using other applications.

4.2 Fully Online Institution

The Open University of Catalonia (UOC) [12] is a fully online university that uses its own VLE for conducting the teaching-learning process. Currently, more than 53,000 students are enrolled in different undergraduate and postgraduate programmes. Present challenges at UOC are to increase the students' mobility and internationalisation. This leads to a situation where maintaining the requirement of a face-to-face, on-site evaluation at the end of each semester becomes inefficient and not cost effective. However, as a certified educational institution, the university cannot ignore the baggage in moving to a fully virtual assessment, since it might heavily impact on its credibility.

The course selected to participate in the first pilot of the TeSLA project was "Computer Fundamentals". The course belongs to the Faculty of Computer Science, Multimedia and Telecommunications, and it is a compulsory course of the Computer Engineering Degree and Telecommunications Technology Degree. In the course, the students acquire the skills of analysis and synthesis of small digital circuits and to understand the basic computer architecture.

The course has a high number of enrolled students, and a low ratio of academic success (40%–50% of enrolled students), mainly for course dropout. This is due to two main factors. On the one hand, the course is placed in the first academic year, i.e. it is an initial course that presents core concepts relevant for more complex courses (e.g. computer organisation, networking and electronic systems). On the other hand, most of the students have professional and familiar commitments, and they can have some problems until they find a balance between these factors, especially when they are unfamiliar with online learning. Nevertheless, the course was considered a suitable course to participate in the pilot due to the following reasons: (1) the feasibility of reaching the expected number of participants with only one course; (2) the course is taught by a researcher involved in the TeSLA project; and (3) students have technical expertise, helping to minimize problems regarding the use of the Moodle.

The delivery mode of the course is fully online, and the assessment model is continuous assessment combined with summative assessment at the end of the semester. Continuous assessment is divided into 3 continuous assessment activities (they assess numeral systems, combinational circuits and sequential circuits, respectively) and one final project (that assesses finite state machines design). Summative assessment is based on a final face-to-face exam. The final mark is obtained by combining the results of the continuous assessment activities, the final project and the exam. The students have to reach a minimum mark of 4 both in the exam and the final project to pass the course (the Spanish grading system goes from 0 to 10, being 5 the lowest passing grade).

Although participation in the pilot worked on a voluntary basis, students were encouraged to participate in the pilot. Firstly, the importance of the pilot was properly contextualised in the case of a fully online university. Secondly, given that participation in the pilot implied a certain workload on the students' side, the minimal mark for the final project was set to 3 instead of 4. Despite this, it was expected a low participation rate and a negative impact of the known dropout issue on the course. Thus, UOC team internally planned to involve at least 120 students in the pilot instead of the 75 participants agreed at the project level.

Table 2. Distribution of instruments on assessment activities at UOC

Assessment activity	Exercise	Face recognition	Voice recognition	Keystroke dynamics	Plagiarism
Continuous assessment activity 2	Short answer			√	√
	Video recording	√	√		
Continuous assessment activity 3	Short answer			√	√
	Video recording	√	√		
Final Project	Short answer			√	√
	Video recording	√	√		

The TeSLA instruments tested in the pilot were face recognition, voice recognition, keystroke dynamics, and plagiarism. In addition to enrollment activities, students performed some exercises included in the second and third continuous assessment activities and the final project (see Table 2). All the students enrolled in the course (independently whether they participated or not in the pilot) performed the same assessment exercises. Differences were related to the way these exercises were performed and submitted (in the Moodle instance with instruments enabled, e.g. keystroke dynamics) and in their format (instead of textual answers included in a file document delivered in the specific assessment space at the UOC VLE, students recorded videos that were uploaded to Moodle for being processed by the corresponding instruments).

5 Pilot Evaluation

This section evaluates the first pilot. For space constraints, the analysis mainly concentrates on preparation and execution phases. Firstly, evaluations for each institution are described independently. Next, a discussion is performed to detect common findings.

5.1 Blended Learning Institution

The students participated as volunteers and their dropout rate was minimal. The achieved final results are better than students' results who do not participate in the piloting courses. Therefore, it may be concluded that the first pilot had a positive impact on the academic success of the involved students.

For the first pilot, the canvas was set to 240 students from different faculties and departments to take part, but for some organisational reasons, the canvas was reduced to 202. TUS planned at least 150 of them to sign the consent form, but in fact 126 of them signed it, the others did not want, pointing out various reasons. For some courses, the TUS team arranged additional assignments (i.e. assignments that were not mandatory for passing the exam), only to test the TeSLA instruments. This is one of the reasons because some students did not want to take part in the pilot. Another reason they claimed was that they felt uncomfortable about cameras and microphones, as if someone was monitoring them, so they could not work calmly. There were also students who worried that someone could abuse their personal and biometric data.

The initial plan was to involve 70 students to test face recognition, but 90 were achieved. The main reason for this success was because the TUS team worked hard to explain to the student what the goal of the TeSLA project was, and assured them that their data would be secured, anonymised and encrypted and no one will be able to misuse their data. Students were made acquainted with the project aims and objectives face-to-face with a presentation. The information letter explaining the purpose of the TeSLA project and the role of TUS as a project partner was uploaded in Moodle. Also, it was distributed via a specially created e-mail distribution list for all piloting courses.

The TUS team thought that the keystroke dynamics instrument will be the most useful in its work and planned 95 students to test it. Finally, 84 students tested this instrument only for enrolment and 73 for real activities. The assessment activity that included quiz with questions from type essay was not planned in the curriculum of the course and such activity had to be additionally designed to satisfy the project requirements related to testing the keystroke dynamics instrument.

Except for the Faculty of Management, there are not many courses in TUS that are suitable for testing instruments like forensic analysis and plagiarism checking. Moreover, in the pilot, only teachers from TeSLA team were involved and this limited the diversity of the piloted courses. The plagiarism instrument was not tested, but the students expressed their desire to do that in the future. Considering this, TUS planned to collect only 10 documents (from a master course in Public Administration) for forensic analysis and not to test plagiarism instrument. All 17 students in the course agreed to test the instrument for plagiarism checking in the upcoming pilots.

Four SEND students were involved in the pilot – 1 student with a physical disability, 2 pregnant students and 1 who was a mother with small child. It is worth noting that they considered the TeSLA system as a new opportunity for the realisation of flexibility in e-assessment, because they would have the possibility to perform their activities online in time and place suitable for them.

During the first pilot, TUS faced different problems. The main problems can be summarised in the following way:

- Some of the students did not have the interest to be educated by new methods and a part of them (a small part) did not have an "intellectual curiosity"; there were students who afraid that new assessment methods would require more time to be spent and more efforts to be made. A small part of students explained that if something was not included in the curriculum they did not want to perform it.
- In some of the piloted courses, the course design was not the most suitable for the opportunity for technology supported performance by TeSLA; TUS is a blended institution and the typical assessment activities are related to standard online quizzes or creation of engineering schemes that not include, for example, voice recording or free text typing (except the students of the Faculty of Management).
- Some technical difficulties were met concerning plugins versioning and their integration in the Moodle instance.
- Additional laboratories for the TeSLA activities had to be arranged. For example, the students studying "Higher Mathematics" did not use any computer laboratories

for online knowledge testing, but with their involvement in the project required computer laboratories equipped with cameras to perform their assessment activities online.

To solve these problems, the TUS team applied different approaches:

- To stimulate students to participate by announcing some stimuli. To motivate students to participate in the first pilot, The TUS team used various stimuli, such as: follow-up activities to contribute to the mark of the final exams; to give the students certificates for participation in the pilot; to publish the best course works done during the project in a virtual library.
- To use more advertisement materials; TUS made a video in Bulgarian for presenting the TeSLA system. In this video, TeSLA members explained the purpose and the functionalities of the TeSLA system to different students. Questions and discussion were also recorded. The project was announced on the TUS website and different online media.
- To discuss the problems with TeSLA members of other universities.

From the first pilot, the TUS team learned various lessons. Some of them are:

- It is very useful to make a good presentation and to involve other media events in explaining the idea of the TeSLA project both to the teachers and to the students.
- There is a need of information dissemination in more and different media channels, especially multimedia, which is important for students at technical universities.
- There is a need for the announcement of proper stimuli to both teachers and students.
- In the next pilot it is natural to involve only courses in which assignments, projects and quizzes are provided during the semester, not only for the end of the semester;
- It is important to involve only teachers that have some experience with Moodle and other VLE.

5.2 Fully Online Institution

UOC exceeded its original plan of 120 students: 154 students signed the consent form (3 were SEND students, they reported mobility or physical impairment), but only 96 performed the enrolment activities (2 were SEND). Here, the effects of the dropout in the first-year course involved in the pilot was noticed in a small period of two weeks between the consent form signature and the enrolment activities processes (in this period students submitted the first continuous assessment activity proposed in the course). The course had more than 500 enrolled students. Thus, only the 30% of students accepted to participate. Most of the students were not interested in participating in a pilot that would imply more workload (their time is limited, they used to have professional and familiar commitments). So, even stimulating them to participate, they evaluated the effort. Moreover, some students were really concerned about sharing their biometric data. Also, some students did not have microphone and webcam on their computer.

When face and voice recognition is analysed, 86 of the 93 students continued the course and did the follow-up activities. Here, the course dropout had less impact in the pilot dropout, i.e. the students who were in the course mostly continued in the pilot.

Related to keystroke dynamics similar numbers were obtained. 90 out of 96 students performed the follow-up activities. Finally, documents of 83 students were collected for plagiarism checking. 2 SEND students completed all the follow-up activities.

For students within the course, not many technical issues were reported, probably their knowledge related to ICT reduced the potential issues. Moreover, some students found workarounds to do the activities when they faced an issue and shared their experience in the TeSLA forum created in the course classrooms in the VLE of the UOC.

The most important issues at UOC were:

- The consent form signature procedure required time and effort both to the students and to the legal department.
- Low involvement of SEND students. UOC has strict rules (related to the Spanish Act of Personal Data Privacy) regarding the communication with SEND students (they cannot be identified nor contacted, unless they share this information).
- Technical issues with the third-party plugin installed the Moodle instance (especially video recording).
- The correction of the follow-up activities (they had an impact in the marks) implied a workload for the teachers. Although the Moodle instance was accessible from the classroom, not all the exercises were delivered in the Moodle (i.e. some exercises were delivered in the devoted space in the UOC VLE). In addition, some students recorded several videos for the same exercise.
- The previous issue is also applicable to the students. They had a certain workload in performing and submitting the activities planned during the course and the pilot.
- The course dropout affected the pilot dropout.

To solve these problems, the UOC team applied different approaches:

- To isolate as much as possible the teachers from the set-up of the technological infrastructure (the Moodle instance) and the design of the enrollment and follow-up activities. This work was assumed by the teacher involved in the TeSLA project.
- Detailed information was provided to teachers and students to reduce overload, –e.g. Frequently Asked Questions (FAQ) and instructions were placed in the Moodle.

The UOC team has also learned several lessons for the upcoming pilots:

- To improve the consent form signing procedure to reduce its negative impact on the pilot participation.
- To design a strategy for the recruitment of SEND students.
- To select a combination of courses with a high number of students (probably with a high dropout) with courses with a lower number of students but with a good ratio of academic success, and promoting learning innovation (e.g. in the activities design).
- To plan extra courses (in the preparation phase) as a contingency plan, if required.
- To prioritise courses that commonly do assessment activities that produce data samples that are useful for testing the TeSLA instruments.
- To find a trade-off between educational and technological needs (e.g. use real activities as enrollment activities).

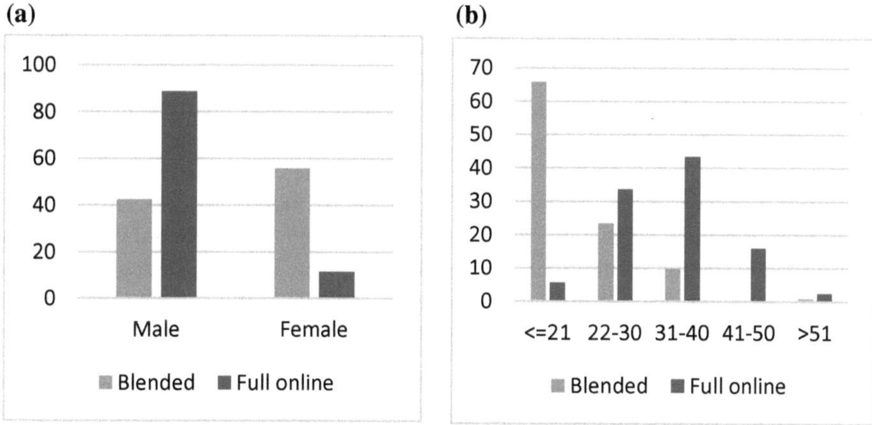

Fig. 2. (a) Gender distribution (%) on the pilot (b) Age distribution (%) on the pilot

- To ensure that follow-up activities have an impact in the marks.
- To guarantee that the TeSLA instruments, as much as possible, work transparently to the student (i.e. in background and integrated into the UOC VLE).
- To have access to the TeSLA system with enough time before the semester starts.
- To create multimedia material for advertising the pilot and the TeSLA project to students and teachers, for providing guidelines and tutorials for conducting the different phases of the pilot, amongst other.

5.3 Discussion

Regarding the demographic characteristics several differences can be observed between both institutions (see Fig. 2a and b). For gender, TUS had a more balanced participation, while at UOC the low presence of women can be observed (13%). This is due to the diversity of the selected courses in TUS. A closer look at the courses in TUS (not shown for space reasons) also shows a gender gap in the courses related to the ICT field ("Internet Technologies" and "Computer Networks") where only the 30% of the participants in the pilot were women. The low presence of women in STEM field and particularly in computer science has been deeply analysed in the literature [13] and cannot be attributed to the pilot. For example, in the case of UOC the 88% of the students enrolled in "Computer Fundamentals" were men, while the percentage of women was 12%. Therefore, women were well represented in the pilot. Concerning the age of participants, different results were also found. While in TUS students mostly enrol when they finish high school and are full-time students (the 63% are aged under 22 and only 12% have a full-time job), UOC students are incorporated into the labour market (the 62% are aged over 30 and the 75% have a full-time job). As in the case of gender, the participation in the pilot was not influenced by the age of the students.

Note that both TUS and UOC exceeded the expected number of participants in the pilot, although they mainly used different strategies. TUS involved 5 courses while UOC only involved one course. Selecting multiple courses in TUS had an added value that different assessment models were covered, but there was a trade-off between more data related to different assessment models and different types of assessment activities, and more complexity in the management of the pilot. As a common strategy, both institutions involved in the first pilot courses taught by teachers involved in the TeSLA project. At the end, both institutions learned that fewer courses improve the execution phase and obtaining more data can be accomplished by deploying different instruments in different activities in the same course. The students' motivation was also a crucial aspect. UOC anticipated that at the preparation phase, while TUS successfully managed it during the execution of the pilot. A shared good practice was to guarantee that the follow-up activities had a small impact in the students' final mark. Finally, the development of the pilot did not negatively affect the academic success of the students that participated in the pilot.

When problems are analysed, similar problems were detected in TUS and UOC. The most relevant ones were the technical issues. The TeSLA system was not ready and the Moodle instance only served as a temporal platform to conduct the piloted courses. It is expected that the technical problems would be mitigated in the upcoming pilots. UOC also pointed out the need of integrating the TeSLA instruments in its own VLE.

Another remarkable problem was the design of the follow-up activities to meet the technical requirements of collecting data for instruments testing. New assessment activities were introduced (sometimes artificially) to collect biometric data, and this is not a real objective of the TeSLA project. Therefore, it is needed that the TeSLA instruments would be transparently integrated into the instructional process. For example, for the next pilots, TUS and UOC plan to select some courses based on the assessment activities where the instruments could be transparently deployed. Another problem was how the TeSLA project should be explained to students and teachers. If the project (and the pilot) is not well explained to students, they may misunderstand the real objectives and they may feel that the university mistrust them. TUS and UOC agree that detailed information in textual and multimedia formats could be a good idea to describe the project to the different users of the project.

Finally, the schedule of the different phases of the pilot also influenced the pilot dropout negatively, especially at UOC. Follow-up activities should be started as soon as possible and this implies that preliminary steps (consent form signature and enrollment activities) should be performed in the first weeks or even before the course starts.

6 Conclusions and Future Work

This paper has presented a case study of a trustworthy based system in two institutions focused on engineering academic programs in two different contexts: blended and fully online learning. Although the system was not ready for the first pilot, a technological solution was found by using a Moodle instance in each university, which allowed that students involved in the pilot may carry out their assessment process without a negative impact on their academic success.

Even though students were significantly different in their demographic characteristics, the results analysis of the preparation and execution phases of the first pilot has pointed out the design of similar strategies, as well as the detection of analogous problems and learned lessons in TUS and UOC.

As future work, the learned lessons will be incorporated in the upcoming pilots of the TeSLA project as best practices in TUS and UOC, and their impact will be analysed. Furthermore, the analysis will be extended with the results of the other institutions of the project participating in the pilots, in order to detect the major issues and to share the best practices. The overall objective is to achieve a better integration of the instructional process with a technological solution oriented to enforce authentication and authorship.

Acknowledgements. This work is supported by H2020-ICT-2015/H2020-ICT-2015 TeSLA project "An Adaptive Trust-based e-assessment System for Learning", Number 688520.

References

1. Herr, N., et al.: Continuous formative assessment (CFA) during blended and online instruction using cloud-based collaborative documents. In: Koç, S., Wachira, P., Liu, X. (eds.) Assessment in Online and Blended Learning Environments (2013)
2. Kearns, L.R.: Student assessment in online learning: challenges and effective practices. J. Online Learn. Teach. **8**(3), 198 (2012)
3. Callan, V.J., Johnston, M.A., Clayton, B., Poulsen, A.L.: E-assessment: challenges to the legitimacy of VET practitioners and auditors. J. Vocat. Educ. Train. **68**(4), 416–435 (2016). https://doi.org/10.1080/13636820.2016.1231214
4. Kaczmarczyk, L.C.: Accreditation and student assessment in distance education: why we all need to pay attention. SIGCSE Bull. **33**(3), 113–116 (2001)
5. Walker, R., Handley, Z.: Designing for learner engagement with e-assessment practices: the LEe-AP framework. In: 22nd Annual Conference of the Association for Learning Technology, University of Manchester, UK (2015)
6. Ivanova, M., Rozeva, A., Durcheva, M.: Towards e-Assessment models in engineering education: problems and solutions. In: Chiu, D.K.W., Marenzi, I., Nanni, U., Spaniol, M., Temperini, M. (eds.) ICWL 2016. LNCS, vol. 10013, pp. 178–181. Springer, Cham (2016). https://doi.org/10.1007/978-3-319-47440-3_20
7. Baneres, D., Rodríguez, M.E., Guerrero-Roldán, A.E., Baró, X.: Towards an adaptive e-assessment system based on trustworthiness. In: Caballé, S., Clarisó, R. (eds.) Formative Assessment, Learning Data Analytics and Gamification in ICT Education, pp. 25–47. Elsevier, New York (2016)
8. The TeSLA Project. http://tesla-project.eu/. Accessed 3 July 2017
9. BOS Online Survey Tool. https://www.onlinesurveys.ac.uk/. Accessed 3 July 2017
10. Jason, C., Foster, H.: Using Moodle: Teaching with the Popular Open Source Course Management System. O'Reilly Media Inc., Sebastopol (2007)
11. The Technical University of Sofia. http://www.tu-sofia.bg/. Accessed 3 July 2017
12. The Universitat Oberta de Catalunya. http://www.uoc.edu/web/eng/. Accessed 3 July 2017
13. Barr, V.: Women in STEM, Women in Computer Science: We're Looking at It Incorrectly. BLOG@CACM, Communications of the ACM (2014). https://cacm.acm.org/blogs/blog-cacm/180850-women-in-stem-women-in-computer-science-were-looking-at-it-incorrectly/. Accessed 3 July 2017

Student Perception of Scalable Peer-Feedback Design in Massive Open Online Courses

Julia Kasch[1], Peter van Rosmalen[1,2(✉)], Ansje Löhr[3(✉)], Ad Ragas[3(✉)], and Marco Kalz[4(✉)]

[1] Welten Institute, Open University of the Netherlands, Heerlen, The Netherlands
julia.kasch@ou.nl
[2] Department of Educational Development and Research, Maastricht University, Maastricht, The Netherlands
p.vanrosmalen@maastrichtuniversity.nl
[3] Faculty Management, Science and Technology, Open University of the Netherlands, Heerlen, The Netherlands
{ansje.lohr,ad.ragas}@ou.nl
[4] Chair of Technology-Enhanced Learning, Institute for Arts, Music and Media, Heidelberg University of Education, Heidelberg, Germany
kalz@ph-heidelberg.de

Abstract. There is scarcity of research on scalable peer-feedback design and student's peer-feedback perceptions and therewith their use in Massive Open Online Courses (MOOCs). To address this gap, this study explored the use of peer-feedback design with the purpose of getting insight into student perceptions as well as into providing design guidelines. The findings of this pilot study indicate that peer-feedback training with the focus on clarity, transparency and the possibility to practice beforehand increases students willingness to participate in future peer-feedback activities and training, increases their perceived usefulness, preparedness and general attitude regarding peer-feedback. The results of this pilot will be used as a basis for future large-scale experiments to compare different designs.

Keywords: MOOCs · Educational scalability · Peer-feedback
Scalable design

1 Introduction

Massive Open Online Courses (MOOCs) are a popular way of providing online courses of various domains to the mass. Due to their open and online character, they enable students from different backgrounds and cultures to participate in (higher) education. Studying in a MOOC mostly means freedom in time, location, and engagement, however differences in the educational design and teaching methods can be seen. The high heterogeneity of MOOC students regarding, for example, their motivation, knowledge, language (skills), culture, age and time zone, entails benefits but also challenges to the course design and the students themselves. On the one hand, a MOOC offers people the chance to interact with each other and exchange information with

E. Ras and A. E. Guerrero Roldán (Eds.): TEA 2017, CCIS 829, pp. 54–68, 2018.
https://doi.org/10.1007/978-3-319-97807-9_5

peers from different backgrounds, perspectives, and cultures [1]. On the other hand, a MOOC cannot serve the learning needs of such a heterogenic group of students [1–3]. Additionally, large-scale student participation challenges teachers but also students to interact with each other. How can student learning be supported in a course with hundreds or even thousands of students? Are MOOCs able to provide elaborated formative feedback to large student numbers? To what extend can complex learning activities in MOOCs be supported and provided with elaborated formative feedback? When designing education for large and heterogeneous numbers of students, teachers opt for scalable learning and assessment and feedback activities such as videos, multiple choice quizzes, simulations and peer-feedback [4]. In theory, all these activities have the potential to be scalable and thus used in large-scale courses, however, when applied in practice they lack in educational quality. Personal support is limited, feedback is rather summative and/or not elaborated and there is a lack in (feedback on) complex learning activities. Therefore, the main motivation of any educational design should be to strive for high *educational scalability* which is the capacity of an educational format to maintain high quality despite increasing or large numbers of learners at a stable level of total [4]. It is not only a matter of enabling feedback to the masses but also and even more to provide high quality design and education to the masses. Thus, any educational design should combine a quantitative with a qualitative perspective. When looking at the term feedback and what it means to provide feedback in a course one can find several definitions. A quite recent one is that of [5] "Feedback is a process whereby learners obtain information about their work in order to appreciate the similarities and differences between the appropriate standards for any given work" (p. 205). This definition includes several important characteristics about feedback such as being a process, requiring learner engagement and being linked to task criteria/learning goals. Ideally, students go through the whole circle and receive on each new step the needed feedback type. In recent years feedback is seen more and more as a process, a loop, a two-way communication between the feedback provider and the feedback receiver [6, 7]. In MOOCs, feedback often is provided via quizzes in an automated form or in forum discussion. Additionally, some MOOCs give students an active part in the feedback process by providing peer-feedback activities in the course. However, giving students an active part in the feedback process requires that students understand the criteria on which they receive feedback. It also implies that students understand how they can improve their performance based on the received feedback. By engaging students more in the feedback process, they eventually will learn how to assess themselves and provide themselves with feedback. However, before students achieve such a high-level of self-regulation it is important that they practice to provide and receive feedback. When practicing, students should become familiar with three types of feedback: feed-forward (where am I going?), feedback (how am I doing?) and feed-forward (how do I close the gap?) [8]. These types of feedback are usually used in formative assessment also known as 'Assessment for Learning' where students receive feedback throughout the course instead of at the end of a course. Formative feedback, hence elaborated, enables students to reflect on their own learning and provides them with information on how to improve their performance [9]. To provide formative feedback, the feedback provider has to evaluate a peer's work with the aim of supporting the peer and improving his/her work. Therefore, positive as well as critical remarks must be given supplemented with suggestions on improvement [10]. In the following sections, we will have a closer look on the scalability of peer-feedback, how it is perceived by students and we will argue that it is not the idea of peer-feedback itself that challenges but rather the way it is designed and implemented in a MOOC.

1.1 Peer-Feedback in Face-to-Face Higher Education

Increased student-staff ratios and more diverse student profiles challenge higher education and influence the curriculum design in several ways such as a decrease in personal teacher feedback and a decrease of creative assignments in which students require personal feedback on their text and or design [1, 5, 11, 12]. However, at the same time feedback is seen as a valuable aspect in large and therefore often impersonalised, classes to ensure interaction and personal student support [13]. Research on student perception of peer-feedback in face-to-face education shows that students are not always satisfied with the feedback they receive [14, 15]. The value and usefulness of feedback is not perceived as high especially if the feedback is provided at the end of the course and therewith is of no use for learning and does not need to be implemented in follow-up learning activities [11]. It is expected that student perception of feedback can be enhanced by providing elaborated formative feedback throughout the course on learning activities that build upon each other. This, however, implies that formative feedback is an embedded component of the curriculum rather than an isolated, self-contained learning activity [5, 13] found that students value high-quality feedback meaning timely and comprehensive feedback that clarifies how they perform against the set criteria and which actions are needed in order to improve their performance. These results correspond to [8] distinction between feedback and feed-forward. Among other aspects, feedback was perceived as a guide towards learning success, as a learning tool and a means of interaction [13]. However, unclear expectations and criteria regarding the feedback and learning activity lead to unclear feedback and thus disappointing peer-feedback experiences [11, 12]. The literature on design recommendations for peer-feedback activities is highly elaborated and often comes down to the same recommendations of which the most important are briefly listed in Table 1 [5, 16, 17].

A rubric is a peer-feedback tool often used for complex tasks such as reviewing essays or designs. There are no general guidelines on how to design rubrics for formative assessment and feedback, however, they are often designed as two-dimensional matrixes including the following two elements: performance criteria and descriptions of student performance on various quality levels [18]. Rubrics provide students with transparency about the criteria on which their performance get reviewed and their level of performance which makes the feedback more accessible and valuable [7, 16, 17]. However, a rubric alone does not explain the meaning and goals of the chosen performance criteria. Therefore, students need to be informed about the performance and quality criteria before using a rubric in a peer-feedback activity. Although rubrics include an inbuilt feed-forward element in the form of the various performance levels, it is expected that students need more elaboration on how to improve their performance to reach the next/higher performance level. Students need to be informed and trained about the rubric criteria in order to be used effectively [17].

Table 1. Common peer-feedback design recommendations in face-to-face education

Peer-feedback design recommendations	Examples
Clarity: regarding instructions, expectations and tools	Students need clear instructions on what they are expected to do, how and why. If tools such as a rubric are used students should understand how to interpret and use them
Practice	Students need the opportunity to practice with feedback tools such as a rubric beforehand
Exemplars	Exemplars make expectations clear and provide transparency
Alignment	Peer-feedback activities should be aligned with the course content to make them valuable for students
Sequencing	Guide students through the peer-feedback process by sequence the activities from simple to complex

1.2 Peer-Feedback in (Open) Online Education

Large student numbers and high heterogeneity in the student population challenge the educational design of open online and blended education [3, 10]. A powerful aspect of (open) online education compared to face-to-face education is its technological possibilities. However, also with technology, large-scale remains a challenge for students to interact with teachers [19]. When it comes to providing students with feedback, hints or recommendations, automated feedback can be easily provided to large student numbers. However, the personal value of automated feedback is limited to quizzes and learning activities in which the semantic meaning of student answers is not taken into account [1]. Providing feedback to essays or design activities even with technological support is still highly complex [20]. When it comes to courses with large-scale student participation, peer-feedback is used for its scalable potential with mainly a quantitative approach (managing large student numbers) rather than a qualitative one [1].

Research focusing on student perceptions regarding the quality, fairness, and benefits of peer-feedback in MOOCs show mixed results [21, 22] ranging from low student motivation to provide peer-feedback [10], students' mistrust of the quality of peer-feedback [23] to students recommending to include peer-feedback in future MOOCs [20].

Although reviewing peers' work, detecting strong and weak aspects and providing hints and suggestions for improvement, trains students in evaluating the quality of work they first need to have the knowledge and skills to do so [3]. This raises the question if and how students can learn to provide and value peer-feedback. Although peer-feedback is used in MOOCs, it is not clear how students are prepared and motivated to actually participate in peer-feedback activities. Research of [18] has shown that students prefer clear instructions of learning activities and transparency of the criteria for example via rubrics or exemplars. Their findings are in line with research of [21] who found that especially in MOOCs the quality of the design is of great importance since participation is not mandatory. MOOC students indicated that they prefer clear and student-focused design: "Clear and detailed instructions. A thorough description of the assignment, explaining why a group project is the requirement rather than an individual activity. Access to technical tools that effectively support group collaboration" [21, p. 226]. The design of peer-feedback is influenced by several aspects such as the technical possibilities of the MOOC platform, the topic and learning goals of the MOOC. Nevertheless, some pedagogical aspects of peer-feedback design such as listed in Table 1 are rather independent of the technological and course context as mentioned above. Similar to research in face-to-face education, literature about peer-feedback in MOOCs shows that clear instructions and review criteria, cues and examples are needed in order to not only guide students in the review process [1, 3, 24] but also to prepare them for the review activity so that they trust their own abilities [25].

To extend our understanding of students' peer-feedback perceptions and how they can be improved by scalable peer-feedback design, we focus on the following research question: "How do instructional design elements of peer-feedback (training) influence students' peer-feedback perception in MOOCs?" The instructional design elements are constructive alignment, clarity of instruction, practice on task and examples from experts (see Table 1). To investigate student's perception, we developed a questionnaire that included four criteria which derived from the Reasoned Action approach by [26]: Willingness (intention); Usefulness (subjective norm), Preparedness (perceived behavioral control) and general Attitude. The four criteria will be explained in more detail further on in the method section. By investigating this research question, we aim to provide MOOC teachers and designer with useful design recommendation on how to design peer-feedback for courses with large-scale participation.

This study explores whether explaining to students the value/usefulness of the peer-feedback activity and embedding it in the course, students will perceive peer-feedback as useful for their own learning. We also expect that their perceived preparedness will increase by giving students the chance to practice beforehand with the peer-feedback tools and criteria and giving them examples. The general attitude regarding peer-feedback should be positively improved by setting up valuable, clearly described learning activities that are aligned with the course.

2 Method

2.1 Background MOOC and Participants

To give an answer on how instructional design elements of peer-feedback training influence students' learning experience in MOOCs, we set up an explorative study which contained a pre- and post-questionnaire, peer-feedback training, and a peer-feedback activity. The explorative study took place in the last week of a MOOC called Marine Litter (https://www.class-central.com/mooc/4824/massive-open-online-course-mooc-on-marine-litter). The MOOC (in English) was offered by UNEP and the Open University of the Netherlands at the EdCast platform. During the 15 weeks runtime students could follow two tracks: (1) the Leadership Track which took place in the first half of the MOOC where students got introduced to marine litter problems and taught how to analyse them and (2) the Expert Track which took place in the second half of the MOOC where more challenging concepts were taught and students learned how to developed an action plan to combat a marine litter problem of choice.

The explorative study took place in the last week of the MOOC from June to August 2017 and was linked to the final assignment in which students were asked to develop an action plan to reduce and or prevent a specific marine litter problem. Students could work in groups or individually on the assignment and would receive a certificate of participation by sending in their assignment. Given the complexity of the assignment, it would be useful for the students to get a critical review and feedback on their work. So, if necessary, they can improve it before handing it in. While tutor feedback was not feasible, reviewing others' assignment would be beneficial to both sender and receiver [19]. Therefore, we added a peer-feedback activity including training. When trying to combat marine litter problems collaboration is important, since often several stakeholders with different needs and goals are included. Being able to receive but also provide feedback, therefore, added value to the MOOC. Participating in the peer-feedback training and activity was a voluntary, extra activity which might explain the low participant numbers for our study (N = 18 out of N = 77 active students). Although not our first choice, this decision suited the design of the MOOC best. There were 2690 students enrolled of which 77 did finish the MOOC.

2.2 Design

The peer-feedback intervention consisted of five components as shown in a simplified form in Fig. 1. Participation in the peer-feedback intervention added a study load of 45 min over a one week period. Before starting with the peer-feedback training, students were asked to fill in a pre-questionnaire. After the pre-questionnaire students could get extra instructions and practice with the peer-feedback criteria before participating in the peer-feedback activity. When participating in the peer-feedback activity students had to send in their task and had to provide feedback via a rubric on their peers work. Whether and in which order students participated in the different elements of the training was up to them but they had access to all elements at any time. After having participated in the peer-feedback activity students again were asked to fill in a questionnaire.

2.3 Peer-Feedback Training

The design of the peer-feedback training was based on design recommendation from the literature as mentioned previously. All instructions and activities were designed in collaboration with the MOOC content experts. In the instructions, we explained to students what the video, the exercise, and the peer-feedback activity are about. Additionally, we explained the value of participating in these activities ("This training is available for those of you who want some extra practice with the DPSIR framework or are interested in learning how you can review your own or another DPSIR."). The objectives of the activities were made clear as well as the link to the final assignment (..it is a great exercise to prepare you for the final assignment and receive some useful feedback!"). An example video (duration 4:45 min) which was tailored to the content of previous learning activities and the final assignment of the MOOC was developed to give students insight into the peer-feedback tool (a rubric) they had to use in the peer-

Fig. 1. Design of the peer-feedback training and activity

feedback activity later on. The rubric was shown, quality criteria were explained and we showed students how an expert would use the rubric when being asked to review a peer's text. The rubric including the quality criteria was also used in the peer-feedback activity and therefore prepared students for the actual peer-feedback activity later on in the MOOC.

Next, to the video, students could actively practice with the rubric itself. We designed a multiple-choice quiz in which students were asked to review a given text exert. To review the quality of the text exerts students had to choose one of the three quality scores (low, average or high) and the corresponding feedback and feed-forward. After indicating the most suitable quality score & feedback students received automated feedback. In the automated feedback, students received an explanation of why their choice was (un)suitable, why it was (un)suitable and which option would have been more suitable. By providing elaborated feedback we wanted to make the feedback as meaningful as possible for the students [8–10, 14]. By providing students with clear instructions, giving them examples and the opportunity to practice with the tool itself we implemented all of the above-mentioned design recommendations given by [1, 3, 18, 21, 24].

2.4 Peer-Feedback Activity

After the peer-feedback exercise students got the chance to participate in the peer-feedback activity. The peer-feedback activity was linked to the first part of the final assignment of the MOOC in which students had to visualize a marine litter problem by means of a framework called DPSIR which is a useful adaptive management tool to analyze environmental problems and to map potential responses. To make the peer-feedback activity for the students focused (and therewith not too time-consuming) they were asked to provide feedback on two aspects of the DPSIR framework. Beforehand, students received instructions and rules about the peer-feedback process. To participate in the peer-feedback activity students had to send in the first part of their assignment via the peer-feedback tool of the MOOC. Then they received automatically the assignment of a peer to review and a rubric in which they had to provide a quality score (low, average or high), feedback and a recommendation on the two selected aspects. There was also space left for additional remarks. Within three weeks of time, students had to make the first part of the final assignment, send it in, provide feedback and if desired could use the received peer-feedback to improve their own assignment. After the three weeks, it was not possible anymore to provide or receive peer-feedback. The peer-feedback activity was tailored to the MOOC set-up in which students could either individually or in groups write the final assignment. To coordinate the peer-feedback process within groups, the group leader was made responsible for providing peer-feedback as a group, sending the peer-feedback in, sharing the received feedback on their own assignment with the group. Students who participated individually in the final assignment also provided the peer-feedback individually.

2.5 Student Questionnaires

Before the peer-feedback training and after the peer-feedback activity, students were asked to fill out a questionnaire. In the pre-questionnaire, we asked students about their previous experience with peer-feedback in MOOCs and in general. Nineteen items were divided among five variables. Seven items were related to students' prior experience, two were related to student's willingness to participate in peer-feedback (training), three items were related to the usefulness of peer-feedback, two items related to the students' preparedness to provide feedback and five were related to their general attitude regarding peer-feedback (training) (see Appendix 1). After participating in the peer-feedback activity, students were asked to fill in the post-questionnaire (see Appendix 1). The post-questionnaire informed us about students' experiences and opinions with the peer-feedback exercises and activities. It also showed whether and to what extent students changed their attitude regarding peer-feedback compared to the pre-questionnaire. The post-questionnaires contained 17 items which were divided among four variables: two items regarding the willingness, five items about the perceived usefulness, five items about their preparedness and another five items about their general attitude. Students had to score the items on a 7-point Likert scale, varying from "totally agree" to "totally disagree".

3 Results

The aim of this study was to get insight into how instructional design elements of peer-feedback (training) influence students' peer-feedback perception in MOOCs. To investigate this questions, we collected self-reported student data with two questionnaires. The overall participation in the peer-feedback training and activity was low and thus the response to the questionnaires was limited. Therefore, we cannot speak of significant results but rather preliminary findings which will be used in future work. Nevertheless, the overall tendency of our preliminary findings is a positive one since student's perception in all five variables increased (willingness, usefulness, preparedness and general attitude).

3.1 Pre- and Postquestionnaire Findings

A total of twenty students did fill in the pre-questionnaire of which two did not give their informed consent to use their data. Of these eighteen students, only nine students did fill in the post-questionnaire. However, from these nine students, we only used the post-questionnaire results of six students since the results of the other three did show that they did not participate in the peer-feedback activities resulting in 'not applicable' answers. Only five of the eighteen students provided and received peer-feedback.

Of the eighteen students who responded on the pre-questionnaire, the majority had never participated in a peer-feedback activity in a MOOC (61.1%) and also had never participated in a peer-feedback training in a MOOC (77.7%). The majority also was not familiar with using a rubric for peer-feedback purposes (66.7%).

The results of the pre- and post-questionnaire (N = 18) show for all items an increase in agreement. Previous to the peer-feedback training and activity, the students already had a positive attitude towards peer-feedback. They were willing to provide peer-feedback and to participate in peer-feedback training activities. Additionally, they saw great value in reading peer's comments. Students (N = 18) did not feel highly prepared to provide peer-feedback but found it rather important to receive instructions/training in how to provide peer-feedback. In general, students also agreed that peer-feedback should be trained and provided with some explanations. Comparing the findings of the pre-questionnaire (N = 18) with student's responses on the post-questionnaire (N = 6), it can be seen that the overall perception regarding peer-feedback (training) improved. Student's willingness to participate in future peer-feedback training activities increased from M = 2.0 to 2.7 (scores could range from −3 to +3). After having participated in our training and peer-feedback activity students found it more useful to participate in a peer-feedback training and activity in the future M = 2.2 to 2.7. Additionally, students scored the usefulness of our training high M = 2.7 because they provided them with guidelines on how to provide peer-feedback themselves. Students felt more prepared to provide feedback after having participated in the training M = 1.9 to 2.3 and they found it more important that peer-feedback is a part of each MOOC after having participated in our training and activity M = 1.4 to 2.7.

3.2 Provided Peer-Feedback

Next, to the questionnaire findings, we also investigated the provided peer-feedback qualitatively. In total five students provided feedback via the feedback tool in the MOOC. To get an overview we clustered the received and provided peer-feedback into two general types: concise general feedback and elaborated specific feedback. Three out of 5 students provided elaborated feedback with specific recommendations on how to improve their peer's work. Their recommendations focused on the content of their peer's work and were supported by examples such as "*Although the focus is well-described, the environment education and the joint action plan can be mentioned.*" When providing good remarks none of the students explained why they found their peer's work good, however when providing critical remarks students gave examples with their recommendations.

4 Conclusions

In this paper, we investigated how instructional design elements of peer-feedback training, influences students' perception of peer-feedback in MOOCs. Although small in number, the findings are encouraging that the peer-feedback training consisting of an instruction video, peer-feedback exercises and examples positively influence student's attitude regarding peer-feedback. We found that student's initial attitude towards peer-feedback was positive and that their perceptions after having participated in the training and the peer-feedback activity positively increased. However, since participation in the peer-feedback training and activity was not a mandatory part of the final assignment we cannot draw any general conclusions. Our findings indicate that by designing a peer-feedback activity according to design principles recommended in the literature, e.g. giving clear instructions, communicating expectations and the value of participating in peer-feedback [5, 13, 16, 17] does not only increase students' willingness to participate in peer-feedback but also increases their perceived usefulness and preparedness. Our findings also seem to support the recommendations by [3, 17] who found that students need to be trained beforehand in order to benefit from peer-feedback by providing them with examples and explaining them beforehand how to use tools and how to interpret quality criteria in a rubric.

In the peer-feedback training, students were informed about how to provide helpful feedback and recommendations before getting the opportunity to practice with the rubric. The qualitative findings show that the feedback provided by students was helpful in a sense that it was supportive and supplemented with recommendations on how to improve the work [10, 27]. Since we were not able to test students' peer-feedback skills beforehand we assume that the peer-feedback training with its clear instructions, examples and practice task supported students in providing valuable feedback [3].

Peer-feedback should be supported by the educational design of a course in such a way that it supports and guides students learning. To some extent design principles are context-dependent, however, we listed a preliminary list of design guidelines to offer MOOC designers and teachers some insight and inspiration:

1. Providing feedback is a skill and thus should be seen as a learning goal students have to acquire. This implies that, if possible, the peer-feedback should be repeated within a MOOC. Starting early on relatively simple assignments and building up to more complex ones later in the course.
2. Peer-feedback training should not only focus on the course content but also on student perception. This means that a training should not only explain and clarify the criteria and requirements but should also explain the real value for students to participate. A perfect design will not be seen as such as long as students are not aware of the personal value it has for them.
3. Providing feedback is a time-consuming activity and therefore should be used in moderation. When is peer-feedback needed and when does it become a burden? Ask students to provide feedback only when it adds value to their learning experience.

Although we were only able to conduct an explorative study we see potential in the preliminary findings. To increase the value of our findings, our design will be tested in a forthcoming experimental study. Next, to self-reported student data, we will add a qualitative analysis of students' peer-feedback performance by analyzing the correctness of the feedback and students' perception of the received feedback. Moreover, learning analytics will provide more insight into student behaviour and the time they invest in the different peer-feedback activities.

Acknowledgements. This work is financed via a grant by the Dutch National Initiative for Education Research (NRO)/The Netherlands Organisation for Scientific Research (NWO) and the Dutch Ministry of Education, Culture and Science under the grant nr. 405-15-705 (SOONER/ http://sooner.nu).

Appendix 1

Pre-questionnaire items				Post-questionnaire items			
Item	Item	M	SD	Item	Item	M	SD
	Willingness				Willingness		
A1	I am willing to provide feedback/comments on a peer's assignment	2.3	1.0	PA1	In the future I am willing to provide feedback/comments on a peer's assignment	2.3	1.2
A2	I am willing to take part in learning activities that explain the peer-feedback process	2.0	1.2	PA2	In the future I am willing to take part in learning activities that explain the peer-feedback process	2.7	0.5
	Usefulness				*Usefulnes*		
B1	I find it useful to participate in a peer-feedback activity	2.2	0.9	PB1	I found it useful to participate in a peer-feedback activity	2.7	0.5
B2	I find it useful to read the feedback comments from my peers	2.3	1.0	PB2	I found it useful to read the feedback/ comments from my peer	2.5	0.5
B3	I find it useful to receive instructions/training on how to provide feedback	2.1	1.0	PB3	1 found it useful to receive instructions/training on how to provide feedback	2.7	0.8
				PB4	I found it useful to see in the DPS1R peer-feedback	2.5	1.2

(*continued*)

(*continued*)

Pre-questionnaire items				Post-questionnaire items			
Item	Item	M	SD	Item	Item	M	SD
					training how an expert would review a DPSIR scheme		
				PB5	The examples and exercises of the DPSIR peer-feedback training helped me to provide peer-feedback in the MOOC	2.7	0.5
	Preparedness				*Preparedness*		
C1	I feel confident to provide feedback/comments on a peer's assignment	1.9	1.5	PC1	I felt confident to provide feedback/comments on a peer's assignment	2.3	1.2
C2	I find it important to be prepared with information and examples/exercises, before providing a peer with feedback comments	1.9	1.5	PC2	1 found it important to be prepared before providing a peer with feedback/comments	2.0	1.3
				PC3	I felt prepared to give feedback and recommendations after having participated in the DPSIR peer-feedback training	2.3	1.2
				PC4	I felt that the DPSIR peer-feedback training provided enough examples and instruction on how to provide feedback	2.3	0.8
				PC5	The DPSIR peer-feedback training improved my performance in the final assignment	1.3	1.5

(*continued*)

(*continued*)

Pre-questionnaire items				Post-questionnaire items			
Item	Item	M	SD	Item	Item	M	SD
	General attitude				*General attitude*		
D1	Students should receive instructions and/or training in how to provide peer-feedback	2.0	1.2	PD1	Students should receive instructions and/or training in how to provide peer-feedback	2.3	1.2
D2	Peer-feedback should be a part of each MOOC	1.7	1.3	PD2	Peer-feedback should be part of each MOOC	3.0	0.0
D3	Students should explain their provided feedback	1.9	1.1	PD3	Students should explain their provided feedback	2.3	0.8
D4	Peer-feedback training should be part of each MOOC	1.4	1.6	PD4	Peer-feedback training should be part of each MOOC	2.7	0.5
D5	Peer-feedback gives me insight in my performance as	−.1	1.9	PD5	Peer-feedback gave me insight in my performance as	−.7	1.2

Pre- and postquestionnaire results with N = 18 for the pre-questionnaire and N = 6 for the post-questionnaire. Students were asked to express their agreement in the questionnaires on a scale of 3 (Agree), 0 (Neither agree/nor disagree) and −3 (Disagree). Excluding item D5 and PD5 where a different scale was used ranging from −3 (a professional) to 3 (a MOOC student).

References

1. Kulkarni, C., et al.: Peer and self-assessment in massive online classes. ACM Trans. Comput. Hum. Interact. **20**, 33:1–31 (2013). https://doi.org/10.1145/2505057
2. Falakmasir, M.H., Ashely, K.D., Schunn, C.D.: Using argument diagramming to improve peer grading of writing assignments. In: Proceedings of the 1st workshop on Massive Open Online Courses at the 16th Annual Conference on Artificial Intelligence in Education, USA, pp. 41–48 (2013)
3. Yousef, A.M.F., Wahid, U., Chatti, M.A., Schroeder, U., Wosnitza, M.: The effect of peer assessment rubrics on learner's satisfaction and performance within a blended MOOC environment. Paper presented at the 7th International Conference on Computer Supported Education, pp. 148–159 (2015). https://doi.org/10.5220/0005495501480159
4. Kasch, J., Van Rosmalen, P., Kalz, M.: A framework towards educational scalability of open online courses. J. Univ. Comput. Sci. **23**(9), 770–800 (2017)
5. Boud, D., Molloy, E.: Rethinking models of feedback for learning: the challenge of design. Assess. Eval. High. Educ. **38**, 698–712 (2013a). https://doi.org/10.1080/02602938.2012.691462

6. Boud, D., Molloy, E.: What is the problem with feedback? In: Boud, D., Molloy, E. (eds.) Feedback in Higher an Professional Education, pp. 1–10, Routledge, London (2013b)
7. Dowden, T., Pittaway, S., Yost, H., McCarthey, R.: Student's perceptions of written feedback in teacher education. Ideally feedback is a continuing two-way communication that encourages progress. Assess. Eval. High. Educ. **38**, 349–362 (2013). https://doi.org/10.1080/02602938.2011.632676
8. Hattie, J., Timperley, H.: The power of feedback. Rev. Educ. Res. **77**, 81–112 (2007)
9. Narciss, S., Huth, K.: How to design informative tutoring feedback for multimedia learning. In: Niegemann, H., Leutner, D., Brünken, R. (eds.) Instructional Design for Multimedia Learning, Münster, pp. 181–195 (2004)
10. Neubaum, G., Wichmann, A., Eimler, S.C., Krämer, N.C.: Investigating incentives for students to provide peer feedback in a semi-open online course: an experimental study. Comput. Uses Educ. 27–29 (2014). https://doi.org/10.1145/2641580.2641604
11. Crook, C., Gross, H., Dymott, R.: Assessment relationships in higher education: the tension of process and practice. Br. Edu. Res. J. **32**, 95–114 (2006). https://doi.org/10.1080/01411920500402037
12. Patchan, M.M., Charney, D., Schunn, C.D.: A validation study of students' end comments: comparing comments by students, a writing instructor and a content instructor. J. Writ. Res. **1**, 124–152 (2009)
13. Rowe, A.: The personal dimension in teaching: why students value feedback. Int. J. Educ. Manag. **25**, 343–360 (2011). https://doi.org/10.1108/09513541111136630
14. Topping, K.: Peer assessment between students in colleges and universities. Rev. Educ. Res. **68**, 249–276 (1998). https://doi.org/10.3102/00346543068003249
15. Carless, D., Bridges, S.M., Chan, C.K.Y., Glofcheski, R.: Scaling up Assessment for Learning in Higher Education. Springer, Singapore (2017). https://doi.org/10.1007/978-981-10-3045-1
16. Nicol, D.J., Macfarlane-Dick, D.: Formative assessment and self-regulated learning: a model and seven principles of good feedback practice. Stud. High. Educ. **31**(2), 199–218 (2007). https://doi.org/10.1080/03075070600572090
17. Jönsson, A., Svingby, G.: The use of scoring rubrics: reliability, validity and educational consequences. Educ. Res. Rev. **2**, 130–144 (2007). https://doi.org/10.1016/j.edurev.2007.05.002
18. Jönsson, A., Panadero, E.: The use and design of rubrics to support assessment for learning. In: Carless, D., Bridges, S.M., Chan, C.K.Y., Glofcheski, R. (eds.) Scaling up Assessment for Learning in Higher Education. TEPA, vol. 5, pp. 99–111. Springer, Singapore (2017). https://doi.org/10.1007/978-981-10-3045-1_7
19. Hülsmann, T.: The impact of ICT on the cost and economics of distance education: a review of the literature, pp. 1–76. Commonwealth of Learning (2016)
20. Luo, H., Robinson, A.C., Park, J.Y.: Peer grading in a MOOC: reliability, validity, and perceived effects. Online Learn. **18**(2) (2014). https://doi.org/10.24059/olj.v18i2.429
21. Zutshi, S., O'Hare, S., Rodafinos, A.: Experiences in MOOCs: the perspective of students. Am. J. Distance Educ. **27**(4), 218–227 (2013). https://doi.org/10.1080/08923647.2013.838067
22. Liu, M., et al.: Understanding MOOCs as an emerging online learning tool: perspectives from the students. Am. J. Distance Educ. **28**(3), 147–159 (2014). https://doi.org/10.1080/08923647.2014.926145
23. Suen, H.K., Pursel, B.K.: Scalable formative assessment in massive open online courses (MOOCs). Presentation at the Teaching and Learning with Technology Symposium, University Park, Pennsylvania, USA (2014)

24. Suen, H.K.: Peer assessment for massive open online courses (MOOCs). Int. Rev. Res. Open Distance Learn. **15**(3) (2014)
25. McGarr, O., Clifford, A.M.: Just enough to make you take it seriously: exploring students' attitudes towards peer assessment. High. Educ. **65**, 677–693 (2013). https://doi.org/10.1007/s10734-012-9570-z
26. Fishbein, M., Ajzen, I.: Belief, Attitude, Intention, and Behavior: An Introduction to Theory and Research. Addison-Wesley, Reading (1975)
27. Kaufman, J.H., Schunn, C.D.: Student's perceptions about peer assessment for writing: their origin and impact on revision work. Instr. Sci. **3**, 387–406 (2010). https://doi.org/10.1007/s11251-010-9133-6

Improving Diagram Assessment in Mooshak

Helder Correia(✉), José Paulo Leal, and José Carlos Paiva

CRACS & INESC-Porto LA, Faculty of Sciences, University of Porto, Porto, Portugal
{up201108850,up201200272}@fc.up.pt, zp@dcc.fc.up.pt

Abstract. Mooshak is a web system with support for assessment in computer science. It was originally developed for programming contest management but evolved to be used also as a pedagogical tool, capitalizing on its programming assessment features. The current version of Mooshak supports other forms of assessment used in computer science, such as diagram assessment. This form of assessment is supported by a set of new features, including a diagram editor, a graph comparator, and an environment for integration of pedagogical activities. The first attempt to integrate these features to support diagram assessment revealed a number of shortcomings, such as the lack of support for multiple diagrammatic languages, ineffective feedback, and usability issues. These shortcomings were addressed by the creation of a diagrammatic language definition language, the introduction of a new component for feedback summarization and a redesign of the diagram editor. This paper describes the design and implementation of these features, as well as their validation.

Keywords: Automated assessment · Diagram assessment
Feedback generation · Language environments · E-learning

1 Introduction

Mooshak [5] is a web-based system that supports assessment in computer science. It was initially designed in 2001 to be a programming contest management system for ICPC contests. Later, it evolved to support other types of programming contests. Meanwhile, it was used to manage several contests all over the world, including ICPC regional contests and IEEExtreme contests. Eventually, it started being used as a pedagogical tool in undergraduate programming courses.

Recently, the code base of Mooshak was reimplemented in Java with Ajax GUIs in Google Web Toolkit. The new version[1] has specialized environments, including a computer science languages learning environment [7]. Although the core of Mooshak is the assessment of programming languages, other kinds of languages are also supported, such as diagrammatic languages. This is particularly important because diagram languages are studied in several computer science

[1] http://mooshak2.dcc.fc.up.pt.

E. Ras and A. E. Guerrero Roldán (Eds.): TEA 2017, CCIS 829, pp. 69–82, 2018.
https://doi.org/10.1007/978-3-319-97807-9_6

disciplines, such as theory of computation – Deterministic Finite Automaton (DFA), databases – Extended Entity-Relationship (EER), and software modeling – Unified Modeling Language (UML), thus it is useful for teaching those subjects. Diagram assessment in Mooshak relies on two components: an embedded diagram editor and a graph comparator. The experience gained with this diagram assessment environment in undergraduate courses revealed shortcomings in both components, that the research described in this paper attempts to solve.

Enki is a web environment that mimics an Integrated Development Environment (IDE). Thus, it integrates several tools, including editors. For programming languages, Enki uses a code editor with syntax highlight and code completion. The diagram editor Eshu [4] has a similar role for diagram assessment. Code editors are fairly independent of programming languages since programs are text files. At most, code editors use language specific rules for highlighting syntax and completing keywords. A diagram editor, such as Eshu, can also strive for language independence since a diagram is basically a graph, although each diagrammatic language has its own node and edge types with a particular visual syntax. Nevertheless, the initial version of Eshu was targeted to Entity-Relationship (ER) diagrams and, although it could be extended to other languages, it required changes to the source code, in order to define the visual syntax.

Diagrams created with Eshu on a web client are sent to a web server, converted into a graph representation and compared with a standard solution. The assessment performed by the graph comparator [12] can be described as semantic. That is, each graph is a semantic representation of a diagram and the differences between the two graphs reflect the differences in meaning of the two diagrams. However, the differences frequently result from the fact that the student attempt is not a valid diagram. A typical error is a diagram that does not generate a fully connected graph, which is not acceptable in most diagrammatic languages. Other errors are language specific and refer to nodes with invalid degrees, or edges connecting wrong node types. For instance, in an EER diagram, an attribute node has a single edge and two entity nodes cannot be directly connected. Hence, feedback will be more effective if it points out this kind of error and refers the student to a page describing that particular part of the language. To enable this kind of syntactic feedback, Kora provides a diagrammatic definition language, that can also be used to relate detected errors with available content that may be provided as feedback.

Another issue with reporting graph differences is the amount of information. On one hand, it provides too much information, that can actually solve the exercise to the student if applied systematically. On the other hand, it is sometimes too much and may confuse some students, as happens with syntactic errors reported by a program compiler invoked from the command line. In either case, from a pedagogical perceptive, detailed feedback in large quantities is less helpful than concise feedback on the most relevant issues. For instance, when assessing an EER diagram, a single feedback line reporting n missing attributes is more helpful than n scattered lines reporting each missing attributes. For the same EER diagram, a line reporting n missing attributes (i.e. condensing n errors on node type) is more relevant than one on m missing relationships (i.e. condensing m errors on another node type), if $n > m$. Nevertheless, if the student persists on the errors, repeating the same message is not helpful. The progressive disclosure of feedback must take into account information provided to the student, to avoid unnecessary repetitions. Thus, new feedback on the same errors progressively focus on specific issues and provides more detail. Also, this incremental feedback must be parsimonious to discourage students from using it as a sort of oracle and avoid thinking for themselves.

This paper reports on recent research to improve diagram assessment in Mooshak and is organized as follows. Section 2 surveys existing systems for diagram edition and assessment. Then, Sect. 3 introduces the components of Mooshak relevant to this research. Three main objectives drove this research: to support a wide variety of diagrammatic languages, to enhance the quality of feedback reported to the student, and to improve usability. The strategy to attain these objectives follows three vectors, each described in its own section: the development of a component to mediate between the diagram editor and the graphs comparator, responsible for reporting on syntactic errors, in Sect. 4; the reimplementation of the diagram editor, to enable the support of multiple diagrammatic languages and mitigate known usability errors, in Sect. 5; and a diagrammatic language definition, capable of describing syntactic features and of configuring the two previous components, in Sect. 6. The outcome of these improvements is analyzed in Sect. 7 and summarized in Sect. 8.

2 Related Work

This research aims to improve Mooshak 2.0 by providing support to the creation and assessment of diagram exercises of any type, with visual and textual feedback. To the best of authors' knowledge, there is only a single tool [14], in the literature, that ensembles most of these features. This tool provides automatic marking of diagram exercises, and it has been embedded in a quiz engine to enable students to draw and evaluate diagram exercises. Although this tool supports the assessment and modeling of multiple types of diagrams, by using free-form diagrams, its feedback consists only of a grade, which is not adequate for pedagogical purposes. Hence, the rest of this section enumerates several works focusing on assessment, editing or critiquing of diagrams.

Diagram Assessment. Most of the existent automatic diagram assessment systems are designed for a specific diagram type. Some examples of these systems are deterministic finite automata (DFA) [2,9], UML class diagrams [1,11,15], Entity-Relationship diagrams [3], among others.

Diagram Editors. Many diagramming software exists from desktop applications, such as Microsoft Visio[2] or Dia[3], to libraries embeddable in web applications, such as mxGraph[4] or GoJS[5]. There is also a growing number of editing tools deployed on the web, such as *Cacoo*[6] and *Lucidchart*[7]. However, most of these tools do not provide validation of the type of diagram being modeled.

Critiquing Systems. From the diagram assessment viewpoint, critiquing features are an important part of diagram editing and modeling tools. A critiquing tool acts on modeling tools to provide corrections and suggestions on the models to be designed. These mechanisms are important, not only to check the syntactic construction of a modeling language, but also to support decision-making and check for consistency between various models within a domain. Much research has been devoted to critiquing tools and they are incorporated in systems such as *ArgoUML* [8], *ArchStudio5*[8] and *ABCDE-Critic* [13].

3 Background

The goal of this research is to make use of new and existing tools to provide support to the creation and assessment of diagram exercises of any type in Mooshak 2.0. Thus, new tools will be created and integrated with those already existent, creating a network of components as depicted in Fig. 1.

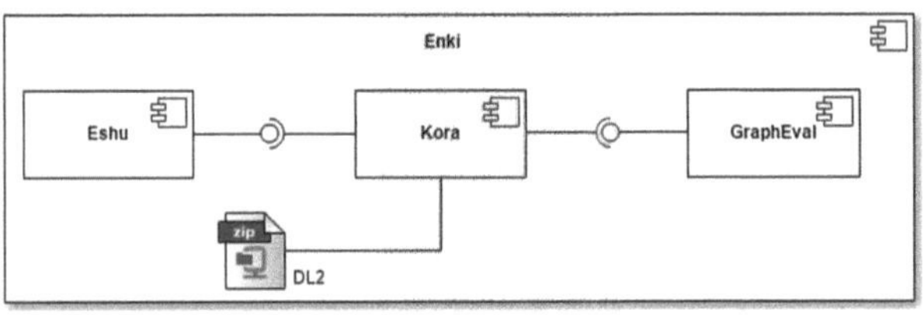

Fig. 1. UML diagram of the components of the system

The next items describe the tools already developed in previous researches that compose the system presented in Fig. 1.

[2] https://products.office.com/en/visio/flowchart-software.
[3] https://wiki.gnome.org/Apps/Dia.
[4] https://www.jgraph.com/.
[5] http://gojs.net/latest/index.html.
[6] https://cacoo.com.
[7] https://www.lucidchart.com/.
[8] https://basicarchstudiomanual.wordpress.com/.

Diagram Editor – Eshu 1.0. The corner stone of a language development environment is an editor. For programming languages, several code editors are readily available to be integrated in Web applications. However, only few editors exist for diagrammatic languages. In project Eshu [4], the authors develop an extensible diagram editor, that can be embedded in web applications that require diagram interaction, such as modeling tools or e-learning environments. Eshu is a JavaScript library with an API that supports its integration with other components, including importing/exporting diagrams in JSON. In order to validate the API of Eshu, an EER diagram editor was created in *Javascript*, using the library provided by Eshu and HTML5 canvas. The editor allows to edit EER diagrams, import/export a diagram into JSON format, apply EER language restrictions in diagram editor (constraints on links) and display visual feedback on EER diagram submissions. The editor has been integrated into Enki [7] (described later on this article) with a diagram evaluator, and validated with undergraduate students in a Databases course.

Diagram Evaluator – GraphEval. Diagrams are schematic representations of information that, ignoring the positioning of its elements, can be abstracted in graphs. Based on this, structure driven approach to assess graph-based exercises was proposed [12]. Given two graphs, a solution and an attempt of a student, this approach computes a mapping between the node sets of both graphs that maximizes the students grade, as well as a description of the differences between the two graphs. Then, it uses an algorithm with heuristics to test the most promising mappings first and prune the remaining when it is sure that a better mapping cannot be computed.

Integrated Learning Environment – Enki. [7] is a web-based IDE for learning programming languages, which blends assessment (exercises) and learning (multimedia and textual resources). It integrates with external services to provide gamification features and to sequence educational resources at different rhythms according to students' capabilities. The assessment of exercises is provided by the new version of Mooshak [5] – Mooshak 2.0, which, among other features, allows the creation of special evaluators for different types of exercises.

4 Kora Component

Kora aims to improve and make feedback extensible to new diagrammatic languages. This tool acts on the diagram editor, by providing corrections and suggestions to submitted diagrams, to help the student solving the exercise. It also makes the bridge between Eshu and Diagram Evaluator.

The Kora component is divided into two parts, `client` and `server`. The `client` part is integrated on the web interface, as shown in Fig. 2, and is responsible for running the Eshu editor, as well as handling user actions and presenting feedback. The `server` part is responsible for evaluating diagrams, generating feedback, and exchanging information with the client side, such as language configurations.

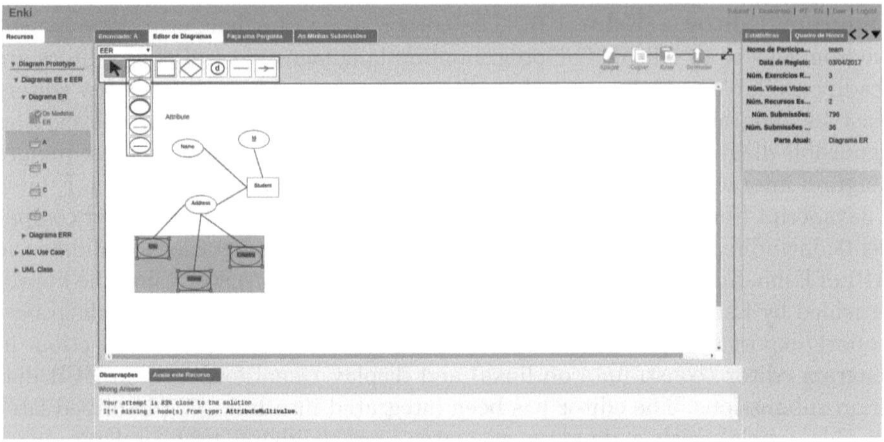

Fig. 2. User interface of Enki integrated with Kora

A diagram is a schematic representation of information. This representation has associated to itself elements that have certain characteristics and a positioning in the space. By abstracting the layout (the position of the elements), the diagrams can be represented as graphs. The approach that is intended to follow for the assessment of the diagrams is the comparison of the graphs. Thus, it is possible to analyze the contents of the diagram without giving relevance to its positioning or graphic formatting.

In Eshu 1.0, the types of connections are checked during creation and editing, that is, if source and target nodes could not be connected it would be reported immediately. However, during the validation of Eshu 1.0, it was noticed that the editor was getting slower as the number of nodes increased, although not all syntactic issues were actually covered. Also, syntactically incorrect graphs were causing problems in the generation of feedback by the evaluator. Due to these issues, syntactic verification was moved to Kora.

The diagram assessment in the system is split into two parts: syntactic assessment and semantic assessment. The syntactic assessment involves the conversion of the JSON file to a graph structure, and validation of the language syntax. It consists of validating the structural organization of the language, based on the set of rules defined in the configuration file. In this phase, the following tasks are done: validation of the types for the language; validation of the edges – for each edge it is checked if the type, source and target are valid; validation of the nodes – check if in and out degree are valid; validation of the number of connected components in the graph. The semantic assessment consists of comparing the attempt and the solution diagrams, following the graph assessment algorithm [12]. The evaluator receives a graph as an attempt to solve a problem and compares it with a graph solution to find out which mapping of the solution nodes in attempt nodes minimizes the set of differences, and therefore maximizes the classification. The feedback is generated based on these differences, and presented in Eshu, both in visual and textual form. However, when the student's attempt is far from the solution, it reports too many differences.

To cope with this problem Kora uses an incremental feedback generator to generated a corrective feedback [10]. The generator uses several strategies to summarize a list of differences in a single message. The most general message that was not yet presented to the user is then selected as feedback.

Kora uses a repertoire of strategies to summarize a list of differences. Some strategies manage to condense several differences. For instance, several differences reporting a missing node of the same type may be condensed in the message "n missing nodes of type T". Another strategy may select one of these nodes and show its label. An even more detailed strategy may show the actual missing node on the diagram. A particular strategy may not be applicable to some list of differences. In this case no message is produced.

The resulting collection of feedback messages is sorted according to generality. General messages have precedence over specific messages. However, if a message was already provided as feedback than it is not repeated. The following message is reported instead. Using this approach, messages of increasing detail are provided to the student if she or he persist on the same exact error.

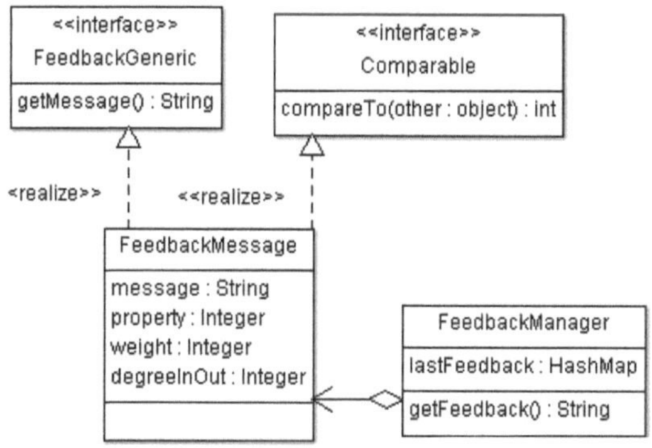

Fig. 3. UML class diagram of the feedback manager

Figure 3 presents the UML class diagram of the feedback manager implementation. The class `FeedbackMessage` contains the feedback information, including message, property number, weight, and in/out degrees (if it is a node). The property number indicates the property to which the message refers, the weight defines how much important is the mistake of the student, the degree of input/output allows to determine the importance of the node comparing to other nodes (i.e. higher degree, generally, means higher importance), and the message is the message itself. The class `FeedbackManager` generates and selects the feedback to be sent to the student. From the list of differences that is returned by the graph evaluator, it is generated a list of `FeedbackMessage`. From this list, the feedback already sent to the student is removed, and the remaining is sorted based on the fields of the `FeedbackMessage` class. The first `FeedbackMessage` from the list is selected and sent to koraClient with `FeedbackMessage` (id,properties). In the `KoraClient`, the `FeedbackMessage` is converted to text and its text is presented, according to the selected language (Portuguese or English) and when possible it is presented with visual feedback in Eshu.

5 Eshu 2.0

A diagram is composed of a set of `Node` and a set `Edge`; each `Node` has a position and a dimension; each `Edge` connects a source and a target node. Although Eshu 2.0, similarly to Eshu 1.0 [4], follows an object-oriented approach for *Javascript*, it separates the data part from the visualization and editing part.

Eshu 2.0 consists of three packages: `eshu`, `graph` and `commands`. The package `graph` has the classes responsible for creating nodes and edges, storing the graph (`Quadtree`) and operating on the data of the graph (insert, remove, save changes and select an element). Package `eshu` contains the classes responsible for the user interface, including handlers for user interaction, methods to export and import the diagram in JSON format, methods to present visual feedback in the diagram editor, among many others. The package `commands` contains the classes that are responsible for the implementation of operations, such as undo, redo, paste, remove or resize.

One of the main improvements of Eshu 2.0 is the extensibility of nodes and edges. In Eshu 1.0, the creation of a new type of node (or edge) involves the creation of a new class that extends `Vertice` (or `Edge` for edges) and defines the method `draw`. With Eshu 2.0, a new type of node (or edge) can be inserted by only adding a `nodeType` (or `edgeType`) element to `diagram`, in the configuration file. This element contains general information for a node (or edge), such as its SVG image path (used to represent it in the UI), type name, constraints on connections, among others.

Eshu is a pure JavaScript library, hence it can be integrated in most web applications. However, some frameworks, such as Google Web Toolkit (GWT), use different languages to code the web interfaces, in this case Java. To enable the integration of Eshu in GWT applications, a binding to this framework was also developed. The binding is composed of a Java class (that is converted to JavaScript by GWT) with methods to use the API, implemented using the JavaScript Native Interface (JSNI) of GWT.

The undo and redo commands are very important to the user while editing the graph. These two operations were not included in the first version of Eshu [4], but were now added. To facilitate the integration of these operations, a set of classes that implement the command design pattern were developed. Now, operations, such as insert, delete and paste, are encapsulated as an object allowing to register them in a stack, and thus pop or push them.

Also, the API allows the host application to send feedback in the form of changes to the existing diagram. For example, if a change is an insertion of an element, then it is presented in the editor, selected, and its size is increased to

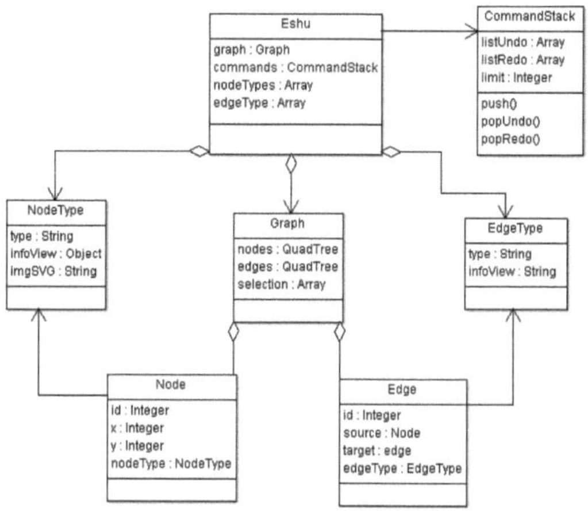

Fig. 4. UML class diagram of Eshu

highlight. If these changes are deletions, modifications or syntax errors, they can be rendered by displaying that nodes and edges with a lower transparency and selected (Fig. 4).

6 Diagrammatic Language Configuration

Both Kora and Eshu were designed to be extensible, to be able to incorporate new kinds of diagrams. A new kind of diagram is defined by an XML configuration file following the Diagrammatic Language Definition Language (DL^2). This file specifies features and feedback used in syntax validation, such as types of nodes, types of edges and language constraints. They also include editor and toolbar style configurations to be used in Eshu.

The language configuration files are set in Mooshak's administration view and must be valid according to DL^2 XML Schema definition. Figure 5 summarizes this definition in an UML class diagram, where each class corresponds to an element type. It should be noted that some element types are omitted for the sake of clarity.

The configuration file has two main types: `Style` and `Diagram`. An element of type `Style` contains four child elements, namely `editor`, `toolbar`, `vertice`, and `textbox`. The element `editor` contains the styles of the editor, such as height, width, background, and grid style properties. Element `toolbar` defines the styles of the toolbar, such as height, width, background, border style, and orientation. The `textbox` element contains attributes to configure the style of the labels for nodes and edges, such as font type and color, text alignment, among others. Finally, `vertice` contains general styles of the nodes, particularly the width, height, background, and border.

Type `Diagram` specifies the syntax of the language, including a set of `nodeType`, which describes the allowed nodes, a set of `edgeType`, that details

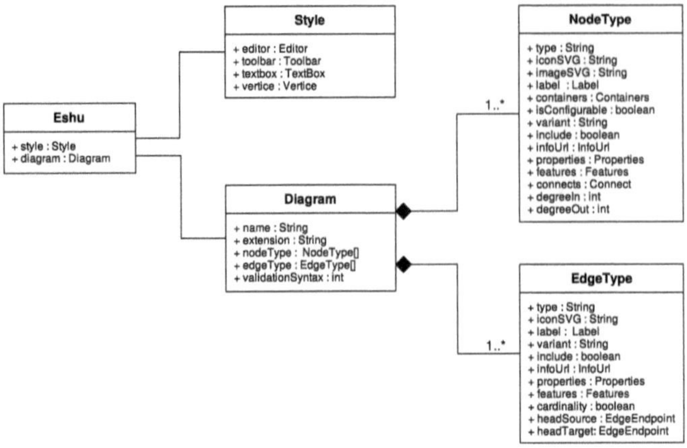

Fig. 5. UML class diagram of DL^2 XML Schema definition

the supported edges, and three attributes: name of the language (`name`), extension associated with the language (`extension`) and type of syntax validation (`validationSyntax`), which can be 0 to disable validation, 1 to validate syntax only in Kora, 2 to validate in Kora and Eshu, or 3 to validate only in Eshu.

Each `nodeType` has a path for the SVG image in the toolbar (`iconSVG`), a path for the SVG image of the node (`imageSVG`), the name of the group to which the node belongs in the toolbar (`variant`), the default properties of the label (`label`), a group of parts of the container that can have labels (`containers`), a set of properties available in the configuration window (`properties`), an `infoURL` with information about the node, a set of possible connections that the node can have (`connects`), the `degreeIn` and `degreeOut` of the node, and a boolean attribute `include` which indicates if an overlap of two nodes should be considered a connection between them.

An `edgeType` contains the configuration of an edge. The majority of its properties are similar to the existent in a `nodeType` (`type`, `iconSVG`, `label`, `variant`, `include`, `properties`, `features` and `infoUrl`). However, it has specific attributes, such as `cardinality`, that indicates whether the edge should have cardinality, and `headSource` and `headTarget` which specify how are both endpoints of the edge.

7 Validation

The goal of features presented in the previous sections is to improve diagram assessment in Mooshak. In particular, the new features are expected to enable the support of multiple diagrammatic languages, enhance feedback quality and solve usability issues. The following subsections present the validations performed to assess if these objectives were met.

7.1 Language Definition Expressiveness

An important objective of this research is to enable the support of new diagrammatic languages. For that purpose, a new XML norm for the specification of diagrammatic languages, named DL^2, was developed. To validate the expressiveness of the proposed specification language, several diagrammatic languages were configured with it.

This language defines the syntactic features of a diagrammatic language and it is instrumental in the configuration of the diagram editor, in the conversion to/of the diagram to a graph representation, and in the generation of feedback.

Mooshak already supported the concept of language configuration for programming assessment. However, the available configurations were designed for programming languages. They include, among other, compilation and execution command lines for each language. To support the configuration of diagrammatic languages, an optional configuration file was added. In the case of diagrammatic languages this field contains a DL^2 specification.

The previous version supported only EER diagrams. Hence, this language was the first candidate to test DL^2 expressiveness. It has twelve types of nodes and three types of edges, and none of them has posed any particular difficulty. In particular, all the node types were easy to draw in SVG and both the node and edge types have a small and simple set of properties. In result, the ZIP archive with the DL^2 specifications contains SVG files of nodes and edges, and an XML with configuration of elements.

UML is a visual modeling language with several diagram types that are widely used in computer science. To validate the proposed approach we selected class and use case diagrams since these are frequently used in courses covering UML. Each of these two languages has characteristics that required particular features of DL^2. Use cases diagram define relationships among nodes without using edges: the system is represented as a rectangle containing use cases. The `include` element of DL^2 allows the definition of connections between overlapping nodes and was used to create these implicit relationships. Classes in class diagram are also particularly challenging since they have complex properties, such as those representing attributes and operations. The `container` element of DL^2 definitions proved its usefulness in structuring these lists of complex attributes.

7.2 Usability and Satisfaction

The experiment conducted to evaluate the usability and satisfaction of the previous version consisted of using the system in the laboratory classes of an undergraduate Databases course, at the *Department of Computer Science of the Faculty of Sciences of the University of Porto (FCUP)*. After the experiment, the students were invited to fill-in an online questionnaire based on the Nielsen's model [6], in Google Forms. The answers have revealed deficiencies in speed, reliability and flexibility. Students complained mostly of difficulties on building the diagrams, and the high delay when evaluating their diagrams.

To check impact of the changes, the validation of the usability of the current version followed a similar approach. The experiment took place on 16th and 19th of June of 2017, also with undergraduates enrolled in same course. The number of participants was 21, of which 7 were females, and the mean of their ages was 20.83 years. They attempted to solve a set of 4 ER exercises and 2 EER exercises.

The questionnaire was very similar to the used before but, this time, it was embedded in Enki, as a resource of the course. Also, the new questionnaire includes a group of questions specifically about feedback, to evaluate whether Kora helps the students in their learning path while not providing them the solution directly.

Figure 6 shows the results grouped by Nielsen's heuristics of the previous and new versions. The collected data is shown in two bar charts, with heuristics sorted in descending order of user satisfaction.

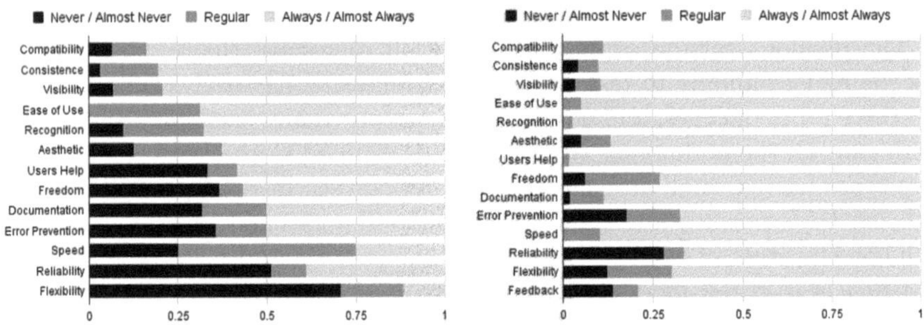

Fig. 6. Acceptability evaluation - on the left side the results of the previous version, and on the right side the results of the new version

It is clear that the usability of the system and satisfaction of the users have improved. In fact, all the heuristics got better results. Also, the results show that, with the new version, the heuristics with higher satisfaction are users' help, recognition, and ease of use. On the other side, reliability, error prevention, and flexibility were the areas with worse results. Some students complained that the feedback with Kora is too explicit, which can allow them to solve the problem by trying several times while following the feedback messages.

The last question of the questionnaire is an overall classification of the system in a 5 values Likert-type scale (very good, good, adequate, bad, very bad). The majority of the students (57.1%) classified it as very good, while the rest (42.9%) stated that it was good.

8 Conclusion

Mooshak is a system that supports automated assessment in computer science and has been used both for competitive programming and e-Learning.

Recently, it was complemented with the assessment of Entity-Relationship (ER) and Extended ER (EER) diagrams. Diagrams in these languages are created with an embed diagram editor and converted to graphs. Graphs from student diagrams are assessed by comparing them with graphs obtained from solution diagrams. The experience gained with this tool revealed a number of shortcomings that are addressed in this paper.

One of the major contributions of this research is the language DL^2. The XML documents using this configuration language decouple syntactic definitions from the source code and simplify the support of new diagrammatic languages. Configurations in the DL^2 are used both on client and server sides. On the client side, they are used by the Eshu diagram editor to configure the GUI with the visual syntax of the node and edge types of the selected languages. On the server side, they are used by the Kora component to perform syntactic analysis as a prerequisite to the semantic analysis. These configurations are also instrumental in the integration with static content describing the language syntax, that can be used as feedback when errors are detected. The expressiveness of DL^2 was validated by reimplementing ER and EER editors, as well as a couple of UML diagrams, namely class and use case.

Another contribution of this research are the approaches used by the Kora component on the server side. In complement to those related to diagram syntax and driven DL^2, mentioned in the previous paragraph, feedback message summarization also contributes to improving feedback quality. The graph comparator used for semantic analysis produces a large amount of errors that confuse the students as much they help. The proposed summarization manages to generate terse and relevant messages, starting with general messages aggregating several errors, and advancing to more focused and particular errors if the student's difficulty persists. In the latter case, feedback is generated in the diagram edition window using the diagrammatic language visual syntax.

In an upcoming version of Mooshak, this work may be used in a new assessment model that transforms the diagram of the student into program code and executes the standard evaluation model. This would allow students to "code" their solutions using diagrams, and the evaluation to be based on input/output test cases. Another assessment model could do the opposite (i.e., transform program code into a diagram) to evaluate the structure of the program, thus improving the feedback quality.

Last but not least, Mooshak with Kora is available for download at the project's homepage. A Mooshak installation configured with a few ER exercises in English are also available for online testing[9].

Acknowledgments. This work is financed by the ERDF – European Regional Development Fund through the Operational Programme for Competitiveness and Internationalisation – COMPETE 2020 Programme, and by National Funds through the FCT – Fundação para a Ciência e a Tecnologia (Portuguese Foundation for Science and Technology) within project POCI-01-0145-FEDER-006961.

[9] http://mooshak2.dcc.fc.up.pt/kora.

References

1. Ali, N.H., Shukur, Z., Idris, S.: A design of an assessment system for UML class diagram. In: International Conference on Computational Science and its Applications, ICCSA 2007, pp. 539–546. IEEE (2007). https://doi.org/10.1109/ICCSA.2007.31
2. Alur, R., D'Antoni, L., Gulwani, S., Kini, D., Viswanathan, M.: Automated grading of DFA constructions. IJCAI **13**, 1976–1982 (2013). https://doi.org/10.5120/18902-0193
3. Batmaz, F., Hinde, C.J.: A diagram drawing tool for semi-automatic assessment of conceptual database diagrams. In: Proceedings of the 10th CAA International Computer Assisted Assessment Conference, pp. 71–84. Loughborough University (2006)
4. Leal, J.P., Correia, H., Paiva, J.C.: Eshu: An extensible web editor for diagrammatic languages. In: OASIcs-OpenAccess Series in Informatics, vol. 51. Schloss Dagstuhl-Leibniz-Zentrum fuer Informatik (2016). https://doi.org/10.4230/OASIcs.SLATE.2016.12
5. Leal, J.P., Silva, F.: Mooshak: a web-based multi-site programming contest system. Softw. Pract. Exp. **33**(6), 567–581 (2003). https://doi.org/10.1002/spe.522
6. Nielsen, J.: Finding usability problems through heuristic evaluation. In: Proceedings of the SIGCHI Conference on Human Factors in Computing Systems, pp. 373–380. ACM (1992)
7. Paiva, J.C., Leal, J.P., Queirós, R.A.: Enki: a pedagogical services aggregator for learning programming languages. In: Proceedings of the 2016 ACM Conference on Innovation and Technology in Computer Science Education, pp. 332–337. ACM (2016). https://doi.org/10.1145/2899415.2899441
8. Ramirez, A., et al.: ArgoUML user manual a tutorial and reference description. Technical report, pp. 2000–2009 (2003)
9. Shukur, Z., Mohamed, N.F.: The design of ADAT: a tool for assessing automata-based assignments. J. Comput. Sci. **4**(5), 415 (2008)
10. Shute, V.J.: Focus on formative feedback. Rev. Educ. Res. **78**(1), 153–189 (2008)
11. Soler, J., Boada, I., Prados, F., Poch, J., Fabregat, R.: A web-based e-learning tool for UML class diagrams. In: 2010 IEEE Education Engineering (EDUCON), pp. 973–979. IEEE (2010). https://doi.org/10.1109/EDUCON.2010.5492473
12. Sousa, R., Leal, J.P.: A structural approach to assess graph-based exercises. In: Sierra-Rodríguez, J.-L., Leal, J.P., Simões, A. (eds.) SLATE 2015. CCIS, vol. 563, pp. 182–193. Springer, Cham (2015). https://doi.org/10.1007/978-3-319-27653-3_18
13. Souza, C.R.B., Ferreira, J.S., Gonçalves, K.M., Wainer, J.: A group critic system for object-oriented analysis and design. In: The Fifteenth IEEE International Conference on Automated Software Engineering, Proceedings of ASE 2000, pp. 313–316. IEEE (2000). https://doi.org/10.1109/ASE.2000.873686
14. Thomas, P.: Online automatic marking of diagrams. Syst. Pract. Act. Res. **26**(4), 349–359 (2013). https://doi.org/10.1007/s11213-012-9273-5
15. Vachharajani, V., Pareek, J.: A proposed architecture for automated assessment of use case diagrams. Int. J. Comput. Appl. **108**(4) (2014). https://doi.org/10.5120/18902-019

A Framework for e-Assessment on Students' Devices: Technical Considerations

Bastian Küppers[1,2](✉) and Ulrik Schroeder[2]

[1] IT Center, RWTH Aachen University,
Seffenter Weg 23, 52074 Aachen, Germany
kueppers@itc.rwth-aachen.de
[2] Learning Technologies Research Group, RWTH Aachen University,
Ahornstraße 55, 52074 Aachen, Germany
schroeder@cs.rwth-aachen.de

Abstract. This paper presents FLEX, a framework for electronic assessment on students' devices. Basic requirements to such a framework and potential issues related with these requirements are discussed, as well as their state of the art. Afterwards, the client-server architecture of FLEX is presented, which is designed to meet all requirements previously identified. The FLEX client and the FLEX server are discussed in detail with focus on utilized technologies and programming languages. The results of first trials with the existing prototype are discussed in relation to the identified basic requirements. Thereafter, assessment of programming courses is discussed as use case of FLEX, which makes use of the extensibility of client and server. The paper closes with a summary and an outlook.

Keywords: Computer based examinations · Computer aided examinations e-Assessment · Bring You Own Device · BYOD · Reliability Equality of Treatment

1 Introduction

E-Assessment is a topic of growing importance for institutes of higher education. Despite being a valuable tool for diagnostic and formative assessments, e-Assessment has not yet been well established for summative assessments [1–4]. This is, among other reasons, caused by financial issues: building and maintaining a centrally managed IT-infrastructure for e-Assessment is costly [5, 6]. Since most students already possess suitable devices [7–9], Bring Your Own Device (BYOD) is a potential solution for this particular issue. BYOD, however, poses new challenges to security and reliability of e-Assessment. There are already existing solutions for carrying out e-Assessment on students' devices, but these have some drawbacks, as further discussed in Sect. 4.1.

This paper presents **FLEX** (**F**ramework **F**or **FLE**xible **E**lectronic **EX**aminations), a framework for e-Assessment on students' devices, which relies on BYOD and tackles new challenges and the drawbacks in existing solutions.

The paper is organized as follows: First, basic requirements to examinations are discussed. Second, an overview of the actual state of research is given and identified

E. Ras and A. E. Guerrero Roldán (Eds.): TEA 2017, CCIS 829, pp. 83–95, 2018.
https://doi.org/10.1007/978-3-319-97807-9_7

problems are discussed. Third, a general overview of FLEX is given, followed by a discussion of the technical details and first evaluation results. Fourth, programming assessment is presented as a use case. The paper closes with a summary and an outlook.

2 Basic Requirements

In order to carry out legally conformant examinations, at least the following conditions have to be fulfilled, which can be deduced by existing laws and regulations. The two requirements that are discussed in the next paragraphs have implications for a technical implementation. Therefore, we consider these as technical conditions, despite the requirements itself being more of an ethic nature.

2.1 Reliability

Assessments have to be reliable. That requirement implies that additional conditions have to be satisfied. On the one hand, these conditions concern the storage of the results of the assessment, allowing for correction and a later review of the correction, and, on the other hand, the conditions concern the secure conduction of the assessment. The results have to be stored in a way that data sets cannot be modified after the assessment [10] and can be safely retrieved for an appropriate amount of time after the assessment, for example ten years at RWTH Aachen University [11]. Additionally, it has to be possible to relate a data set unambiguously to a particular student [10]. Furthermore, the completion of the examination has to be reliable, i.e. cheating has to be prevented to be able to give meaningful marks for each student [10]. That means especially, that the authorship of a set of results has to be determinable.

2.2 Equality of Treatment

In an assessment, every student has to have the same chances of succeeding as every other student [10]. Besides being ethically important, this principle can be required by law. For example, in Germany Article 3 of the Basic Law for the Federal Republic of Germany demands an equality of treatment for all people (‘Equality before the law’) [12]. Since the students’ devices expectedly differ from each other, it is practically impossible to let every student have the exact same circumstances than every other student. However, even in a traditional paper-based assessment, the conditions differ between the students. For example, the students use different pens, sit at different locations in the room and may have different abilities regarding the speed of their handwriting. Hence, it can be concluded that the external conditions do not have to be exactly the same, but similar enough to not handicap particular students.

To obey these requirements, a technical implementation of an e-Assessment framework has to include technical measures that ensure the previously discussed conditions. Besides *Reliability* and *Equality of Treatment*, other conditions, like usability of the developed software tools, are part of the software development process.

However, since these have no counterpart in a traditional paper-based examination, these will not be discussed in this paper, which focuses on the basic requirements that hold for both, e-Assessment and paper-based examinations.

3 State of the Art

3.1 Reliability

Some approaches to prevent cheating during an examination have already been developed. Quite recently, surveillance over a camera, e.g. a built-in webcam, or online proctoring using a remote desktop connection, are of growing interest for distance assessment [13]. These methods could also be applied to on-campus assessment, but introduce a lot of effort, since plenty of invigilators have to be available to monitor the webcams or remote desktop sessions. So-called lockdown programs are an alternative to human invigilators. These programs allow only certain whitelisted actions to be carried out on the students' devices during an examination, for example visiting particular webpages. An example for a lockdown program is the Safe Exam Browser (SEB) [14], which is developed at ETH Zürich as an open source project. Commercial products are also available, for example Inspera Assessment [15], WISEflow [16] or Respondus LockDown Browser [17].

Dahinden proposed in his dissertation an infrastructure for reliable storage and accessibility of assessment results [18]. We enhanced Dahinden's system and introduced versioning of the assessment results by utilizing the version control software git [19].

3.2 Equality of Treatment

Especially in the field of mobile computing, the limited resources of mobile devices, e.g. processing power and battery time, have led to approaches for computational offloading [20, 21]. The same principles can also be applied to desktop computation, for example with applications working in a software as a service (SaaS) paradigm [22]. These treat all user equally, since only a web browser is required to render the user interface, while computationally intensive tasks are offloaded to a server. Web browser, like Google Chrome [23] or Mozilla Firefox [24], are available for every major platform and have hardware requirements that are expected to be matched by every device bought in the last years. The performance of the application depends more on the server's capabilities and the speed of the network connection, than on the client's device. Since the server of a SaaS application is the same for every user, all users can be expected to have a very similar performance for their application.

3.3 BYOD

In [25] we presented a review of existing BYOD approaches to e-Assessment in 2016. As e-Assessment is a very actively researched topic, several universities have published their approach to e-Assessment and BYOD since our review paper was published.

Since then, several universities have started to conduct online assessment with a secure browser: Brunel University uses the commercial product WISEflow [26], which uses the LockDown Browser by Respondus to secure the exam environment according to its vendor UNIwise[1]. The University of Basel, the Swiss Distance University of Applied Sciences, Zurich University of Applied Sciences and Thurgau University of Teacher Education, all located in Switzerland, use the Safe Exam Browser [27–30]. Finally yet importantly, the University of Agder recently started to use the Inspera Assessment software [31], after having used WISEflow before [32].

4 Identified Problems

Considering the presented state of the art, some problems can be identified, which are described in the following paragraphs.

4.1 Reliability

The first problem concerns the security of using lockdown software in a BYOD scenario to ensure reliability of the assessment. Since students' devices have to be considered as *untrusted platform* in principle, there exist doubts about the security of lockdown approaches [33] and about their applicability in a BYOD setting. Thus, there is no guarantee that the software on the students' devices, which shall ensure reliability, is itself reliable. Especially if the software is deployed asynchronously, i.e. the students can download and install the software prior to the exam, the software could have been altered on a student's device to provide an unfair advantage. As long as the software leads the server, for example a server running a LMS that is used to conduct an assessment, to believe that everything is all right, a tampered version of the software cannot be technically determined without further effort. In general, this method of cheating requires a lot of overhead, because the software has to be reverse engineered first to be able to alter it without the server noticing it. Therefore, in practice, this may be a negligible threat, however, in theory it is possible. The situation is different for SEB, because it is available open source. Thus, everyone can compile an own version of it and include any changes that are desirable.

Furthermore, it is not possible to prevent every possible unwanted action without administrative privileges on a device and even with administrative privileges, there is no guarantee that every unwanted action is effectively prevented. There may be bugs or conceptual flaws in the lockdown software, which leave a backdoor open. Additionally, requiring administrative privileges may be delicate, because student would have to grant administrative privileges to a software that could be theoretically harmful to their device. As a side note, the importance of a valid software signature of a software that is deployed by an institute of higher education can be concluded.

[1] UNIwise was contacted via email.

4.2 Equality of Treatment

Security tools, like the previously described lockdown software, are not available for every platform: To our knowledge, currently it exists no lockdown software that runs on a Linux-based operating system, but only on MacOS and Windows. Especially in a computer science study program, this could turn out to be a problem, since a higher diversity of operating systems among the students' devices can be expected. Therefore, some students may be handicapped because they use a not supported operating system.

5 FLEX

The previously identified problems were considered when designing the software architecture of FLEX in a design research workflow [34]. That means FLEX was planned in a way that the previously discussed basic requirements are fulfilled in a way that overcomes the issues in existing software solutions. Furthermore, the existing prototype is used to validate that the intended goals were actually met.

5.1 Meeting the Basic Requirements

To be able to conduct reliable examinations, each student has to be identifiable and results have to be relatable to a particular student unambiguously. Normally, a student is identified by checking her ID and her results are related to her by her handwriting. Checking the ID still works for e-Assessment, but relating results to students by their handwriting does not work anymore, obviously. Therefore, it was chosen to utilize digital signatures [35] in order to ensure authorship and integrity of the results of the assessment. These digital signatures, however, have to be relatable to a student likewise. In other scenarios, for example checking marks in an online system, authentication methods like Shibboleth [36] are used to determine a person's identity and relate it to the digital data set that exists for that person in the university's identity management (IdM). Therefore, information about the digital signature can be - or rather have to be - stored in the IdM, for example the public key of the corresponding certificate. As described in [19], students can deploy their public keys to the IdM themselves. Later on, the students' public keys will also be used to establish secure communication channels during an assessment.

Because of the previously identified problems regarding the reliability of e-Assessment scenarios using lockdown software, we proposed an alternative approach that does not prevent all unwanted actions, but makes extensive use of logging [37], which is a lot easier to achieve even without administrative privileges. If something suspicious happens on a student's device, this action will be logged on the FLEX server (see Sect. 5.4) and one of the invigilators present at the examination room will be informed. However, this does not solve the problem that the FLEX client (see Sect. 5.3) could have been altered. To prevent this, remote attestation techniques are utilized [38, 39] to check the integrity of the FLEX client.

To meet the requirement *Equality of Treatment,* a programming language and software architecture have to be chosen appropriately. As already mentioned, SaaS fulfills the requirement quite well, since it can be designed in a way that only the frontend, i.e. the user interface, runs on the students' devices with rather low requirements and everything else, especially computationally intensive tasks, can be offloaded to a server. Since this server is the same for all students, this scenario can be considered to fulfill the requirement. A second advantage of SaaS is the portability to different platforms, since only a web browser is needed in order to execute the application. Therefore, supporting the major desktop platforms (Windows, Linux, MacOS) and even mobile platforms (Android, iOS, ChromeOS) later on is easy.

Another requirement, which came up, was the relinquishment of administrative privileges on the students' devices. In addition to the previously mentioned concerns about security, to make the deployment of the client software as easy as possible, it should be runnable as portable software without administrative privileges. Thus, a regular user account should be sufficient to run the software properly. This requirement is of importance, because the students do not have necessarily administrative privileges on the devices used during an assessment. This could be, for example, the case if a student employee is allowed to use a device that is provided by her employer.

5.2 Basic Architecture

FLEX consists of a FLEX client (see Sect. 5.3) and a FLEX server (see Sect. 5.4), which have to communicate periodically throughout the assessment. In order to secure the communication between client and server, a client authenticated TLS-secured connection between client and server is utilized. Therefore, the server and the client use certificates to verify their identity to each other.

The basic architecture is depicted in Fig. 1.

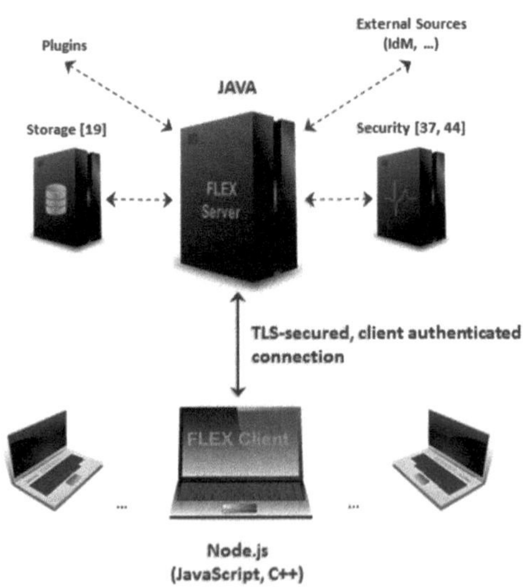

Fig. 1. Basic architecture of FLEX.

5.3 FLEX Client

To fulfill the previously discussed requirements, it was decided to implement the FLEX client using the electron framework [40], which is based on Node.js [41]. Therefore, the programming language used is JavaScript. The electron framework offers the ability to develop cross platform applications using web technologies, therefore keeping the applications lightweight. It is, however, also possible to make use of native features of the operating system, which is important for integrating security features into the client. In case, the API provided by electron does not support particular operations, it can be extended by plugins, which are provided in form of shared libraries. These shared libraries are implemented in C++ in order to have the native APIs of the different operating systems available. Logging and remote attestation are implemented as native plugins, because these mechanisms have to be platform dependent.

The Node.js runtime environment already offers functionalities for cryptographic operations. Therefore, a TLS-secured connection to the server and a digital signature of the assessment results, using the previously described certificate, can be implemented with the available API.

The client application itself is also extensible via plugins. Therefore, the client can be extended in order to integrate new features, for example new types of assignments or new storage backends.

5.4 FLEX Server

The implementation of the FLEX server is done in JAVA [42]. Mainly intended to be used on a Linux-based server, the implementation in JAVA potentially allows for the change of the server's operating system later on.

The server has different purposes. It identifies the students by their certificates, it distributes the assignments of the assessment and it collects the students' (intermediate) results. Additionally, it implements a part of the security mechanism described in [37] and provides capabilities for computational offloading. Depending on the plugins that may be used in the client, the server potentially has to be extended as well if a particular plugin requires a counterpart on the server. Therefore, the server uses a micro services architecture [43] to be easily extensible.

Additionally, the server communicates with external systems in order to retrieve information that are needed throughout an examination. Such a system could be, for example, the IdM to verify the students' certificates.

6 First Results

While FLEX is still in development, a first functional prototype is available. Therefore, we were able to conduct first evaluations regarding the question whether FLEX fulfills the postulated requirements. For the first trials, we concentrated on the requirement *Equality of Treatment*, since it had to be ensured this basic requirement is fulfilled by the chosen technologies and architecture. More on the *Reliability* of FLEX can be found in [19, 44].

To check whether all users would have a similar user experience in terms of the performance of FLEX, we measured the timing of crucial steps within the workflow of the FLEX client. We considered three steps, because these are the most computationally intensive ones for the FLEX client: starting the application (*start*), loading and initializing an exam (*init*), and finishing an exam (*finish*). The steps *init* and *finish* include network latency, because they contain communication between FLEX client and FLEX server.

We had six different test systems available and conducted 1000 runs of the FLEX client on each system in order to smooth out random fluctuations in the time measurement, e.g. caused by the operating system scheduling. The setup of the test systems can be found in Table 1.

Table 1. Configuration of the test systems.

System ID	CPU	RAM	OS
1	Quad Core (3.1 GHz)	8 GB	MacOS (High Sierra)
2	Quad Core (1.8 GHz)	8 GB	MacOS (High Sierra)
3	Quad Core (2.5 GHz)	8 GB	Windows 10
4	Quad Core (2.5 GHz)	8 GB	Ubuntu (GNOME 3)
5	Quad Core (2.5 GHz)	4 GB	Windows 10
6	Quad Core (2.5 GHz)	4 GB	Ubuntu (GNOME 3)

The obtained results are shown in Table 2.

Table 2. Obtained results.

System ID	Start	Init	Finish	$\sum$
1	1370 ms	176 ms	52 ms	1598 ms
2	1585 ms	217 ms	52 ms	1854 ms
3	1657 ms	35 ms	1037 ms	2729 ms
4	1523 ms	43 ms	42 ms	1608 ms
5	1630 ms	39 ms	1036 ms	2705 ms
6	1365 ms	38 ms	43 ms	1446 ms

From the obtained results, we conclude that the chosen technologies and architecture is suited to fulfill the requirement of *Equality of Treatment* in principle. Admittedly, there are differences in the measured timings for the different test systems, however, these can be considered negligible, since the differences are in the order of a few hundred milliseconds. Interesting to note, though, that not only the used hardware but also the used operating system seems to make a difference.

7 Use Case: Programming Assessments

Despite FLEX being designed as a flexible system in general, this chapter discusses assessment in the field of computer science respectively its subfield programming. In this section, assessment for programming courses will be discussed as a representative use case for FLEX. In a programming assessment, the students are obliged to write a program in JAVA using the FLEX client. The students' performance in this assignment is assessed by the quality of the source code that is delivered as their solutions.

7.1 FLEX Client

To be able to carry out programming assessments, a plugin for the FLEX client was developed. This plugin offers a user interface that resembles a programming integrated development environment (IDE). Therefore, a text editor with syntax highlighting is available and the possibilities to execute and debug the entered program code. Additionally, it is possible to load a code fragment provided by the examiner from the storage backend as a starting point. The editor is implemented based on CodeMirror [45], which is a freely available open source project, which was chosen, because it is extensible via plugins. Additionally to the code editor, webpages can be provided to the students, for example a programming API.

The functionality to execute and debug programs has to be realized in a way that ensures *Equality of Treatment*. Therefore, the code is not executed or debugged on the students' devices, which could result in different time consumption due to different hardware capabilities, but the code is transmitted to the server and executed or debugged there [46].

A screenshot of the FLEX client using the developed plugin for programming assessment is shown in Fig. 2.

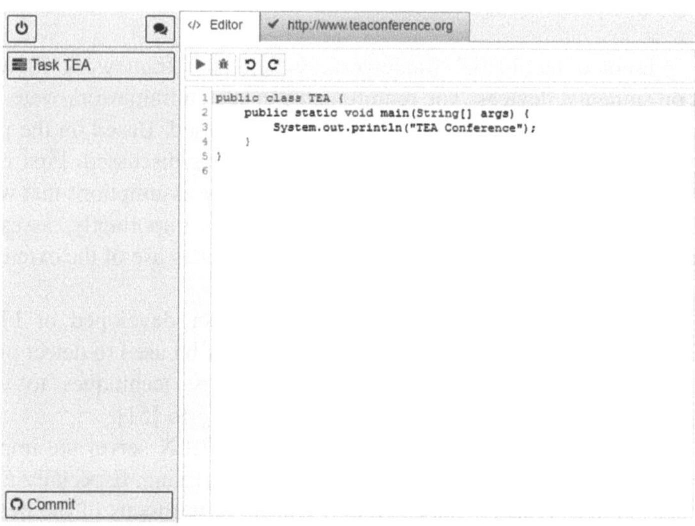

Fig. 2. Screenshot of the FLEX client.

7.2 FLEX Server

The server provides the capabilities to execute and debug code. The possibility to execute code is offered via a RESTful webservice [47]. The client sends the code to the webservice, which executes this code and sends the generated output, for example error messages or printings to the standard output, back to the client. In case the code shall be debugged, the connection between server and client is established over a websocket, which is, in difference to connections to a RESTful webservice, stateful. Statefulness is important for debugging, since several commands could be sent to the server, which are potentially related to each other.

In both cases, the code is executed in a Docker container [48] in order to prevent the execution of malicious code directly on the server. Therefore, in the worst case, the malicious code infects or destroys the Docker container, but the integrity of the server itself is preserved.

7.3 Assessment

The solutions that are handed in by the students are checked for the ability to solve the given assignment successfully. First, it has to be determined whether the source code successfully compiles. This should be the case, since the students can verify this before handing in using the FLEX client. However, if the source code does not compile it has to be determined why this is the case, which has to be done manually by the corrector. If the source code compiles successfully, the expected functionality of the resulting program is verified automatically using unit tests [49]. Based on the successful compilation and the number of unit tests that the compiled program passes, a grade can be obtained. Several approaches for assigning a grade already exist [50].

8 Summary and Outlook

This paper presented the FLEX framework, which is a framework for electronic assessment on students' devices. The requirements to such a framework were presented and the state of the art for those requirements was discussed. Based on the postulated requirements, the basic architecture of the framework was discussed. First evaluation results were presented and their discussion implied that the assumptions that were made about the chosen technologies are justified. Finally yet importantly, assessment of programming courses was presented as a use case that makes use of the extensibility of FLEX client and FLEX server.

To provide additional security measures, the further developed of FLEX will include additional software tools on the server, which can be used to detect plagiarism. Especially for the assessment of programming courses, techniques to verify the authorship of source code will be implemented according to [51].

In the actual state of the project, FLEX client and FLEX server are implemented prototypically. The next steps will be beta testing and bug fixing. Especially *Equality of Treatment* and *Reliability* as discussed before will be in the focus of the beta test.

References

1. Themengruppe Change Management & Organisationsentwicklung: E-Assessment als Herausforderung - Handlungsempfehlungen für Hochschulen. Arbeitspapier Nr. 2. Berlin: Hochschulforum Digitalisierung. (2015). https://hochschulforumdigitalisierung.de/sites/default/files/dateien/HFD%20AP%20Nr%202_E-Asessment%20als%20Herausforderung%20Handlungsempfehlungen%20fuer%20Hochschulen.pdf
2. James, R.: Tertiary student attitudes to invigilated, online summative examinations. Int. J. Educ. Technol. High. Educ. **13**, 19 (2016). https://doi.org/10.1186/s41239-016-0015-0
3. Berggren, B., Fili, A., Nordberg, O.: Digital examination in higher education–experiences from three different perspectives. Int. J. Educ. Dev. Inf. Commun. Technol. **11**(3), 100–108 (2015)
4. JISC: Effective Practice with e-Assessment (2007). https://www.webarchive.org.uk/wayback/archive/20140615085433/http://www.jisc.ac.uk/media/documents/themes/elearning/effpraceassess.pdf
5. Biella, D., Engert, S., Huth, D.: Design and delivery of an e-assessment solution at the University of Duisburg-Essen. In: Proceedings of EUNIS 2009 (2009)
6. Bücking, J.: eKlausuren im Testcenter der Universität Bremen: Ein Praxisbericht (2010). https://www.campussource.de/events/e1010tudortmund/docs/Buecking.pdf
7. Brooks, D.C., Pomerantz, J.: ECAR Study of Undergraduate Students and Information Technology (2017). https://library.educause.edu/~/media/files/library/2017/10/studentitstudy2017.pdf
8. Poll, H.: Student Mobile Device Survey 2015: National Report: College Students (2015). https://www.pearsoned.com/wp-content/uploads/2015-Pearson-Student-Mobile-Device-Survey-College.pdf
9. Willige, J.: Auslandsmobilität und digitale Medien. Arbeitspapier Nr. 23. Berlin: Hochschulforum Digitalisierung. (2016). https://hochschulforumdigitalisierung.de/sites/default/files/dateien/HFD_AP_Nr23_Digitale_Medien_und_Mobilitaet.pdf
10. Forgó, N., Graupe, S., Pfeiffenbring, J.: Rechtliche Aspekte von E-Assessments an Hochschulen (2016). https://dx.doi.org/10.17185/duepublico/42871
11. RWTH Aachen University: Richtlinien zur Aufbewahrung, Aussonderung, Archivierung und Vernichtung von Akten und Unterlagen der RWTH Aachen (2016). http://www.rwth-aachen.de/global/show_document.asp?id=aaaaaaaaaatmzml
12. German Bundestag: Basic Law for the Federal Republic of Germany (2012). https://www.btg-bestellservice.de/pdf/80201000.pdf
13. Frank, A.J.: Dependable distributed testing: can the online proctor be reliably computerized? In: Marca, D.A. (ed.) Proceedings of the International Conference on E-Business. SciTePress, S.l (2010)
14. Safe Exam Browser. https://www.safeexambrowser.org/
15. Inspera Assessment. https://www.inspera.no/
16. WISEflow. https://europe.wiseflow.net/
17. LockDown Browser. http://www.respondus.com/products/lockdown-browser/
18. Dahinden, M.: Designprinzipien und Evaluation eines reliablen CBA-Systems zur Erhebung valider Leistungsdaten. Ph.D. thesis (2014). https://dx.doi.org/10.3929/ethz-a-010264032
19. Küppers, B., Politze, M., Schroeder, U.: Reliable e-assessment with git practical considerations and implementation (2017). https://dx.doi.org/10.17879/21299722960
20. Akherfi, K., Gerndt, M., Harroud, H.: Mobile cloud computing for computation offloading: issues and challenges. Appl. Comput. Inform. **14**, 1–16 (2016). https://doi.org/10.1016/j.aci.2016.11.002. ISSN 2210-8327

21. Kovachev, D., Klamma, R.: Framework for computation offloading in mobile cloud computing. Int. J. Interact. Multimed. Artif. Intell. **1**(7), 6–15 (2012). https://doi.org/10.9781/ijimai.2012.171
22. Buxmann, P., Hess, T., Lehmann, S.: Software as a service. Wirtschaftsinformatik **50**(6), 500–503 (2008). https://doi.org/10.1007/s11576-008-0095-0
23. Google Chrome. https://www.google.com/intl/en/chrome/browser/desktop/
24. Mozilla Firefox. https://www.mozilla.org/en-US/firefox/
25. Küppers, B., Schroeder, U.: Bring Your Own Device for e-Assessment – a review. In: EDULEARN 2016 Proceedings, pp. 8770–8776 (2016). https://dx.doi.org/10.21125/edulearn.2016.0919. ISSN 2340-1117
26. About Digital Assessment @Brunel (2017). http://www.brunel.ac.uk/about/education-innovation/Digital-Assessment-Brunel/About
27. eAssessment an der Universität Basel, Basel (2017). https://bbit-hsd.unibas.ch/medien/2017/10/EvaExam-Betriebskonzept.pdf
28. Sadiki, J.: E-Assessment with BYOD, SEB and Moodle at the FFHS (2017). https://www.eduhub.ch/export/sites/default/files/E-Assessment_eduhubdays_showtell.pdf
29. Kavanagh, M.; Lozza, D.; Messenzehl, L.: Moodle-exams with Safe Exam Browser (SEB) on BYOD (2017). https://www.eduhub.ch/export/sites/default/files/ShowTell_ZHAW.pdf
30. Die ersten «BYOD» E-Assessments an der PHTG (2016). http://www.phtg.ch/news-detail/456-260216-laessig-die-ersten-byod-e-assessments-an-der-phtg/
31. Written examinations. https://www.uia.no/en/student/examinations/written-examinations
32. WISEflow implemented on the University of Agder, Norway. http://uniwise.dk/2014/07/31/wiseflow-uia/
33. Søgaard, T.M.: Mitigation of Cheating Threats in Digital BYOD exams. Master's thesis (2016). https://dx.doi.org/11250/2410735
34. March, S.T., Smith, G.F.: Design and natural science research on information technology. Decis. Support Syst. **15**(4), 251–266 (1995). https://doi.org/10.1016/0167-9236(94)00041-2. ISSN 0167-9236
35. Kaur, R., Kaur, A.: Digital signature. In: 2012 International Conference on Computing Sciences, pp. 295–301 (2012). https://doi.org/10.1109/ICCS.2012.25
36. Morgan, R.L., Cantor, S., Carmody, S., Hoehn, W., Klingenstein, K.: Federated security: the Shibboleth approach. EDUCAUSE Q. **27**(4), 12–17 (2004)
37. Küppers, B., Kerber, F., Meyer, U., Schroeder, U.: Beyond lockdown: towards reliable e-assessment. In: GI-Edition - Lecture Notes in Informatics (LNI), P-273, pp. 191–196 (2017). ISSN 1617-5468
38. Seshadri, A., Luk, M., Shi, E., Perrig, A., van Doorn, L., Khosla, P.: Pioneer: verifying code integrity and enforcing untampered code execution on legacy systems. ACM SIGOPS Oper. Syst. Rev. **39**(5), 1–16 (2005). https://doi.org/10.1145/1095810.1095812
39. Garay, J.A., Huelsbergen, L.: Software integrity protection using timed executable agents. In: Proceedings of the 2006 ACM Symposium on Information, Computer and Communications Security, pp. 189–200 (2006). https://dx.doi.org/10.1145/1128817.1128847
40. Electron Framework. https://electron.atom.io/
41. Node.js. https://nodejs.org/en/
42. JAVA. https://www.java.com/de/
43. Namiot, D.; Sneps-Sneppe, M.: On micro-services architecture. Int. J. Open Inf. Technol. **2** (9) (2014)
44. Küppers, B., Politze, M., Zameitat, R., Kerber, F., Schroeder, U.: Practical security for electronic examinations on students' devices. In: Proceedings of SAI Computing Conference 2018 (2018, in Press)
45. CodeMirror. https://codemirror.net/

46. Zameitat, R., Küppers, B.: JDB – Eine Bibliothek für Java-Debugging im Browser (in Press)
47. Fielding, R.T., Taylor, R.N.: Principled design of the modern Web architecture (2002). https://dx.doi.org/10.1145/514183.514185
48. Docker. https://www.docker.com/
49. Langr, J., Hunt, A., Thomas, D.: Pragmatic unit testing in Java 8 with Junit, 1st edn. Pragmatic Bookshelf, Raleigh (2015). ISBN 978-1-94122-259-1
50. Queirós, R., Leal, J.P.: Programming exercises evaluation systems - an interoperability survey. In: Helfert, M., Martins, M.J., Cordeiro, J. (eds.) CSEDU (1), pp. 83–90. SciTePress (2012)
51. Caliskan-Islam, A., Liu, A., Voss, C., Greenstadt, R.: De-anonymizing programmers via code stylometry. In: Proceedings of the 24th USENIX Security Symposium (2015). ISBN 978-1-931971-232

Online Proctoring for Remote Examination: A State of Play in Higher Education in the EU

Silvester Draaijer[1(✉)], Amanda Jefferies[2], and Gwendoline Somers[3]

[1] Faculty of Behavioural and Movement Sciences,
Department of Research and Theory in Education, Vrije Universiteit Amsterdam,
De Boelelaan 1105, 1081 HV Amsterdam, The Netherlands
s.draaijer@vu.nl

[2] School of Computer Science,
Centre for Computer Science and Informatics Research,
Hertfordshire University, Hatfield, Hertfordshire, UK
a.l.jefferies@herts.ac.uk

[3] Dienst onderwijsontwikkeling, diversiteit en innovatie, Universiteit Hasselt,
Martelarenlaan 42, 3500 Hasselt, Belgium
gwendoline.somers@uhasselt.be

Abstract. We present some preliminary findings of the Erasmus+ KA2 Strategic Partnership project "Online Proctoring for Remote Examination" (OP4RE). OP4RE aims to develop, implement and disseminate up to par practices for remote examination procedures. More specifically, OP4RE strives to develop guidelines and minimum standards for the secure, legal, fair and trustworthy administration of exams in a remote location away from physical exam rooms in a European context. We present findings and issues regarding security, cheating prevention and deterrence, privacy and data protections as well as practical implementation.

Keywords: Proctoring · Invigilation · Remote examination
Distance education · e-Assessment · Technology-enhanced assessment

1 Introduction

Online proctoring involves technologies and procedures to allow students to take exams securely in a remote location away from a physical exam room. In the US, the term *proctoring* is used to describe the oversight and checking of students and their credentials for an examination. In the UK and other English-speaking countries, this is referred to as *invigilation*. With secure online proctoring, exams can now for example be taken at home. Cheating, collusion and/or fraudulently acquiring answers to tests are the core phenomena that proctoring must prevent during the examination process. It is expected that a future secure level of online proctoring will contribute to increasing access to higher education (HE) for various groups of (prospective) students. Online proctoring is expected to increase the opportunity for 'anytime, anyplace' examination processes once security and privacy issues have been resolved to the satisfaction of the HE institution (HEI) and the student.

E. Ras and A. E. Guerrero Roldán (Eds.): TEA 2017, CCIS 829, pp. 96–108, 2018.
https://doi.org/10.1007/978-3-319-97807-9_8

Online proctoring must be seen as part of the complete assessment cycle, which combines systems and processes to author test items and tasks, to assemble test items into tests, to administer these tests to students under correct and controlled conditions, to collect responses and to execute scoring and grading. Online proctoring itself involves technologies, processes and human observers (proctors, examiners, exam board members) to record and view test-takers as they take their tests [1]. A graphical overview of the systems and individuals involved is depicted in Fig. 1.

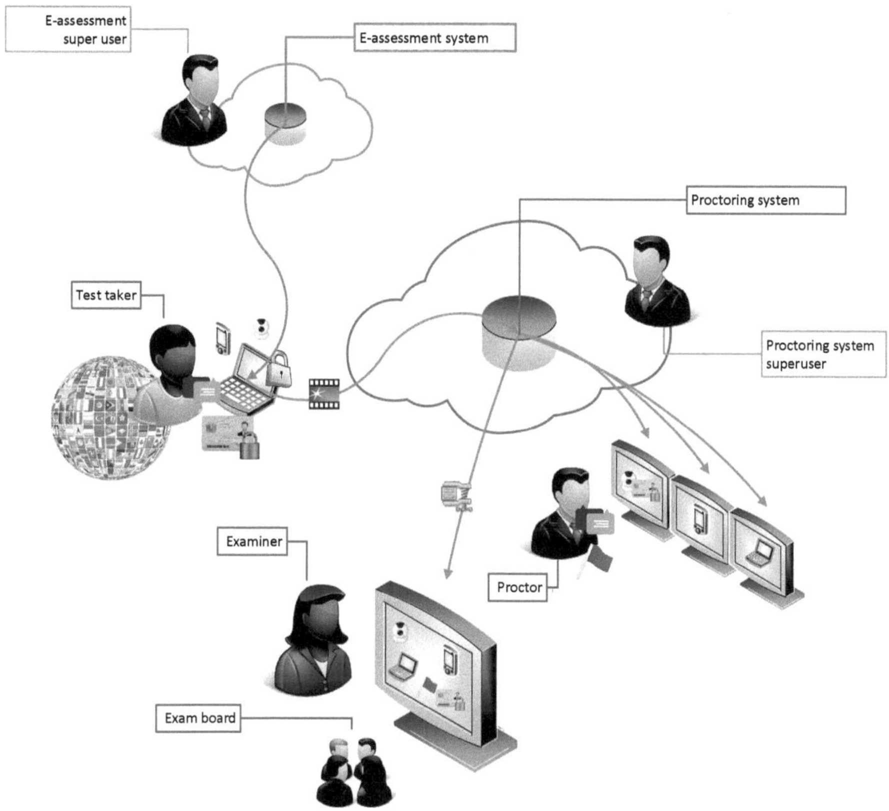

Fig. 1. Overview of systems and individuals involved in online proctoring.

The importance of online remote examination is clear in relation to goals of the European Union (EU) and HEI's in general. It is for example an Erasmus+ priority to enable 'supporting the implementation of the 2013 communication on opening up education' [2] along with the directive of 'open and innovative education, training, and youth work in the digital era' [3]. The priorities of Erasmus+ address the ultimate objective of using the current strides in technological advancements to increase access to HE for citizens. HEIs in the EU are increasingly seeking to attract students from all over Europe and the world to be attractive and competitive in current education and research.

In this paper, we present some preliminary findings of the Erasmus+ KA2 Strategic Partnership project "Online Proctoring for Remote Examination" (OP4RE), which started in September 2016. In the project, seven HEIs and a proctoring technology provider collaborate to study the possibilities for and limitations of remote examination in HE. OP4RE aims to develop, implement and disseminate innovative practices for remote examination procedures. More specifically, OP4RE will strive to develop guidelines and minimum standards to minimise the impact of the key barriers to the uptake of remote examination in higher education in a European context:

- Issues related to the validity and reliability of remote examination in view of accreditation and the student experience
- Issues related to security and cheating
- Issues related to practical and technical issues for the implementation of online proctoring
- Issues related to privacy and data protection.

The preliminary phase from the first year is almost done (June 2017) and this paper will share some of the dissemination of the project achievements to date.

2 Assessment

The prevailing European and US cultural view on any accredited educational programmes in HE is that summative tests are needed in many cases to assess student achievement in a reliable and valid way [4]. Summative tests can be divided into low, medium- or high-stakes exams, depending on the extent of the consequences or importance of the decision made based on the outcome of the assessment [5]. High stakes imply that for both the test-taker and the educational institution, much depends on the successful outcome of an exam. High-stakes exams tend to result in issuing course credits, course certificates, diplomas and degrees. High-stakes exams may involve the release of funds or access to HE or the workplace.

3 Possible Applications

It is clear that distance education students can benefit from online remote proctored examination as the need for travel and physical presence in exam rooms are removed. In this line of thinking there are specific applications under study in the OP4RE project. For example, experiments geared towards students with disabilities and students studying for a limited time in a foreign country but needing to resit exams. Other, more large-scale examples, are also under consideration:

Example 1: Selection Tests for Entrance into Bachelor Programmes with Numerus Fixus. Experiments for remote proctoring are set-up in the OP4RE project for bachelor study programmes that require the selection of students (numerus fixus programmes). Dutch HEIs are obliged to offer students living in the so-called 'overseas islands' (Bonaire, Saba and Sint Eustatius) the possibility to take these selection tests under the same conditions as mainland Dutch students without any possible financial barriers. As travelling to the Netherlands can be costly, online proctoring can provide a solution to this problem both for the HEI's as well as the prospective students.

Example 2: Mathematics Proficiency Tests for International Students. The second example is concerned with offering remote examinations to international students who want to enter an international bachelor study programme in the Netherlands, but lack evidence of having sufficient mathematical skills. Currently, students need to come to the Netherlands to take mathematics ability tests. Improved access to HE can be realised if these students could take these tests online. Conducting an experiment within the OP4RE project could provide additional empirical evidence to support such a business case. In such a business case, the possible outcomes for remote examination (in terms of increased student enrolment from specific countries and chances of successful study careers) are weighted against the costs of designing, maintaining and administering high-quality homemade mathematics tests.

Example 3: Online Proctoring in a MOOC Context. The final example is related to online proctoring in the context of massive open and online education. A few experiments have already been undertaken in the past with the current MOOC providers such as Coursera <ref>, but up to now online proctoring in that context has not taken off fully. This is amongst others due to problems of the sheer number of test-takers in relation to too low protecting against uncontrolled exposure and dispersion of exams and exam questions. In that context, authenticating students and ensuring a secure and fraud resistant form of summative examination is under study in the OP4RE project.

4 Trust

Trust is one of the main concepts when it comes to assessment. HEIs and society place a strong emphasis on the accreditation of trustworthy diplomas and degrees awarded and hence in the trustworthiness of examination processes. The higher the stakes of an exam, the higher the trustworthiness of the exam and exam procedures that is required. When HEIs are exposed to and confronted by (suspicions of) unethical behaviour, malpractice or otherwise fraudulently acquired course credits, diplomas or certificates, trust is undermined.

The trustworthiness of online proctored exams has been called into question in a number of reports. In particular, problems have been uncovered by mystery test-takers who tried actively ‘to game’ the system [6, 7]. Publishing stories involving such mystery guests and uncovered breaches in cheating prevention in the national media or social media are often presented in terms of a ‘loss-frame’ [8], emphasizing the grave consequences the identified problem causes. These stories can induce a large setback for the uptake and acceptance of online proctoring. Serious consequences can arise. These consequences can include nullified diplomas, damaged reputations and declining student numbers [7, 9].

An interesting comparable situation can be seen in the area of e-voting. In recent years, a number of experiments have involved implementing e-voting for national elections. These experiments did not all run well. For example, in the Netherlands, an attempt to implement e-voting was made, but a group of computer specialists identified possible security risks in the process and technical chains. This fuelled intensive political and public debate, eventually leading to the abandonment of the idea of e-voting in the Netherlands altogether [10].

Online assessment including proctoring calls, in the light of trustworthiness, for even more stringent application and communication of possible problems and remedies than traditional proctoring already does. In the eyes of the public, teachers and examiners, the fact that an examination is held in a remote location of the student's choosing instead of at an accredited assessment location means that much stronger guarantees regarding the prevention of fraud or cheating must be in place.

5 Online Proctoring in the US in HE

With the advent in 2001 of service providers for online remote proctoring [11], the apparent number of identified cheating possibilities in online examinations has been reduced substantially. Kryterion was the first company to offer online proctoring services and systems (WebAssessor™). Later, a number of other software solutions and service providers entered the market [12, 13]. Each combination of software solutions, offering additional services, such as fingerprint authentication or data forensic and proctoring options (live proctoring or recorded proctoring), raises the bar with an extra layer of security and cheating deterrence and detection [14, 15].

Example 1. A well-known example of an HEI using online proctoring is Western Governors University (WGU) based in Salt Lake City. Since 2009, WGU has used amongst others WebAssessor™ in their distance education programmes [16]. Currently, more than 36,000 assessments per month are administered at WGU [17]. Case and Cabalka were of opinion in an evaluation report of the pilot practices at WGU, that no significant differences with respect to performance between students taking an exam on-site or online were detected and no significant differences in occurrences of cheating. Their findings however are not extensively documented or supported by detailed evidence.

Example 2. An initiative focused on part of the complete e-assessment process is the EU-funded project TeSLA. TeSLA's aim is to develop and deliver methods and techniques for the authentication of test-takers via biometric approaches [18]. The project involves research on facial recognition, voice recognition, keystroke analysis and fingerprint analysis to ensure that test-takers are not impersonators and that the answers are provided by the actual test-taker. The technologies developed are intended to become building blocks for use with managed learning environments, such as Moodle, or with proctoring solutions that are more general, such as ProctorExam.

6 Online Proctoring in the EU in HE

While developments in and the employment of online remote proctoring in HE have gained substantial ground in the US, this is not yet the case in both distance and residential education in the EU [1]. In the countries involved in the OP4RE project (United Kingdom, Germany, Belgium, France, The Netherlands), only limited number of applications are known and most of them are in pilot or early phases. It is only the distance education department of VIVES University College in Belgium that applies online remote proctoring to a more large scale of approximately a thousand examinations per year [19] using dedicated support staff. A few reasons for this limited uptake of online proctoring in a European context can be pointed out.

First, no EU-based technology and service provider existed previously. Most proctoring companies are US-based, and only a few HEIs in the EU have piloted online proctoring with US-based companies [20, 21]. This hindered a more trust-based collaboration between HEIs in the EU and proctoring service providers. It was not until 2013 that a few European companies entered the market, including ProctorExam (Netherlands) and TestReach (Ireland). ProctorExam was established in Amsterdam to allow for closer collaboration in designing technology and fitting in with the European educational culture of examination at, for example, the University of Amsterdam [22].

Second, HEIs need to become familiar with the concept of online proctoring and they require new procedures and protocols. It is essential to determine who is responsible for which part of the process in the institution in terms of execution, governance, administration, finance, legal issues, exam procedures, standards, etc. Implementing online proctoring in a traditional HEI will also likely require internal organisational change and development, as individuals and organisational units need restructured funding, expertise and processes.

Third, HEIs are increasingly obliged by law to comply fully with privacy and data protection legislation. Legislation regarding privacy and data security has become increasingly restrictive within and outside of Europe in the past decade. With the advent of the EU General Data Protection Regulation (GDPR), there will be many changes to data privacy regulations. It will enter into force on 25 May 2018 [23]. HEIs must be cautious when collecting data and employing service providers, data processors and technologies if the HEI cannot oversee the possible consequences that these legislative rules imply. In particular, this relates to the required rules of conduct (in detail) and potential high fines that data authorities can issue when there is a failure to comply with regulations.

Finally, the cost of online proctoring cannot be neglected [24]. For example, in the legislation of some EU countries, charging extra fees for students to take exams is prohibited by law. Therefore, any extra out-of-pocket cost for HEIs arising from deploying online proctoring is not yet accounted for in the regular budgeting practices. Of course, current exam facilities and proctoring procedures also cost money, but these costs are already factored into many long-term financial plans, and the internal setup of a central authority for managing assessments across individual HEIs is not so separately visible. This problem can be enlarged in situations in which HEIs must ensure equal access to all groups, not only distant or specials groups. The latter could imply that when an HE offers an online proctored examination to distance students, they are obliged to offer this service to all regular students.

7 Security

Preventing and reacting to security breaches is one the main preliminary conditions for successful and trustworthy online proctoring. Possible security problems in technical systems can be identified in numerous process steps, technological devices, software and organisational structures in the proctoring chain. Security issues can relate to manipulating the flow of information through the system with fraudulent intent on the one hand. On the other hand, security issues can relate to processes that cause malfunctioning of proctoring or assessment systems. Therefore, in the OP4RE project, close analysis and testing of the proctoring system of the technology vendor ProctorExam is part of the project. For this activity, the Threat Assessment Model for Electronic Payment Systems (TAME) will be used [25]. The TAME is a third-generation threat assessment methodology that uses organisational analysis and a four-phase analysis and trial approach as the core activities to assess the nature and impact of security threats and measures to minimise or inhibit these threats. In the OP4RE Start Report [1], a further outline of the TAME model can be found. Figure 2 illustrates the high-level phases of the TAME.

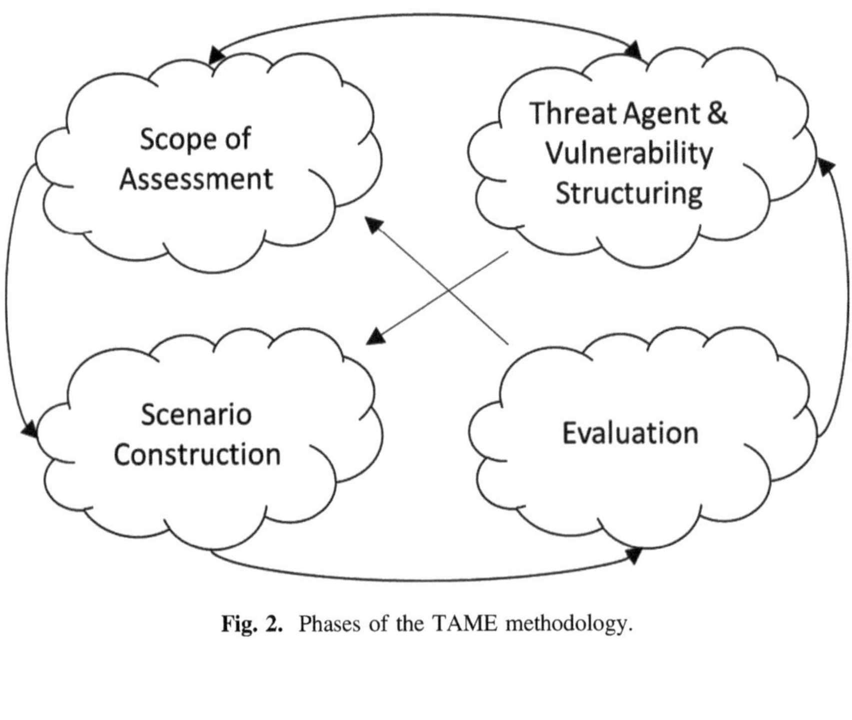

Fig. 2. Phases of the TAME methodology.

8 Cheating

One of the primary goals of online proctoring is to deter and detect cheating. Possibilities for cheating can be identified at various stages and phases of the examination process, comprising in general (1) prior sight of exam questions, (2) unfair retaking or grade changing for assessments and (3) unauthorised help (impersonation, illegal assistance, illegal resources) during the assessment [4, 11]. With online proctoring, phase (3) specifically is subject of scrutiny.

More and more 'tips and tricks' are available on the Internet that show how to cheat in online and face-to-face exams, and new methods arise constantly [26, 27]. One could conclude that deterring and detecting cheating is a mission impossible. Based on Foster and Layman [12] and on Kolowich [13], however, the number of incidences of serious suspicions of online cheating in online proctoring is below five or 2.7%. Foster and Layman conclude that this constitutes neither more nor less incidences than during regular face-to-face proctoring. Therefore, there seems to be no objective reason why the public or accreditation bodies should be more concerned with the problem of cheating in online proctoring as compared to the current processes involved in face-to-face proctoring.

9 Technology in a Practical e-Assessment Context

Given high demands for security and preventing and detecting cheating, yet allowing for a smoothly run, uninterrupted exam process, exams must be designed and administered in a manner that is easy to understand and control, but at the same time requires high personal and academic standards of behaviour from all stakeholders involved in the examination process. These stakeholders include students, academic faculty members, examiners, exam boards and proctors, as well as information technology (IT) and administrative staff. On all levels and throughout the complete infrastructure, all possible negatively impactful events should be faced up front. This calls for closely aligned and orchestrated procedures and responsibility assignments.

Example 1. Case and Cabalca [16], Beust et al. [20] and Beust and Duchatelle [28] concluded that the first time that students take an online proctored test, anxiety levels with respect to following correct procedures and the adequate use and reliability of technology are high. They reported a fair number of incidents in which procedures failed and a number of incidents in which students declined from participating in an online exam altogether. However, in subsequent tests, anxiety levels and procedural failures drop much lower due to familiarisation with procedures and technologies. It can be concluded that there is a steep learning curve for test-takers in taking online exams, but there is also a steep reduction in anxiety in later situations after the first run of proctoring has been successfully executed.

Example 2. The language spoken by the test-takers and that spoken by the proctors should be compatible. Beust and Duchatelle [28] reported that French-speaking students were dissatisfied that communication with a proctor of ProctroU could only be conducted in English and that language issues caused problems during proctoring. As it cannot be expected that all test-takers are able to speak or read English, live proctors must be able to speak the mother tongue of the test-takers preferably, and the user interface of the proctoring software should be adaptable to the language of the test-taker.

Example 3. The WebAssessor™ suite includes such technologies as data forensics (searching and immunising online illegal repositories of exams), digital photography, biometric facial recognition software, automated video analysis or keystroke analysis to ensure the identity of the test-taker and the ownership of the test data. All these technologies result in the identification of possible misconduct. However, not all identified issues are necessarily related to actual cheating. For that reason, for example, Software Secure (another proctoring solution provider) identifies three sorts of incidents according to Kolowich [13]: "minor suspicions" (identified in about 50% of reported issues), "intermediate suspicions" (somewhere between 20 and 30% of reported issues) and "major incidents" (2–5% of reported issues). Interestingly enough, after the initial implementation of high-level technologies, such as biometric authentication and keystroke analysis, Western Governors University currently does not use these high-level features anymore. WGU found that any additional technology to detect possible cheating leads to more occurrences of failure in executing a proctoring session successfully. Equally important, the technologies lead to far too many instances of false-positives for cheating suspicion [17]. WGU now always uses live proctoring with as little as possible technological features. WGU places most trust at this moment in human proctors who invigilate test-takers in real time. At WGU, a dedicated team of multiple full-time equivalents is responsible for the whole process of online proctoring. By ensuring thorough training and monitoring of the quality of the human proctors, malpractice is most effectively deterred and detected, according to WGU.

10 Privacy and Data Protection

Given the wider political, legal and public concern for privacy, data protection is becoming more and more important: students want to know who is collecting data, for what goal, how will it be stored and in what kind of system accessible by whom, etc. Incidents in which personal data are accessed illegally or made public are still presented in the media as 'big events', causing damage to the reputation of the institution at hand. As well, in view of the new European and international legislation, institutions can face serious fines.

The data stored for online proctoring contain the personal information of a test-taker (for example, the ID card shown and photographed with the webcam) or the examinee's home interior. Camera images and video footage fall into a separate category under the GDPR: namely, that of sensitive personal data. In particular, camera images can be used to detect medical conditions (e.g. 'wears glasses'), race and ethnicity. This personal data may not in principle be processed unless the law provides specific or general exceptions.

The legislation can be more or less restrictive on these points in different countries. In France, for instance, the national institution for personal data protection and individual liberties (CNIL) allows an HEI to store identity information and full video recordings using a webcam, but it does not allow easily the use or storage of biometric data. Being knowledgeable about these rules and guidelines is of great importance for HEIs to go forward with implementing online proctoring.

Any institution wanting to begin using online proctoring should consider the concept of *privacy by design*. A flow chart is in development that can be used to communicate the steps to ensure privacy by design. See Fig. 3.

This flow chart can be of assistance in designing processes and agreements with that goal. Therefore, after identifying opportunities for online proctoring, each institution will have to develop and implement privacy and data protection policies, regardless of any proctoring system being used. The relevant officers must be identified and the relevant procedures and agreements should be drawn up and agreed upon. This privacy by design approach must be used, along with other aspects of online proctoring that are of importance, such as raising awareness, practical procedures, security, fraud detection etc. Hence, multiple streams of policies and technical studies must be executed when an institution wants to begin using online proctoring and comply with data protection regulations.

Some general—and relatively easy and obvious—guidelines have already been identified when conducting any form of online proctoring. We will provide a few examples:

- When performing an online exam, candidates need to be informed in advance of the nature of the exam, and their consent to use the data is needed. Consent information must be as clear as possible. Candidates need to be made explicitly aware of what is going to happen with the data and their rights (ownership, data protection, etc.). In some institutions, these kinds of experiments (with students) even need to be submitted to an ethical commission. In the OP4RE project, templates for consent forms will be developed.
- When collecting ID information, ensure the test-takers cover any information on their ID cards that refers to, for example, passport, social security or driver license numbers.
- Ensure that obvious rules-of-conduct for superusers of systems, proctors and examiners are in place, such as not viewing videos in a public place, not downloading videos to personal or unprotected devices, not downloading ID cards and photographs to personal or unprotected devices, etc.
- Ensure that any video or ID material that is stored will be erased by default from all systems after a set time in case that no suspicions of fraud had been detected.

Issues concerning data protection when multiple and/or foreign countries are involved in a proctoring situation should be resolved as well (cross border flow of data). The problem that arise from this are not easy to oversee. For example, HEIs in one country organising online proctoring for a remote examination for test-takers in other countries and the ID and video data are stored in yet another country must comply with all three local regulations. How do international regulations (i.e. foreign laws, local laws) and institutional procedures match? Which specific regulations are applicable? It is important to know all specific regulations and act accordingly to be able to comply fully.

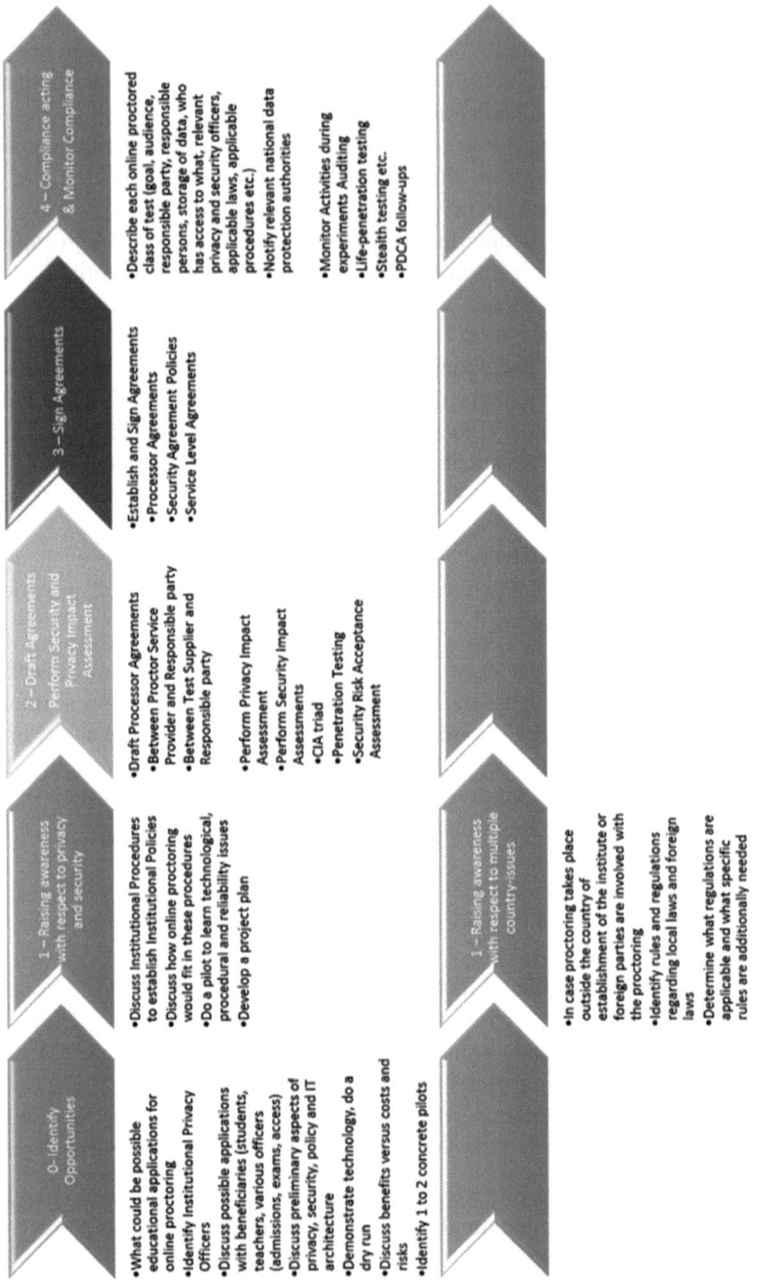

Fig. 3. Flow chart of privacy by design for online proctoring.

11 Conclusion

In this paper, we described the current understanding in de Erasmus+ project ‘Online Proctoring for Remote Examination’ (OP4RE) of the concept of online remote proctoring in a European HE context. Online remote proctoring can increase access to higher education for various target groups and applications. We posited that trust is the main concept in thinking about the broad acceptance of online proctoring. Trust can be built by developing technologies and procedures in close collaboration with all stakeholders. Current practices, in particular in the US, show that large scale online proctoring is possible, provided that the organisations adapt to it. For distance education institutions, this seems easier to accomplish than for residential focused HIE’s. Many issues related to security, cheating and data protection need to be addressed to allow for a larger uptake of online remote proctoring in higher education. The OP4RE project aims to develop descriptions of best practices, to develop templates, to develop rulebooks and guidelines that can help all HEI’s in the EU to be able increase the speed of utilization of online proctoring technologies in a managed and trustworthy manner.

References

1. Draaijer, S., et al.: Start Report - a report on the current state of online proctoring practices in higher education within the EU and an outlook for OP4RE activities. Online Proctoring for Remote Examination (2017)
2. Abbott, D., Avraam, D.: Opening up education through new technologies. https://ec.europa.eu/education/policy/strategic-framework/education-technology_en
3. Strategic Partnerships in the field of education, training and youth - Erasmus + - European Commission. https://ec.europa.eu/programmes/erasmus-plus/programme-guide/part-b/three-key-actions/key-action-2/strategic-partnerships-field-education-training-youth_en
4. Rowe, N.C.: Cheating in online student assessment: beyond plagiarism (2004)
5. NCME: Glossary of Important Assessment and Measurement Terms. http://www.ncme.org/ncme/NCME/Resource_Center/Glossary/NCME/Resource_Center/Glossary1.aspx?hkey=4bb87415-44dc-4088-9ed9-e8515326a061#anchorH
6. Bonefaas, M.: Online proctoring, goed idee? (Online proctoring, a good idea?) (2016). http://onlineexamineren.nl/online-proctoring-goed-idee/
7. Töpper, V.: IUBH führt On-Demand-Online-Klausuren ein: So einfach war Schummeln noch nie. (IUBH implements On-Demand-Online-Exams: cheating has never been so easy) (2017). http://www.spiegel.de/lebenundlernen/uni/iubh-fuehrt-on-demand-online-klausuren-ein-so-einfach-war-schummeln-noch-nie-a-1129916.html
8. Tewksbury, D., Scheufele, D.A., Bryant, J., Oliver, M.B.: News framing theory and research. Media Eff. Adv. Theory Res. 17–33 (2009)
9. Dagblad, A.: Grootschalige fraude door eerstejaars economie UvA. (Large scale fraud by freshmen Economics University of Amsterdam) (2014). http://www.ad.nl/ad/nl/1012/Nederland/article/detail/3635930/2014/04/15/Grootschalige-fraude-door-eerstejaars-economie-UvA.dhtml
10. Loeber, L., Council, D.E.: E-voting in the Netherlands; from general acceptance to general doubt in two years. Electron. Voting **131**, 21–30 (2008)

11. Rodchua, S., Yiadom-Boakye, M.G., Woolsey, R.: Student verification system for online assessments: bolstering quality and integrity of distance learning. J. Ind. Technol. **27**, 1–8 (2011)
12. Foster, D., Layman, H.: Online Proctoring Systems Compared. Webinar (2013)
13. Kolowich, S.: Behind the Webcam's Watchful Eye, Online Proctoring Takes Hold. Chronicle of Higher Education (2013)
14. Mellar, H.: D2.1 – Report with the state of the art February 29th, 2016 (2016)
15. Li, X., Chang, K., Yuan, Y., Hauptmann, A.: Massive open online proctor: protecting the credibility of MOOCs certificates. In: Proceedings of the 18th ACM Conference on Computer Supported Cooperative Work & Social Computing, pp. 1129–1137. ACM, New York (2015)
16. Case, R., Cabalka, P.: Remote proctoring: results of a pilot program at Western Governors University (2009). Accessed 10 June 2010
17. Lelo, A.: Online Proctoring at Western Governors University (2017)
18. Noguera, I., Guerrero-Roldán, A.-E., Rodríguez, M.E.: Assuring authorship and authentication across the e-Assessment process. In: Joosten-ten Brinke, D., Laanpere, M. (eds.) TEA 2016. CCIS, vol. 653, pp. 86–92. Springer, Cham (2017). https://doi.org/10.1007/978-3-319-57744-9_8
19. Verhulst, K.: EXAMEN OP AFSTAND. Reach Out Session 1 - Online Proctoring for Remote Examination (OP4RE) project (2017)
20. Beust, P., Cauchard, V., Duchatelle, I.: Premiers résultats de l'expérimentation de télé surveillance d'épreuves. http://www.sup-numerique.gouv.fr/cid100211/premiers-resultats-de-l-experimentation-de-telesurveillance-d-epreuves.html
21. Dopper, S.: Toetsing binnen open education. Dé Onderwijsdagen (2013)
22. Brouwer, N., Heck, A., Smit, G.: Proctoring to improve teaching practice. MSOR Connect **15**, 25–33 (2017)
23. European Commission: Regulation (EU) 2016/679 of the European Parliament and of the Council of 27 April 2016 on the protection of natural persons with regard to the processing of personal data and on the free movement of such data, and repealing Directive 95/46. Off. J. Eur. Union OJ. **59**, 1–88 (2016
24. Draaijer, S., Warburton, B.: The emergence of large-scale computer assisted summative examination facilities in higher education. In: Kalz, M., Ras, E. (eds.) CAA 2014. CCIS, vol. 439, pp. 28–39. Springer, Cham (2014). https://doi.org/10.1007/978-3-319-08657-6_3
25. Vidalis, S., Jones, A., Blyth, A.: Assessing cyber-threats in the information environment. Netw. Secur. **2004**, 10–16 (2004)
26. Quora: What are some particularly creative ways that students cheat? – Quora. https://www.quora.com/What-are-some-particularly-creative-ways-that-students-cheat
27. Tweedy, J.: The ingenious ways people cheat in exams…. http://www.dailymail.co.uk/femail/article-3582576/Sophisticated-ways-modern-students-CHEAT-exams-including-using-ultra-violet-pens-flesh-coloured-earphones-Mission-Impossible-style-glasses.html
28. Beust, P., Duchatelle, I.: Innovative practice relating to examination in distance learning. Presented at The Online, Open and Flexible Higher Education Conference, Università Telematica Internazionale UNINETTUNO, 19 October 2016

Student Acceptance of Online Assessment with e-Authentication in the UK

Alexandra Okada(✉), Denise Whitelock, Wayne Holmes, and Chris Edwards

The Open University, Milton Keynes, UK
{alexandra.okada,denise.whitelock,wayne.holmes, chris.edwards}@open.ac.uk

Abstract. It has been suggested that the amount of plagiarism and cheating in high-stakes assessment has increased with the introduction of e-assessments (QAA 2016), which means that authenticating student identity and authorship is increasingly important for online distance higher education. This study focuses on the implementation and use in the UK of an adaptive trust-based e-assessment system known as *TeSLA* (*An Adaptive Trust-based e-Assessment System for Learning*) currently being developed by an EU-funded project involving 18 partners across 13 countries. *TeSLA* combines biometric instruments, textual analysis instruments and security instruments. The investigation reported in this paper examines the attitudes and experiences of UK students who used the *TeSLA* instruments. In particular, it considers whether the students found the e-authentication assessment to be a practical, secure and reliable alternative to traditional proctored exams. Data includes pre- and post- questionnaires completed by more than 300 students of The Open University, who engaged with the *TeSLA* keystroke analysis and anti-plagiarism software. The findings suggest a broadly positive acceptance of these e-authentication technologies. However, based on statistical implicative analysis, there were important differences in the students' responses between genders, between age groups and between students with different amounts of previous e-assessment experiences. For example, men were less concerned about providing personal data than women; middle-aged participants (41 to 50 years old) were more aware of the nuances of cheating and plagiarism; while younger students (up to 30 years old) were more likely to reject e-authentication.

Keywords: Trust in e-assessment · e-Authentication · Cheating Plagiarism · Responsible Research and Innovation

1 Introduction

Data collected by QAA (2016) from UK Universities revealed that British education is experiencing an epidemic of academic dishonesty [1, 2]. However, traditional proctored tests have not experienced any notable increase in academic fraud [3, 4]. Instead, the amount of plagiarism and cheating in high-stakes assessments has increased with the introduction of e-assessments [5].

E. Ras and A. E. Guerrero Roldán (Eds.): TEA 2017, CCIS 829, pp. 109–122, 2018.
https://doi.org/10.1007/978-3-319-97807-9_9

The authentication of student identities and authorship in high stakes assessments has become especially important for online distance education universities, where the use of online assessments has raised concerns over fraud [1]. For example, students can easily plagiarize the Internet. They can find information on the web and cut-and-paste ideas without attribution or they can use an online bespoke essay-writing service and claim authorship for someone else's work. Other forms of cheating are also possible in digital environments. For example, students can send text messages via mobile phones to ask a friend to help during an online examination or to take the e-assessment on their behalf by using their username and password.

Whitelock [6] has advocated the use of new technologies to promote new assessment practices, especially by means of the adoption of more *authentic* assessments. This paper builds on that work by focusing on the findings from a pilot study undertaken by the Open University, UK, (OU) as part of the EU-funded *TeSLA* project (*An Adaptive Trust-based e-Assessment System for Learning*, http://tesla-project.eu). The *TeSLA* system has been designed to verify student authentication and checking authorship through the following instruments:

- **Biometric Instruments:** facial recognition for analysing the face and facial expressions, voice recognition for analysing audio structures, and keystroke analysis for analysing how the user uses the keyboard.
- **Textual analysis instruments:** anti-plagiarism for using text matching to detect similarities between documents and forensic for verifying the authorship of written documents.
- **Security instruments:** digital signature for authenticating and time-stamp for identifying when an event is recorded by the computer.

Our investigation examines student perceptions of plagiarism and cheating, and their disposition to provide personal data when requested for e-authentication. Such findings might be useful both for e-authentication technology developers and for online distance educational institutions.

1.1 Cheating

Cheating in online assessments has been examined at various levels. For example, Harmon and Lambrinos' study [3] investigated whether online examinations are an invitation to cheat, and found that more mature students who have their direct experience or working with academics are less likely to cheat. This group were also found to be more open to e-authentication systems, believing that they will assure the quality of the online assessment and will contribute to a satisfactory assessment experience. Meanwhile, Underwood and Szabo [4] highlight an interrelationship between gender, frequency of Internet usage, and maturity of students, and an individuals' willingness to commit academic offences. Their study, which focused on UK students, found that new undergraduates are more likely to cheat and plagiarise than students in later years of their degree. Finally, here, Okada et al. [7] stressed that reliable examinations, credible technologies, and authentic assessments are key issues for quality assurance (reducing cheating) in e-assessments.

1.2 e-Authentication Systems and Instruments

There are various studies that examines security and validity of online assessment supported by technology. Some of these research papers have recommended that online distance universities use traditional proctored exams for high-stakes and summative purposes [8, 9]. However, this recommendation, while understandable from an organizational and authentication point of view, brings self-evident difficulties. For some online students (for example, those who have mobility difficulties, those who are in full-time employment, and those who live at a considerable distance) having to attend an examination centre in person can be especially challenging [10]. Some recent studies (e.g. [11, 12]) have focused on commercial e-authentication systems (such as *Remote Proctor, ProctorU, Kryterion, and BioSig-ID;* see Table 1) that have been adopted by several universities.

Table 1. e-Authentication assessment systems and instruments (adapted and extended from Karim and Shukur 2016 [13])

e-Authentication assessment	What you know *(Knowledge)*	Who you are *(Biometrics)*		Where you are *(Other)*	What you do *(Production)*
		(Behavioural)	(Psychological)		
Remote Proctor	-	-	Fingerprint	-	-
ProctorU	Username and password ID photo	-	-	Human proctor audio and video monitoring	-
Kryterion	-	Keystroke rhythms	Face recognition	Secure browser video monitoring	-
BioSig-ID	Username and password	Signature	-	-	-
TeSLA	Username and password	Voice recognition keystroke analysis	Face recognition	Timestamp	Anti-plagiarism forensic textual analysis

Some authors [12] highlight that e-assessment systems are perceived as secure and appropriate when the instruments successfully identify (*Who are you?*) and authenticate (*Is it really you?*) the examinee. Other authors [13] draw attention to four groups of instruments for online authentication, which they term: *knowledge, biometric, possession* and *others.* To this, in the *TeSLA* project, we add a fifth group: *product.*

- **What you know (Knowledge).** Here, authentication is based on the students' knowledge of private information (e.g. their name, password, or a security question). Advantages of *knowledge group tools* include that they can be easy-to-use and inexpensive, while disadvantages include that they provide low-levels of security because they rely on knowledge that is susceptible to collusion and impersonation [14].

- **Who you are (Biometrics).** Here, authentication is based on physiological and behavioural characteristics. Physiological characteristics include facial images (2D or 3D), facial thermography, fingerprints, hand geometry, palm prints, hand IR thermograms, eye iris and retina, ear, skin, dental, and DNA. Behavioural characteristics include voice, gait, signature, mouse movement, keystroke and pulse [15]. Advantages of *biometric group tools* include that they can be effective and accurate, while disadvantages include that they can be technically complex and expensive.
- **What you have (Possession).** Here, authentication is based on private objects that the examinee has in their possession, such as memory cards, dongles, and keys [16]. This tends to be the least popular e-authentication group of instruments, mainly because they can be stolen or copied by other examinees.
- **Where you are (other).** Here, authentication is based on a *process*, such as the examinee's location, a timestamp, or their IP address.
- **What you do (learning).** Here, authentication is based on what the student has written and how the writing has been structured, for example by means of anti-plagiarism software and forensic textual analysis.

1.3 User Interfaces

Studies that have examined a number of e-authentication technologies show that user interfaces have an important effect on users' disposition to accept and use the systems [13]. The user interface often determines how easy the system is to use, whether it is used effectively and whether or not it is accepted [17]. In addition, the user interface can affect different users (those who have different characteristics or preferences, based on their individual backgrounds and culture) in different ways. This might also impact upon the users' acceptance and usage of the system [18].

There is a limited literature on user interfaces using biometric authentication in the context of learning that examines real scenarios with students. Examples that do exist and that focus on technology include [15]: random fingerprint systems for user authentication [19], continuous user authentication in online examinations via keystroke dynamics [20], face images captured on-line by a webcam to confirm the presence of students [21], fingerprints for e-examinations [15, 22], and combination of different biometric instruments [23, 24].

User interfaces also have particular relevance for students with certain disabilities. Ball [25] drew attention to the importance of inclusive e-assessment. In particular, Ball emphasised the importance of *'accessibility'* (to improve the overall e-assessment experience for disabled users) and *'usability'* (which, instead of targeting someone's impairment, should focus on good design for all learners based on their individual needs and preferences).

Finally, here, Gao [15] also drew attention to *credential sharing problems*. Some of the commercial systems presented in Table 1 require a webcam for video monitoring the students while they are taking an online examination. Alternatively, if a webcam is not available, a frequent re-authentication of the student's live biometrics becomes necessary for the duration of their e-assessment. Biometric systems, however, present two key issues: error and security. The systems must be configured to tolerate various amounts of error (they are at least currently incapable of error-free analysis, and two measurements of the same biometric might give similar but different results). Data security and privacy must also be assured since the data will be saved in a central database. Students might be unwilling to give out their biometric data when they are unsure how data will be used or saved.

1.4 Research Questions

This study investigates student attitudes by means of the following research questions: What are the preliminary opinions of students on cheating in online assessments? Do students consider e-assessment based on e-authentication to be a practical, secure, reliable and acceptable alternative to traditional face-to-face (proctored) assessments? Do gender, age and previous experience with e-authentication have an impact on their views?

2 Method

The *TeSLA* project http://tesla-project.eu conducted various studies during the first semester of 2017. This involved seven universities across Europe, including the OU in the UK, and approximately 500 students per university. The pilot studies were designed to check the efficacy of the *TeSLA* instruments while gathering feedback from users about their experiences using the instruments. The *TeSLA* instruments piloted by the OU were keystroke analysis and anti-plagiarism (future studies in the UK will include the other *TeSLA* instruments).

2.1 Participants

The OU invited by email four tranches of up to 5,000 OU undergraduate students (the OU carefully manages the number of research requests put to students), to participate in the pilot study. The invitees were selected from 11 modules (those that had among the largest cohorts at the OU at the time of the study, see Table 2) and were studying towards a range of different qualifications (49 different qualifications in total, including a BA (Hons) in Combined Social Sciences, a BSC (Hons) in Psychology and a BSc (Hons) in Health Sciences). The students were allocated randomly to either the keystroke analysis tool or the anti-plagiarism tool. Of the 13,227 students who were invited to participate, a total of 648 participants completed the pilot (thus creating a self-selected unsystematic sample). This paper analyses a selection of data from the 328 participants who also answered both the pre- and post-questionnaire. TeSLA pilot studies received local ethics committee approval and all of the data were anonymized. The OU UK students accessed the video about TeSLA e-authentication instruments (https://vimeo.com/164100812) to be aware of the various ways used to verify identity and checking authorship. They were randomly allocated to each of the two tools used – Keystroke and Anti-Plagiarism, which were available in the Moodle system and adapted by the OUUK technical team. The decision to ask participants to only attempt to use one tool, rather than two or more, was based on a concern about the time commitment required for our geographically dispersed online distance learning students.

Table 2. Modules from which students were invited to participate in the study

Open University module name	Number of invited students
Investigating psychology 1	4,663
Introducing the social sciences	2,777
My digital life	1,692
Discovering mathematics	1,253
Essential mathematics 1	950
Children's literature	656
Software engineering	354
Investigating the social world	306
Adult health, social care and wellbeing	226
Why is religion controversial?	212
Health and illness	138
Total	**13,227**

2.2 Procedures

The participants were asked to complete the following steps (it was made clear to the participants that they were free to drop out of the study either before, during or after any step):

1. **Log in.** Participants were asked to use their OU username and password to access the secure *TeSLA* Moodle environment.
2. **Consent form.** Participants were asked to read and sign a 1-page document that included information about relevant legal and ethical issues, including data protection and privacy related to their participation in *TeSLA* project. If participants declined to sign this consent form, their involvement in the pilot finished here.
3. **Pre-questionnaire.** Participants were asked to complete a 20-question questionnaire about their previous experience with e-assessment, their views on plagiarism and cheating, their opinions of e-authentication systems, their views on trust and e-authentication, and their willingness to share personal data such as photographs, video and voice recordings for e-authentication.
4. **Enrolment task.** Those participants allocated to the keystroke analysis tool were asked to complete an activity to initialize (set a baseline for) the system. This involved the participant typing 500 characters. There was no enrolment task for the anti-plagiarism tool.
5. **Assessment task.** Those participants allocated to the keystroke analysis tool were asked to complete a task that involved typing answers to some simple questions. The participants allocated to the anti-plagiarism tool were asked to upload a previously assessed module assignment.

6. **Post-questionnaire.** Finally, participants were asked to complete a 15-question post-questionnaire about their experience with the *TeSLA* system, their opinions of e-authentication systems, their views on trust and e-authentication, and their willingness to share personal data such as keyboard use and previously marked assessments for e-authentication.

2.3 Data Collection and Analysis Tools

The data analysed in this study are drawn from the pre- and post- study questionnaires (Steps 3 and 6 described above), which were developed by the *TeSLA* consortium and administered via a secure online system. The responses recorded were exported to a csv file, converted into variables with binary values in Microsoft Excel, then imported into the software tool CHIC - Cohesive Hierarchical Implicative Classification, for SIA - Statistical Implicative Analysis, which is a method for data analysis focused on the extraction and the structuration of quasi-implications [26]. CHIC was used to identify associations between variables and to generate cluster analysis visualizations by means of a similarity tree (also known as dendrogram), which is based on the similarity index [26, 27] and is used to identify otherwise unobvious groups of variables. Similarity index is a measure to compare objects and variables and group them into significant classes or clusters based on likelihood connections [27]. Gras and Kunts (2008: 13) explain that SIA help users "*discover relationships among variables at different granularity levels based on rules to highlight the emerging properties of the whole system which cannot be deduced from a simple decomposition into sub-parts*". CHIC was used in this study because it enables researchers to extract association rules from data that might be surprising or unexpected.

3 Findings

3.1 Descriptive Statistical Analysis

A descriptive statistical analysis was used to address the first and second research questions (about students' views on e-authentication, on cheating, and on the viability of using e-authentication in lieu of traditional proctored assessments).

Description of Participants. Data presented in Table 3 reveal that the sample was broadly comparable with overall OU student demographics [28]. The sample comprised 41% male and 59% female participants. 30% of the sample were aged up to 30 years old (henceforward we refer to this group as 'young students'), 26% were between 31 and 40 years old and 23% were between 41 and 50 years old ('middle-aged'), and 23% were more than 51 years old ('senior age') (figures have rounded to the nearest integer). Cross-referencing with anonymous OU data showed 26% of the participating students classified themselves as having special educational needs or disabilities, which is important data for further studies on accessibility and adaptability in e-assessment [25, 29]. The data also show that 39% of the sample had previous experience of e-assessment, while 61% did not.

Table 3. Questionnaire responses for 328 participants

Categories	Indicators	Values	Pre-survey		Post-survey	
Demographics	Gender	Female	193	59%		
		Male	135	41%		
	Age	<21	25	8%		
		22–30	71	22%		
		31–40	84	26%		
		41–50	74	23%		
		>51	74	23%		
	Occupation	Student	26	8%		
		Employed	218	66%		
		Retired	23	7%		
		Not working (e.g. disabled)	20	6%		
		Other	41	13%		
	Level of education	Vocational	92	28%		
		Secondary school	80	24%		
		Bachelor's degree	41	13%		
		Master's degree	28	9%		
		Other	87	27%		
	Special needs	Disabled	85	26%		
Previous experiences	Experience with e-assessment (during the whole module)	Yes	129	39%		
		No	199	61%		
Preliminary opinion	Is it plagiarism if I help or work together with a classmate in an individual activity and the work we submit is similar or identical?	Strongly agree, agree	256	78%		
		Neutral	26	8%		
		Strongly disagree, disagree	46	14%		
	Is it cheating if I copy-paste information from a website in a work developed by me without citing the original source?	Strongly agree, agree	311	95%		
		Neutral	3	1%		
		Strongly disagree, disagree	14	4%		
Acceptance	e-Authentication & quality	Strongly agree, agree	296	90%	297	91%
	Trust online assessment	Strongly agree, agree	254	77%	259	79%
	University does NOT trust students	Strongly disagree, disagree	311	95%	311	95%
	What personal data would you be willing to share in order to be assessed online	Video of my face	103	31%	—	—
		Still picture of my face	223	68%	—	—
		Voice recording	195	59%	—	—
		Keystroke dynamic	210	64%	235	71%
		A piece of written work	—	—	225	69%

(continued)

Table 3. (*continued*)

Categories	Indicators	Values	Pre-survey		Post-survey	
Rejection potential issues	e-Authentication and quality	Strongly disagree, disagree	8	2%	4	1%
	Trust online assessment	Strongly disagree, disagree	32	10%	28	9%
	University does NOT trust students	Strongly agree, agree	15	4%	15	4%
	What personal data would you be willing to share in order to be assessed online	None	18	0.05	29	0.09
Practical issues	I am satisfied with the assessment	Strongly gree, agree			251	77%
		Strongly disagree, disagree			77	23%
	The workload is greater than I expected	Strongly agree, agree			95	29%
		Strongly disagree, disagree			233	71%
	I felt an increased level of surveillance	Strongly agree, agree			48	15%
		Strongly disagree, disagree			280	85%
	I felt more stressed	Strongly agree, agree			33	10%
		Strongly disagree, disagree			295	90%
Security and reliability	My personal data was treated in a secure way	Strongly agree, agree			253	77%
		Strongly disagree, disagree			75	23%
	I received technical guidance	Strongly agree, agree			106	32%
		Strongly disagree, disagree			222	68%
	Issues were quickly and satisfactorily solved	Strongly agree, agree			60	57%
		Strongly disagree, disagree			16	15%

Participants' Preliminary Opinion on Plagiarism and Cheating. The questionnaire also investigated the participants' prior opinions on academic plagiarism and cheating. Participants were asked to provide their opinion by answering "Is it plagiarism if I help or work together with a classmate in an individual activity and the work we submit is similar or identical?" 78% of students agreed while 8% of participants were not sure and 14% disagreed. Students also appeared to be aware of some aspects of 'cheating' in e-assessments based on their opinions about "Is it cheating if I copy-paste information from a website in a work developed by me without citing the original source?". 95% of students agreed, while only 4% were unsure and 1% disagreed.

Participants' Opinions on e-Authentication. Questions also investigated the participants' opinions, before and after they engaged with the *TeSLA* tasks, on the importance of e-authentication for enhancing the quality of assessment in online distance universities. Pre- and post- questionnaire answers were very similar. First, participants were asked whether or not they agreed that "the university is working to ensure the quality of the assessment process". Responses of both questionnaires (pre- and post-) were very similar, 90% of students agreed, while 7% were unsure and 2% disagreed. The participants were also asked whether "they would trust an assessment system, in which all assessment occurs online". Again, the difference between pre- and post- questionnaires was very small. 77% participants agreed while13% were either unsure and 10% disagreed. Finally here, participants were asked whether they agreed or disagreed with the statement "the use of security measures for assessment purposes makes you feel that the university does not trust you". On both questionnaires, only a small number, 5% of students, agreed with this statement while most disagreed, 95% of students.

Students' Disposition to Submit Personal Data for e-Authentication. Participants were also asked about which types of personal data they were willing to share as part of an e-authentication process. 16% were willing to share all the types of personal data that they were asked about and only 31% were willing to share video. Yet, 68% of participants were willing to share their photograph and 59% were willing to share a voice recording. Additionally, data from post-questionnaire revealed that 64% were willing to share their keystrokes and 69% were willing to share a piece of their written work.

Participants' Opinions on Practical Issues with e-Authentication. Considering data from post-questionnaire, participants were asked whether they were "satisfied with the assessment"; most participants agreed (77%). They were also asked whether "the workload is greater than I expected", whether they "felt an increased level of surveillance due to the *TeSLA* pilot", and whether they "felt more stressed when taking assessments due to the use of security". Most participants disagreed with each of these statements (71%, 85% and 90%, respectively). Finally, participants were asked questions about security and reliability. Most (77%) agreed that their "personal data was treated in a secure way". However, while 69% disagreed that they had "received technical guidance", 79% of respondents (n = 76) agreed that "issues were quickly and satisfactory solved".

3.2 Statistical Implicative Analysis

Impact of Gender, Age and Previous Experience. Figure 1 presents an extract of the similarity tree, showing various indexes of similarity (IoS) generated by the CHIC software, between the various questionnaires items (the full similarity tree is too large for inclusion in this paper). Figure 1 shows a high similarity between female participants and those who said that they did not receive technical guidance (IoS = 0.768) when using the *TeSLA* system; and a high similarity between male participants and those who were willing to share personal data: voice and video recordings

(IoS = 0.997) and photographs (IoS = 0.953). Male participants also had a smaller but noteworthy similarity (IoS = 0.401) with those who are willing to share keystrokes after using the *TeSLA* system. The similarity tree shown in Fig. 1 also suggests that participants aged over 51 years who are retired and have completed masters-level education have limited previous experience of online assessment (IoS = 0.850). Finally, here, the full similarity tree shows a high similarity between senior women who were more than 50 years old and retired participants, who hold a master degree and middle age (from 41 to 50) who have a full-time job and a vocational qualification with those who have not previously experienced an online module with online assessments.

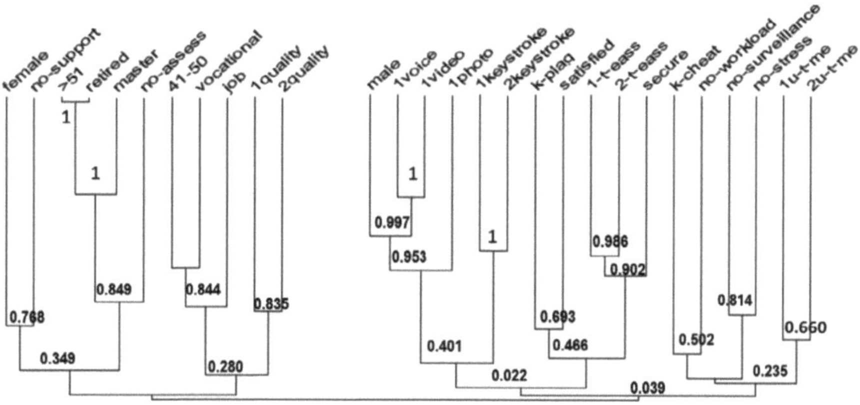

Fig. 1. Extract of the similarity tree created in CHIC to analyse the impact of gender.

Trust and Security. Figure 1 also suggests two clusters related to plagiarism and cheating. The first cluster shows participants who were aware of what constitutes plagiarism and satisfied with the online experience (IoS = 0.694). The second cluster includes those participants who expressed trust in online assessments and those who believe that their personal data are treated in a secure way (IoS = 0.902). Further, these two clusters have a smaller but noteworthy connection with each other (IoS = 0.466). Finally, those participants who do not "feel an increased level of surveillance" are linked to those who do not feel more stressed when taking assessments due to the use of security procedures (IoS = 0.814), and to those who have trust in their institution (IoS = 0.661).

The CHIC similarity tree analysis also suggested other noteworthy clusters. A first such cluster includes young students (<22 years old), all of whom had previous experience with online assessment (IoS = 1.000), with those who requested technical guidance and had all their technical issues solved (IoS = 0.897). A second cluster includes young students (22–30 years old) who were strongly linked (IoS = 0.996) with those who disagreed that e-authentication will improve the quality of e-assessment systems. This group were also strongly linked (IoS = 1.000) with those who agreed that universities using e-authentication did not trust them, those who felt more stressed and those who felt an increased level of surveillance (IoS = 1.000). They were also strongly linked (IoS = 0.991) with those who were unsure about trust or security and did not want to share their personal data, those who were not satisfied with the assessment experience and did not have their technical issues solved, and those (IoS = .882) who did not agree with the examples provided about plagiarism and cheating. A third cluster includes middle-aged students (31 to 40 years old) who were strongly linked with those who were unsure about the examples provided on plagiarism and cheating (IoS = 0.986). A fourth cluster includes students who hold a bachelor's degree who were strongly linked with those who indicated that the e-authentication system had a higher workload than expected.

4 Discussion and Conclusion

This study investigated student acceptance of online assessment with e-authentication in the UK, with a sample that was self-selecting (comprising those participants in the *TeSLA* UK pilot study who also answered both the pre- and post-questionnaire), effectively random and broadly representative of the OU UK student body.

Findings related to the first research question indicated a large majority of participants who were aware of what constituted cheating in online assessments. The outcomes related to the second and third question, however, were more interrelated. The overall findings suggest a positive acceptance of e-authentication for e-assessments by both participants women and men. In addition, neither group finding the e-authentication instruments to be either stressful or onerous. In general, findings show that the women participants, trusted online assessments more than men, and they were more confident that e-assessment based on e-authentication has the potential to enhance the quality of online assessments. However, although opinions about sharing personal data for e-assessment based on e-authentication indicated that half of the sample were willing to share all the named types of personal data and half were unwilling, men were on average more willing to share. This indicates an issue that e-authentication must address: if students do not want to share the types of information for e-authentication then how can e-assessment work?

Yet, as noted, attitudes to e-authentication were positive in general, there were some nuances by age, supporting the earlier findings [3, 4, 7]. While older students, who typically had limited prior experience with e-assessments, were more willing to trust e-authentication instruments, some younger students were unconvinced that e-authentication had the potential to enhance e-assessment. Findings revealed that many of the younger students saw the university' use of e-authentication as an indicator that the university did not trust the examinees not to cheat. It is perhaps for this reason that the younger students were also more likely to reject the use of e-authentication in assessments. Finally, although e-authentication makes e-assessment potentially easier for institutions, the disabled students presented on average a negative opinion to e-authentication for online assessments.

The outcomes of this quantitative study presented the need for the e-authentication technology teams and teaching staff to identify the distinctive nature of students to anticipate any potential barrier. The Responsible Research and Innovation – RRI approach implies that computer scientists, technology developers, course teams and students must interact during the whole process of RRI to better align both its outcomes and process with the needs, expectations and values of whole community as highlighted by the European Commission. Society and technology innovators, through RRI, become more responsive to each other by examining together the ethical acceptability and sustainability of the innovation process [30]. The lack of qualitative data is considered as a limitation of this study. Our next research work will examine the updated TeSLA e-authentication system based on mixed-method approach with a larger group of OU students.

Acknowledgements. The authors would like to thank colleagues in the *TeSLA* project for their support and the reviewers of TEA conference. This work is supported by the H2020-ICT-2015/H2020-ICT-2015, Number 688520.

References

1. QAA: Plagiarism in Higher Education - Custom essay writing services: an exploration and next steps for the UK higher education sector (2016)
2. Bermingham, V., Watson, S., Jones, M.: Plagiarism in UK law schools: is there a postcode lottery? Assess. Eval. HE **35**(1), 1–14 (2010)
3. Harmon, O.R., Lambrinos, J.: Are online exams an invitation to cheat? J. Econ. Educ. **39**(2), 116–125 (2008)
4. Underwood, J., Szabo, A.: Academic offences and e-learning: individual propensities in cheating. Br. J. Educ. Technol. **34**(4), 467–477 (2003)
5. Chew, E., Ding, S.L., Rowell, G.: Changing attitudes in learning and assessment: cast-off 'plagiarism detection' and cast-on self-service assessment for learning. Innov. Educ. Teach. Int. **52**(5), 454–463 (2015)
6. Whitelock, D.: Activating assessment for learning: are we on the way with Web 2.0? In: Lee, M.J.W., McLoughlin, C. (eds.) Web 2.0-Based-E-Learning: Applying Social Informatics for Tertiary Teaching, pp. 319–342. IGI Global (2011)
7. Okada, A., Mendonca, M., Scott, P.: Effective web videoconferencing for proctoring online oral exams: a case study at scale in Brazil. Open Prax. – Int. J. OECD **7**(3), 227–242 (2015)
8. Edling, R.J.: Information technology in the classroom: experiences and recommendations. Campus - Wide Inf. Syst. **17**(1), 10–15 (2000)
9. Rovai, A.P.: Online and traditional assessments: what is the difference? Internet High. Educ. **3**(3), 141–151 (2001)
10. Hanna, D.E.: Higher education in an era of digital competition: emerging organizational models. J. Asynchronous Learn. Netw. **2**(1), 66–95 (1998)
11. Harmon, O., Lambrinos, J., Buffolino, J.: Assessment design and cheating risk in online instruction. Online J. Distance Learn. Adm. **13**(3) (2010). https://www.westga.edu/~distance/ojdla/Fall133/harmon_lambrinos_buffolino133.html. Accessed 24 July 2018
12. Apampa, K, Wills G., Argles, D.: User security issues in summative e-assessment. Secur. Int. J. Digit. Soc. (IJDS) (2010). https://infonomics-society.org/wp-content/uploads/ijds/published-papers/volume-1-2010/User-Security-Issues-in-Summative-E-Assessment-Security.pdf

13. Karim, N.A., Shukur, Z.: Proposed features of an online examination interface design and its optimal values. Comput. Hum. Behav. **64**, 414–422 (2016)
14. Ullah, A., Xiao, H., Barker, T., Lilley, M.: Evaluating security and usability of profile based challenge questions authentication in online examinations. J. Internet Serv. Appl. **5**(1), 2 (2014)
15. Gao, Q.: Biometric authentication to prevent e-cheating. Instr. Technol. (2012). https://www.researchgate.net/publication/315643312_Biometric_Authentication_to_Prevent_e-Cheating
16. Hastings, N.E., Dodson, D.F.: Quantifying assurance of knowledge based authentication. In: 3rd European Conference on Information Warfare and Security, ECIW (2004)
17. Figueroa, A.M., Juarez-Ramirez, R., Inzunza, S., Valenzuela, R.: Implementing adaptive interfaces: a user model for the development of usability in interactive systems. Comput. Syst. Sci. Eng. **29**(1), 95–104 (2014)
18. Rau, P.-L.P., Choong, Y.-Y., Salvendy, G.: A cross cultural study on knowledge representation and structure in human computer interfaces. Int. J. Ind. Ergon. **34**(2), 117–129 (2004)
19. Levy, Y., Ramin, M.: A Theoretical Approach for Biometrics Authentication of e-Exams (2007). http://telem-pub.openu.ac.il/users/chais/2007/morning_1/M1_6.pdf
20. Flior, E., Kowalski, K.: Continuous biometric user authentication in online examinations. In: Seventh International Conference on Information Technology, pp. 488– 492 (2010)
21. Penteado, B.E., Marana, A.N.: A video-based biometric authentication for e-Learning web applications. In: Filipe, J., Cordeiro, J. (eds.) ICEIS 2009. LNBIP, vol. 24, pp. 770–779. Springer, Heidelberg (2009). https://doi.org/10.1007/978-3-642-01347-8_64
22. Alotaibi, S.: Using biometrics authentication via fingerprint recognition in e-exams in e-learning environment. In: The 4th Saudi International Conference. The University of Manchester, UK (2010)
23. Asha, S., Chellappan, C.: Authentication of e-learners using multimodal biometric technology. In: International Symposium on Biometrics and Security Technologies, pp. 1–6, Islamabad (2008)
24. Rabuzin, K., Baca, M., Sajko, M.: E-learning: biometrics as a security factor. In: Multi-Conference on Computing in the Global Information Technology, pp. 64–64 (2006)
25. Ball, S.: Accessibility in e-assessment. Assess. Eval. High. Educ. **34**(3), 293–303 (2011)
26. Gras, R., Kuntz, P.: An overview of the statistical implicative analysis (SIA) development. Stud. Comput. Intell. (SCI) **127**, 11–40 (2008)
27. Lerman, I.C.: Foundations and Methods in Combinatorial and Statistical Data Analysis and Clustering. Springer, Heidelberg (2016). https://doi.org/10.1007/978-1-4471-6793-8
28. Jelfs, A., Richardson, J.T.: The use of digital technologies across the adult life span in distance education. Br. J. Educ. Technol. **44**(2), 338–351 (2013)
29. Baneres, D., Baró, X., Guerrero-Roldán, A., Rodríguez, M.: Adaptive e-assessment system: a general approach Int. J. Emerg. Technol. Learn. (2016). http://online-journals.org/index.php/i-jet/article/view/5888. Accessed 24 July 2018
30. von Schomberg, R.: Prospects for technology assessment in a framework of responsible research and innovation. In: Dusseldorp, M., Beecroft, R. (eds.) Technikfolgen abschätzen lehren, pp. 39–61. Springer, Heidelberg (2011). https://doi.org/10.1007/978-3-531-93468-6_2

The Dilemmas of Formulating Theory-Informed Design Guidelines for a Video Enhanced Rubric

Kevin Ackermans(✉), Ellen Rusman, Saskia Brand-Gruwel, and Marcus Specht

Welten Institute, Open Universiteit,
Valkenburgerweg 177, 6419 AT Heerlen, The Netherlands
{Kevin.Ackermans,Ellen.Rusman,Saskia.Brand-Gruwel,
Marcus.Specht}@ou.nl

Abstract. Learners aiming to master a complex skill may benefit from the combination of abstract information found in a text-based analytical rubric and concrete information provided by a video modeling example. In this paper, we address the design dilemmas of combining video modeling examples and rubrics into a Video Enhanced Rubric. We propose a model to address these design dilemma's and develop our first prototype based on this model. We review the first prototype through a two-stage international expert validation session. In the first stage, 20 experts are asked to design a user interface for the Video Enhanced Rubric. In the second stage, 20 experts are asked to perform an expert appraisal of our first prototype. The preliminary results of the expert validation session are subsequently analyzed using Sauli, Cattaneo and van der Meij's Framework for Developing Instructional Hypervideo to detect common design suggestions. Following the results of the expert validation, we developed a second prototype of the Video Enhanced Rubric. With the design guidelines of a Video Enhanced Rubric, we aim to improve the formative assessment and mastery of complex skills by fostering learner's mental model development and the quality (consistency, concreteness) of both given as well as received feedback. On a more general note, we expect the design dilemmas addressed in this paper to inform researchers who aim to apply theoretical multimedia design guidelines to formative assessment practices with rubrics.

Keywords: Video · Rubrics · (Formative) assessment · Complex skills
Mental models

1 Introduction

A text-based analytic rubric can be an effective instrument for the formative assessment of complex skills, providing a detailed description of each level of complex skill mastery. This detailed description provides structured and transparent communication of the assessment criteria, providing a uniform assessment method that fosters insight into complex skills acquisition and fosters learning [1]. Apart from being an effective instrument, the rubric is an instrument that can be implemented to address the lack of

E. Ras and A. E. Guerrero Roldán (Eds.): TEA 2017, CCIS 829, pp. 123–136, 2018.
https://doi.org/10.1007/978-3-319-97807-9_10

explicit, substantial and systematic integration of complex skills in the Dutch curriculum [2, 3]. While a transparent description of a complex skill can be presented to a learner using a text-based analytic rubric, such a textual rubric has three deficiencies [4]. First, it provides a fragmentary textual framework, because a rubric describes a complex skill using a subdivided set of constituent (sub)skills that are identified by the expert. This may result in insufficient attention to the necessary integration of constituent skills during task execution. Second, a text-based rubric lacks the contextual information needed to convey the real world attributes and natural context of skills' execution and represent the dynamic information (such as gesturing in the complex skill of presenting) that can be extracted from dynamic stimuli such as a video [5, 6]. Third, rubrics may not provide the procedural information needed to support the automation of constituent skills, risking the formation of an incomplete mental model. This paper proposes a design that may address the afore mentioned deficiencies of a textual analytic rubric by combining them with video modeling examples, introducing a format called 'Video Enhanced Rubrics' (VER). VER are a synthesis of the concrete information of video modeling examples and the abstract information of a textual analytic rubric into a single format. We expect that video modeling examples can provide the lacking contextual and dynamic information, may foster inter-task and sub-skill coordination and the formation of a richer mental model than a text-based rubric alone.

From a pedagogical perspective, the information carried by both rubric and video may offer a platform to engage the learner in a more emotional and motivational manner by offering an educational narrative [7]. From a didactical viewpoint, emotional and motivational engagement may foster deeper learning [8, 9].

In this paper, we aim to take one step closer to the practical implementation of the VER by answering the research question: *"How to formulate design guidelines for a Video Enhanced Rubric to improve the formative assessment of complex skills by fostering learner's mental model development, feedback quality, and complex skill mastery?* With practical implementation within Dutch lower secondary education in mind, the preliminary validation and prototype sections will question the ecological validity of the first prototype Video Enhanced Rubric using a two-part validation with multimedia experts. We value the ecological validity of our prototype because we aim for real-life applicability in Dutch classrooms. The first part instructed the participants to design a user interface according to the design requirements, conditions, and guidelines set by the Viewbrics project. The second part consisted of an audio-recorded expert appraisal with 20 participants. During this appraisal, the participants provided detailed feedback on the first prototype and the associated design decisions. The design guidelines resulting from the analysis of this two-step ecological validation were then used to formulate the second prototype.

Having addressed the outline of this paper, we conclude the introduction with a definition of the concepts used in this paper. Although the VER may support the development of a wide range of complex skills, we limit the design guidelines to the complex skills of presentation, collaboration, and information literacy as these are the complex skills addressed by the Viewbrics project. For this paper, we limit the concept of feedback quality to consistency and concreteness of both given as well as received expert- and peer feedback [10]. As stated in our research question, we aim to foster a rich mental model of a complex skill with the VER, which in turn is expected to affect feedback quality. To define a 'rich' mental model, the Viewbrics project identified 11 constituent skills within the three skill clusters of presenting, 14 constituent skills within the four skill clusters of information literacy and 20 constituent skills within the four skill clusters of collaboration. Having described the background, outline and defined the applicable concepts of this paper, we move on to the identification of design guidelines.

2 Identification of Design Goals and Roles

Using the ISO 9241-210 standard for Human-centred design processes for interactive systems, we identified two roles and two goals the VER may fulfill following the evolving growth of the learner in the formative assessment cycle [11, 12].

The first goal of the VER is to foster the development of complex skills. To support learners' achievement of this goal, the feedback and transparent assessment qualities of a textual analytic rubric and the dynamic and contextual qualities of an expert modeling example need to be accessible throughout the VER. To foster this goal, navigation and motivating the learner to explore both video and rubric are key. The control feedback principle may motivate the learner to explore by giving the learner control over the VER [13]. As our video of the complete complex skill of collaboration has a runtime of thirteen minutes, we also consider Keller's Attention, Relevance, Confidence, and Satisfaction (ARCS) model to foster the learner's motivation. Motivation may be of importance for self-regulation of complex multimedia learning, as it may mediate the cognitive load impact of the VER as well as foster whole-task learning [9, 14–17]. Guidelines for developing complex skill instruction can be found in Four Component Instructional Design Theory (4C/ID) [18]. We choose this particular complex skill instructional design methodology for its integration with multimedia theory and SDT as found by Van Merriënboer and Kester [18] and Van Merriënboer and Sluijsmans [19]. The integration of 4C/ID with SDT is essential for the VER as the formative assessment context of the VER requires the learner to formulate a self-directed goal concerning a complex skill.

The second goal of the VER is to visualize every constituent (sub-) skill in both the rubric and the video modeling example. This may allow the learner to recognize and mentally connect the constituent skills within the video modeling example and may help them to form a rich mental model from both textual and Visio-spatial information. To foster this goal, the location of each constituent skill in both rubric and video must be clear [20]. As this goal concerns the physical placements of multimedia elements and their effect on learning, we choose to rely on Mayer's principles. Using the effect size of Mayer's principles to quantify the learning effect of design decisions, the choice for the design guidelines with the best transfer score can be made [21].

As formative assessment facilitates the growth of the learner, the VER will be used by beginning and advanced learners. To support learners with different levels of prior knowledge, we identify two distinct roles for the VER, the orientation role, and the preparation role.

In the *orientation role*, we aim to support the learner's first orientation on the complete complex skill. The learners participate in Dutch lower secondary education where one teacher guides approximately thirty learners aged 12–14 years old. The learners have limited experience in explicitly practicing and assessing complex skills. Assuming little experience in the complex skills as an attribute of our learners, we can also assume that their current mental model of the complex skill is of limited complexity. By familiarizing the learner with a whole task performed by a modeling example, we aim to foster the formulation of a rudimentary mental model. As stated by van Merrienboer [22], such a modeling example operationalises his mastery mental model into the performance of the complex skill. Although this is the learners first viewing of the video, we aim to guide the learner in unraveling the underlying mastery mental model of the expert modeling example during the use of the VER using the performance criteria in the rubric to offer insight.

In the *preparation role*, we aim to support practicing a complex skill by fostering self-assessment and self-directed goal selection and improving the feedback quality of received expert- and peer assessment through the use of the VER [10]. The transparent and descriptive performance criteria in a rubric may allow the learner to review the received feedback with the help of the rubric. Moreover, it may help the learner to provide (self- and peer) feedback based on the rubric [23, 24].

3 Prototype 1

When combining the design guidelines derived from various feasible theories, several design dilemmas emerged. It turned out to be challenging to formulate a single set of design guidelines for the VER. In Fig. 1, we illustrate several dilemmas we have encountered. Figure 1 shows the tension between motivational and complex skill developmental guidelines as derived from 4CID, ARCS, SDT and Cognitive Load Theory on the left hand, with the multimedia learning guidelines as derived from the cognitive theory of multimedia learning on the right hand.

We have addressed the design dilemmas by focussing on the roles defined using the ISO guidelines for User Centred Design. The orientation role of prototype 1 has the primary goal to support learners during their orientation on the complex skill. This also defines our position in the method versus media debate as placing the methods that foster complex skill development first, and the media carrying the method second. Therefore, according to 4C/ID guidelines, The orientation role must represent a whole task [19]. Several guidelines can then be used to support this primary goal. Showing a whole task of a complex skill may take longer than the working memory of a learner can facilitate. We will take a working memory limitation of approximately four items into account to prevent errors in the learner's memory retrieval. We choose approximately four items in line with Cowan's four, Miller's magical number 7 (plus or minus two) and most importantly, research from Luck and Vogel, finding visual items are retained in three or four independent object 'slots' in working memory [25, 26]. Although the existence of transport time between working memory and long-term

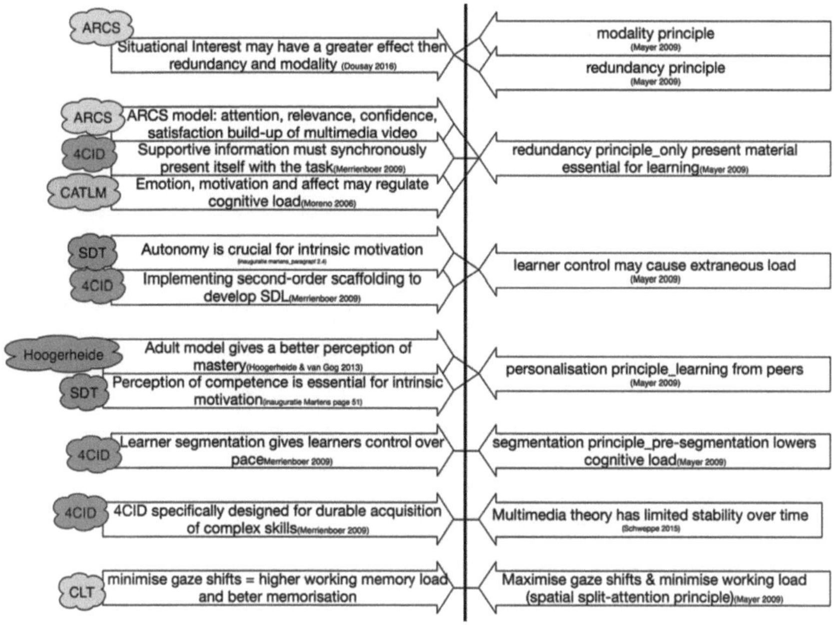

Fig. 1. Encountered design dilemmas for the design of a VER

memory is still a matter of discussion, we do aim to support this process in the VER using fading between each (sub)-skill-cluster of approximately four items [19, 21, 27].

To foster the learner's motivation regarding watching the video, the video is scripted using the ARCS method. Firstly, grabbing the learner's Attention (A) by using recognizable and identifiable role models and scenario's within the video modelling examples, secondly establishing Relevance (R) by illustrating a school-related real-world task, thirdly by inspiring Confidence that learners can learn the skills themselves by using identifiable peer actors and voice-overs that reveal procedural information and emotion, and concluding with a successful ending.

As we adhere to a method before media standpoint, we lastly elaborate on the used media guidelines. In the orientation role the video of a whole task has priority in the user interface. The orientation role has minimal learner control to limit cognitive load and is designed only to provide stimuli from the medium that is essential for learning at the moment (the redundancy principle). The segmentation principle has already been implemented from a cognitive load standpoint, taking working memory into account. The personalization principle has already been implemented from the ARCS standpoint, using peer-actors and a motivational script. We adhere to Hoogerheide's argument seen in Fig. 1 concerning the 'perception of mastery' providing a better modeling example by only providing a 'mastery' example and working with slightly older actors, able to perform the skill with mastery while remaining within peer appearance [28].

The preparation role of prototype one is designed to support the contextualization of the *received peer- and expert feedback, self-directed goal selection and for practicing a complex* skill. An interactive interface is used to facilitate these features. The

Fig. 2. Prototype 1, the orientation role

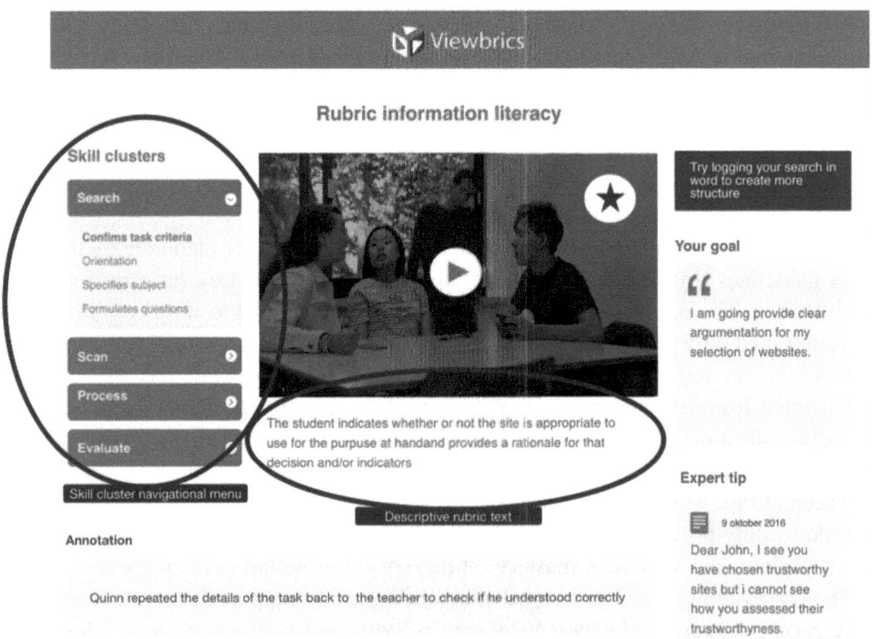

Fig. 3. Prototype 1, the preparation role (Color figure online)

skill cluster is located on the left, functioning as the table of contents. In line with web-ergonomics, the navigational menu is placed in Jakob Nielson's [29] traditional F-shape viewing pattern, illustrated in Fig. 3, fostering navigation through a quick scan of the skill, cluster and selected sub-skill.

Learners may use the table of contents to navigate to the sub-skill they wish to develop. The expert feedback is visible on the right, providing the learner with personal feed forward on the level of the whole complex skill. The learner's goal is visible on the right of the screen to provide input selecting the corresponding sub-skill(s). The red field on the right hand of the screen shows a general tip for all learners, based on the teacher's experience with the complex skill. When the learner selects a constituent skill, a subpage dedicated to only this constituent skill opens as seen in Fig. 2. The subpage plays the specific scene of the video modeling example performing a constituent skill, with the scenes needed to provide the needed context to the constituent skill. The subpage will also show the complete descriptive rubric text as shown in Fig. 3, providing the learner with feedback.

4 Preliminary Validation

The first prototyping was validated with an international expert appraisal workshop. This workshop aimed at gauging how different multimedia and instructional design experts would react to the validity and potential practicality of the first prototype. A two-step approach was used during this workshop. During the first part, participants were instructed to design a user interface according to the design guidelines addressed in paragraph 2, without having seen our first prototype. The second part consisted of an audio-recorded expert appraisal of the prototype design with 20 participants. During this appraisal, the participants provided detailed feedback on the first prototype. In this paper, we focus on the preliminary analysis of the expert designs which were made during the first part of this workshop.

Participants. Twenty international multimedia and instructional design experts were invited to the expert appraisal workshop: five full professors (of ICT, Pedagogics, Educational Psychology, New Media and Learning and Instructional design), two associate professors, one researcher, one junior researcher, one scientific collaborator and one junior instructional designer, one developer, one lecturer and one teacher. The international participants were aged between 26 to 53 years, had 1 to 20 years of design experience and came from Switzerland, Italy, Spain, Germany, the Netherlands, Israel, and Finland.

Procedure. Along with the following assignment at the beginning of the workshop, the participants were given a pencil, one piece of A3 paper and one piece of A4 paper:

"You are the multimedia expert of a secondary school. The school is developing a multimedia application to foster a complex skill for kids aged 12 to 14, for this example we will use the complex skill of presentation. Specifically, the multimedia application must foster the feedback quality, mental model accuracy, and performance of presentation. The application collects peer and teacher-feedback, which is presented to learners to foster their self-directed goal selection. You are specifically hired to develop the screens in which video modeling examples and rubrics are combined. The screens you are asked to develop have to support the formative assessment process, giving learners insight into their development over time."

The participants were then instructed to draw a user interface design (screens) on a piece of A3 paper, and make notes of the considerations and decisions that led to their design on a piece of A4 paper. The participants were given 20 min and where free to form couples and discus their designs as they saw fit.

Analysis. During part one, 20 participants produced 11 user interface designs. For the preliminary analysis of the expert appraisal workshop data, the designs are analyzed using the design features found in Cattaneo, Van Der Meij, Aprea, Sauli, and Zahn's [30] model for designing hyper video-based instructional scenarios as seen in Fig. 4. We use this model as it allows us to categorize the main features of hyper video.

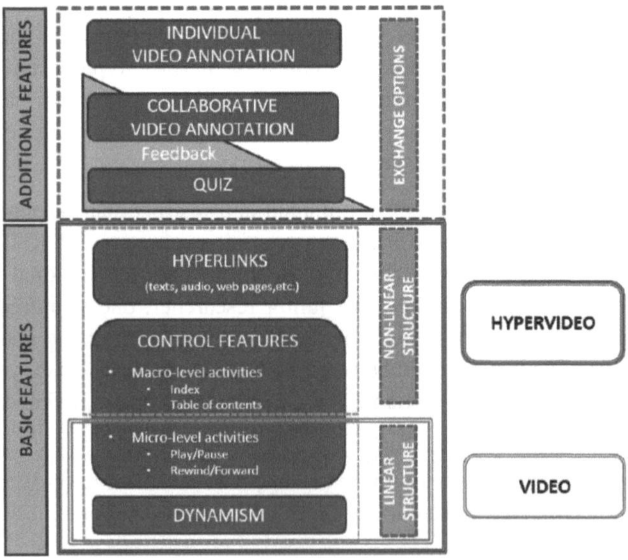

Fig. 4. Cattaneo, Van Der Meij, Aprea, Sauli, and Zahn's model for designing hyper video-based instructional scenarios

The features found in this model are connected to the participants' interface designs using concept mapping software. Using this method, we can quantify the number of times each feature of the model occurs in the user interface designs. The 11 user interface designs are then translated to a table to identify additional design guidelines. In this initial analysis, we can see the features "individual annotation" and "table of content" have been illustrated the most in the 11 user interface designs. On a cluster level, as seen in Table 1. From the analysis on a cluster level, we can see that the participants drew the 22 features on the exchange feature level, followed by 16 features on the non-linear level and 14 features on the linear level. Drawings and three and eight are considered of high quality, as they depict 7 or more elements from Sauli, Cattaneo and van der Meij's Framework for Developing Instructional Hypervideo [30]. Drawing three and eight also represent the most experience, exceeding 20 years of expertise. Drawing 8 (as seen in Fig. 5), has noted the highest amount of design considerations, such as 'annotation,' 'goals,' 'comparison,' 'summery,' 'contents,' 'presentation' and 'key events.'

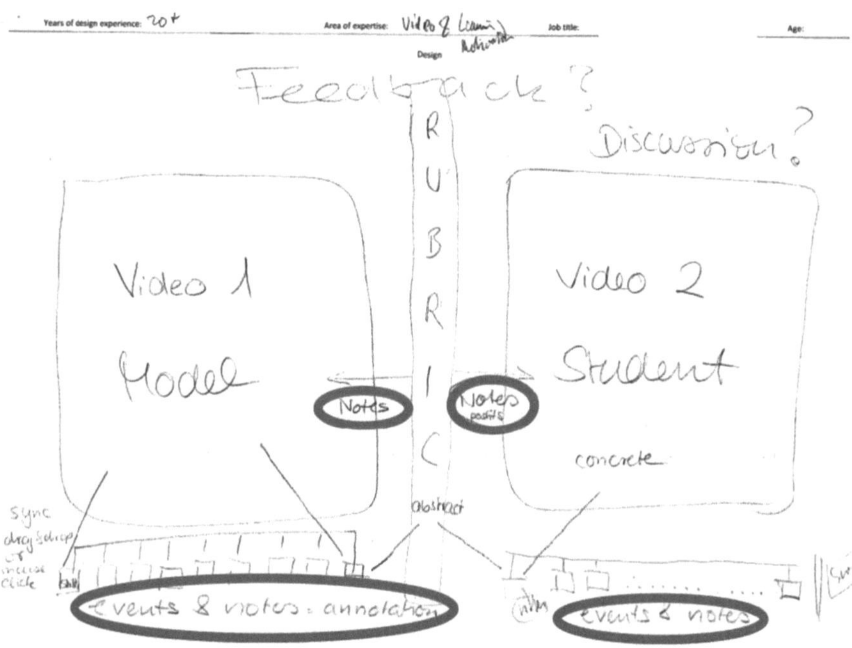

Fig. 5. One of the user interface designs drawn by the participants

Table 1. Preliminary results for additional design guidelines

Feature clusters	Features	Drawing # 1	Drawing # 2	Drawing # 3	Drawing # 4	Drawing # 5	Drawing # 6	Drawing # 7	Drawing # 8	Drawing # 9	Drawing # 10	Drawing # 11	Feature total
Additional features													
Exchange options	Individual annotation	1	3	3	1	1	2		2			2	15
	Collaberative annotation					1							1
	Feedback		1				1	2	1				5
	Quiz			1									1
	Exchange cluster total												22
Basic features													
Non-linear	Hyperlinks			1			1	1				1	4
	Index/table of contents	1	1	2			1	1	2	2	1	1	12
	Non-linear total												16
Linear	Play/pause	1	1	1				1		1			5
	Rewind/forward							1					1
	Dynamism				1	1	1	1	2	1	1		8
	Linear level total												14

The data shows the annotation feature has been referenced 15 times in the drawings. This may suggest an individual annotation as an additional feature compared to prototype 1. For instance, using notes, events, and annotation as highlighted in Fig. 5. The importance of the individual annotation feature may confirm our method before media standpoint, as the results prioritize the complex skill development benefits of the individual annotation function above the possible extraneous load of such a feature. The importance of this feature may resolve the design dilemma is in favor of the methods and underlying theories on the left side of Fig. 1. The data also shows the importance of the content/index menu, being referenced 12 times in the drawings.

The expert appraisal session is recorded in a 17-minute audio file and transcribed in Nvivo 11.4. The session referenced to the design features found Cattaneo, Van Der Meij, Aprea, Sauli, & Zahn's model for designing hyper video-based instructional scenarios on 18 instances, representing a 29.07% coding coverage. The expert appraisal yielded four main areas of interest: Annotation, The Recorded Learner, Gamification and Learner Control.

Annotation is referenced the most in the analysis of the expert appraisal. The function of annotation is found four times and mainly concerns facilitating the learner to connect the abstract knowledge (rubric) to concrete knowledge (video) in the personal language of the learner.

The recorded learner is also referenced four times. The argument made by the experts for recording the learner relies on preface that a recording of the learner may result in a more objective self-assessment. A counter argument is also given by one of the full professors in the expert appraisal, saying:

"(video of the learner) Is more appropriate for VET (vocational educational teaching) then for formal learning of 12–14 years. So, for your target, more formal, you do not need real self-assessment".

Gamification has been found in the designs as well as the expert appraisal. It is argued by the participants that gamification should serve the purpose of making the prototype feel learner-centered, as well as introducing a competitive element.

Considerations. Annotation is referenced the most in both the drawings as the expert appraisal; we will incorporate this feature into the second prototype. Annotation may be of value to the VER because annotation may facilitate the connection between the video and rubric, fostering our design goals. Annotation may be a tool for the learner to regulate learning, positively affecting cognitive load according to Moreno's Cognitive Affective Theory of Learning with Multimedia [7]. Although a counter argument can be made for the increased cognitive load of an annotation feature, we will prioritize the methodological value of annotation over the media guideline in this case and consider this result in the second prototype [21].

Recording the learner may have benefits for more objective self-assessment. However, the technical limitations of the viewbrics project do not allow for this feature to be implemented at the current stage.

Gamification has been found in both the designs and the expert appraisal, aiming to increase personalisation, goal setting, and peer-competition. Learner-centred designs can be theoretically supported with both Mayer's personalisation principle as the ARCS motivational model. As this element is complementary to our current guidelines, we will consider it in the second prototype.

5 Prototype 2

We aim to meet the complementary guidelines from the results by implementing changes in the design of the first prototype 2. For the orientation role, we choose to implement the annotation feature. It is our goal to build the mental model of the learner by linking the video and rubric information. To facilitate this, we implement a Quiz feature to present the learner with a question that may trigger connecting a constituent skill found in both rubric and video such as: 'How did Quinn confirm his task? The answer to this question is then stored into the annotation field of the appropriate constituent skill in the preparation role, where the learner may serve as input for the evaluation, selection and preparation process as seen in Fig. 6.

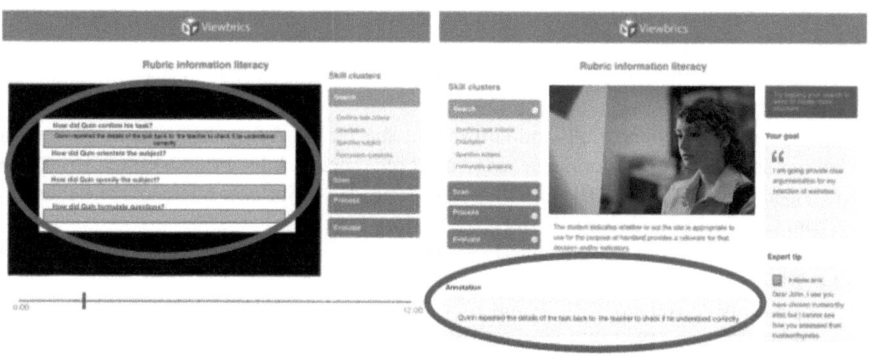

Fig. 6. Prototype 2. Left: orientation role. Right: preparation role

6 Conclusion and Discussion

The question of "How to formulate design guidelines for a Video Enhanced Rubric to improve the formative assessment of complex skills by fostering learner's mental model development, feedback quality, and complex skill mastery?" has presented us with several design dilemmas. We conclude that a thorough analysis of the learner's attributes, the implemented instructional design and the different didactical roles of the VER may greatly decrease the design dilemmas for researchers who aim to foster complex skill development using multimedia.

Considering the complexity of complex skills development, we also found it may prove fruitful to (a) prioritize method over media and (b) facilitate the learner to personally consolidate the connection between the abstract information of a textual analytic rubric and the concrete information of a video modeling example. This connection can be facilitated by implementing features such as notes, events, annotation or a quiz.

We will focus our further work on the more in-depth analysis of our data and the effect of the implementation of the second prototype on the formative assessment and mastery of complex skills of learners in Dutch secondary education. Information on the Viewbrics project can be found on www.viewbrics.nl.

Acknowledgements. We would like to gratefully acknowledge the contribution of the Viewbrics project, that is funded by the practice-oriented research program of the Netherlands Initiative for Education Research (NRO), part of The Netherlands Organisation for Scientific Research (NWO).

References

1. Panadero, E., Romero, M.: To rubric or not to rubric? The effects of self-assessment on self-regulation, performance and self-efficacy. Assess. Educ. Princ. Policy Pract. **21**, 133–148 (2014). https://doi.org/10.1080/0969594X.2013.877872
2. Rusman, E., Martínez-Monés, A., Boon, J., et al.: Gauging teachers' needs with regard to technology-enhanced formative assessment (TEFA) of 21st century skills in the classroom. In: Kalz, M., Ras, E. (eds.) CAA 2014. CCIS, vol. 439, pp. 1–14. Springer, Cham (2014). https://doi.org/10.1007/978-3-319-08657-6_1
3. Thijs, A., Fisser, P., van der Hoeven, M.: 21E Eeuwse Vaardigheden in Het Curriculum Van Het Funderend Onderwijs. Slo 128 (2014)
4. Ackermans, K., Rusman, E., Brand-Gruwel, S., Specht, M.: A first step towards synthesizing rubrics and video for the formative assessment of complex skills. In: Joosten-ten Brinke, D., Laanpere, M. (eds.) TEA 2016. CCIS, vol. 653, pp. 1–10. Springer International Publishing, Cham (2017). https://doi.org/10.1007/978-3-319-57744-9_1
5. Westera, W.: Reframing contextual learning: anticipating the virtual extensions of context **14**, 201–212 (2011)
6. Matthews, W.J., Buratto, L.G., Lamberts, K.: Exploring the memory advantage for moving scenes. Vis. Cogn. **18**, 1393–1420 (2010). https://doi.org/10.1080/13506285.2010.492706
7. Moreno, R., Mayer, R.: Interactive multimodal learning environments. Educ. Psychol. Rev. **19**, 309–326 (2007). https://doi.org/10.1007/s10648-007-9047-2

8. Dousay, T.A.: Effects of redundancy and modality on the situational interest of adult learners in multimedia learning. Educ. Technol. Res. Dev. **64**, 1–21 (2016). https://doi.org/10.1007/s11423-016-9456-3
9. Park, B., Plass, J.L., Brünken, R.: Cognitive and affective processes in multimedia learning. Learn. Instr. **29**, 125–127 (2014). https://doi.org/10.1016/j.learninstruc.2013.05.005
10. Brookhart, S.M., Chen, F.: The quality and effectiveness of descriptive rubrics. Educ. Rev. **1911**, 1–26 (2014). https://doi.org/10.1080/00131911.2014.929565
11. König, C., Hofmann, T., Bruder, R.: Application of the user-centred design process according ISO 9241-210 in air traffic control. Work **41**, 167–174 (2012). https://doi.org/10.3233/WOR-2012-1005-167
12. Clark, I.: Formative assessment: assessment is for self-regulated learning. Educ. Psychol. Rev. **24**, 205–249 (2012). https://doi.org/10.1007/s10648-011-9191-6
13. Eitam, B., Kennedy, P.M., Higgins, E.T.: Motivation from control. Exp. Brain Res. **229**, 475–484 (2013). https://doi.org/10.1007/s00221-012-3370-7
14. Leutner, D.: Motivation and emotion as mediators in multimedia learning. Learn. Instr. **29**, 174–175 (2014). https://doi.org/10.1016/j.learninstruc.2013.05.004
15. Vollmeyer, R., Rheinberg, F.: Motivational effects on self-regulated learning with different tasks. Educ. Psychol. Rev. **18**, 239–253 (2006). https://doi.org/10.1007/s10648-006-9017-0
16. Mayer, R.E.: Incorporating motivation into multimedia learning. Learn. Instr. **29**, 171–173 (2014). https://doi.org/10.1016/j.learninstruc.2013.04.003
17. Schank, R.C., Fano, A., Bell, B., Jona, M.: The design of goal-based scenarios. J. Learn. Sci. **3**, 305–345 (1994). https://doi.org/10.1207/s15327809jls0304_2
18. Van Merriënboer, J.J.G., Kester, L.: The four-component instructional design model: multimedia principles in environments for complex learning. In: Mayer, R. (ed.) Cambridge Handbook of Multimedia Learning, pp. 104–148. Cambridge University Press, Cambridge (2014)
19. Van Merriënboer, J.J.G., Sluijsmans, D.M.A.: Toward a synthesis of cognitive load theory, four-component instructional design, and self-directed learning. Educ. Psychol. Rev. **21**, 55–66 (2009). https://doi.org/10.1007/s10648-008-9092-5
20. Mayer, R.E., Moreno, R.: Nine ways to reduce cognitive load in multimedia learning. Educ. Psychol. **38**, 43–52 (2003). https://doi.org/10.1207/S15326985EP3801_6
21. Mayer, R.E.: Multimedia Learning, 2nd edn. Cambridge University Press, Cambridge (2009). https://doi.org/10.1007/s13398-014-0173-7.2
22. Janssen-Noordman, A.M., Van Merriënboer, J.J.G.: Innovatief Onderwijs Ontwerpen. Wolters-Noordhoff, Groningen (2002)
23. Panadero, E., Jonsson, A.: The use of scoring rubrics for formative assessment purposes revisited: a review. Educ. Res. Rev. **9**, 129–144 (2013). https://doi.org/10.1016/j.edurev.2013.01.002
24. Mertler, C.: Designing scoring rubrics for your classroom. Pract. Assess. Res. Eval. **7**, 1–10 (2001)
25. Ma, W.J., Husain, M., Bays, P.M., et al.: Changing concepts of working memory. Nat. Neurosci. **17**, 347–356 (2014). https://doi.org/10.1038/nn.3655
26. Luck, S.J., Vogel, E.: The capacity of visual working memory for features and conjunctions. Nature **390**, 279–281 (1997). https://doi.org/10.1038/36846
27. Spanjers, I.A.E., Van Gog, T., Wouters, P., Van Merriënboer, J.J.G.: Explaining the segmentation effect in learning from animations: the role of pausing and temporal cueing. Comput. Educ. **59**, 274–280 (2012). https://doi.org/10.1016/j.compedu.2011.12.024

28. Hoogerheide, V., Loyens, S.M.M., van Gog, T.: Effects of creating video-based modeling examples on learning and transfer. Learn. Instr. **33**, 108–119 (2014). https://doi.org/10.1016/j.learninstruc.2014.04.005
29. Mátrai, R., Kosztyán, Z.T., Sik-Lányi, C.: Navigation methods of special needs users in multimedia systems. Comput. Hum. Behav. **24**, 1418–1433 (2008). https://doi.org/10.1016/j.chb.2007.07.015
30. Cattaneo, A., Van Der Meij, H., Aprea, C., et al.: A model for designing hypervideo-based instructional scenarios. Paper submitted for publication

Rubric to Assess Evidence-Based Dialogue of Socio-Scientific Issues with LiteMap

Ana Karine Loula Torres Rocha[1(✉)], Ana Beatriz L. T. Rocha[2], and Alexandra Okada[3]

[1] University of the State of Bahia UNEB, Salvador, Brazil
aklrocha@uneb.br
[2] Catholic University of Salvador UCSAL, Salvador, Brazil
beatriz.rocha@open.ac.uk
[3] The Open University, OU, Milton Keynes, UK
ale.okada@open.ac.uk

Abstract. The aim of this study is to investigate whether the LiteMap application tool helps teachers annotate students' socio-scientific discussion and assess their evidence-based dialogue using a rubric system of inquiry skills for Responsible Research and Innovation (RRI). This study focuses on a set of materials and activities of the European *ENGAGE* project used by Brazilian students from a city affected by the Zika virus to discuss whether the mosquito Aedes Aegypti should be exterminated or not. The Zika virus project was developed by 24 teachers and 478 students from a public professional school in Irecê including also 5 collaborators and 2 researchers. This qualitative study analyses the dialogue of 35 students (21 girls and 14 boys) randomly selected who participated of 1-h debate to discuss their informed views and evidence-based opinions. Findings of this study reveal that the rubric system facilitates the annotation and mapping of questions, claims, arguments and evidence. LiteMap was useful to represent students' evidence based dialogue and provide feedback. The visualization of evidence-based dialogue maps can be used by teachers and students during formative assessment of inquiry skills for RRI. However, the process must be planned and it requires time.

Keywords: Rubrics · Evidence-based dialogue map
Research and responsible innovation · RRI · LiteMap · Formative assessment
Open schooling · ENGAGE

1 Introduction

Digital scientific literacy is increasingly important for students to make sense of scientific innovations that affects their lives and make decisions based on evidence (Okada 2016). To become digitally scientifically literate, students must know concepts and understand processes on how scientific research is constructed and how digital technology can be used. One of the important challenges for educators is to prepare students with knowledge and skills for discussing scientific innovation and reflecting on its applications and implications for society. Teachers must also be prepared to

E. Ras and A. E. Guerrero Roldán (Eds.): TEA 2017, CCIS 829, pp. 137–149, 2018.
https://doi.org/10.1007/978-3-319-97807-9_11

know how to assess and support students to develop informed views and to argue scientifically (Okada 2016).

This exploratory study, aims to investigate whether a system of rubrics with LiteMap tool can help teachers annotate and assess students' evidence-based dialogue of socio-scientific issues and whether the visual representations of students' arguments can be used for teachers to provide feedback to enhance learning. This study focuses on the system of rubrics developed for the *ENGAGE* project by Okada (2015) to guide teachers to map argumentative discussions on topical dilemmas and support students to develop inquiry skills for Responsible Research and Innovation (RRI).

ENGAGE, funded by the European Commission, aims to help teachers prepare the next generation for RRI through inquiry based learning, by offering Open Educational Materials (OER) on topical science and MOOC (Massive Open Online Courses) on pedagogical strategies for educators. ENGAGE is an open schooling portal that reached more than 18,000 members in 80 countries: teachers, lecturers, researchers, topical science educators and scientists. This community has been reusing and recreating OER for learners to develop 10 inquiries based learning skills for RRI.

The purpose of RRI is to engage society and scientists to work together considering that the responsible development of science and technology is the base for a better future. Therefore, innovations must be carefully planned to address societal needs by engaging all societal actors. This interaction must consider societal values in order to maximize the benefits and reduce any harmful impact for people's life and the environment.

The relevance of this work is to examine whether LiteMap - cloud-based application for collaborative mapping - can help teachers annotate and map students' evidence-based dialogue for formative assessment of inquiry skills for RRI.

The following Sect. 2 presents the literature about the use of evidence-based dialogue maps and rubrics to support formative assessment of argumentation as well as challenges related to the uses of mapping tools by teachers and students. Based on these challenging issues, Sect. 3 introduces the research questions and Sect. 4 describes the qualitative approach based on participatory action-research including findings. Finally, Sect. 5 presents a brief discussion and conclusions.

2 Literature

The word "rubric" derives from the Latin whose meaning is "red ochre" to mark part of a text to emphasize it. Rubric is used in education for assessment, as an approach to establish a system of criteria and requirements to address these criteria. It also refers to a list of expectations for an assignment, or a set of assignments, including levels of quality in relation to each of these expectations (Reddy and Andrade 2010). Rubric for assessment is formally defined as a scoring guide, consisting of specific pre-established criteria, used to assess students' work or their performance.

Rubric can be used as an assessment instrument, which has been increasingly adopted by educators in universities (Simon and Forgette-Giroux 2001) and widely used in secondary school as well (Reddy 2007). One of its popular benefits is to enhance the psychometric properties of performance assessment and also support the process of formative assessment, particularly when rubric is used to inform students about their progress to help them in their development (Black and Wiliam 2009; Wiliam 2011).

Visual representation of knowledge such as knowledge mapping (Okada et al. 2008) is a pedagogical strategy to support students' learning and assess students' domain knowledge and skills, such as concept maps (Novak and Canas 2006; Nesbit and Adesope 2006); argumentative maps (Rider and Thomason 2006) and evidence-based dialogue maps (Okada 2008; 2014). The use of visual representation to map knowledge has been studied previously in combination with metacognitive activities (e.g., Hilbert and Renkl 2009) and with the use of rubrics to enhance learning including the reliability and validity of students' self- and peer assessment (Besterfield-Sacre et al. 2004).

The evidence-based dialogue map is a technique created by Okada (2006) to support scientific thinking for inquiry based learning. It is grounded on IBIS created for Information Systems and Toulmin scheme usually applied in Law. Table 1 shows the common components of these three approaches. IBIS is used to represent shared understanding of complex issues called "wicked problems". Toulmin scheme is used to represent argumentation often in Law. Evidence-based dialogue represents components of a discussion supported by data, facts or knowledge. Table 1 shows the key- components and the fundamentals that support this approach.

Table 1. Components of evidence-based dialogue, Okada 2006

Evidence-based dialogue map	IBIS Issues Based Information Systems	Toulmin scheme
Question: is related to a socio-scientific issue	**Question:** is related to a wicked problem	
Idea: is a claim that responds a socio-scientific issue	**Idea:** is a claim that responds a wicked problem	
Argument: includes pros that support the idea and cons that refute the idea	**Argument:** includes pros that support the idea and cons that refute the idea	**Argument:** includes pros that support the idea and cons that refute the idea
Substantive evidence: is based on knowledge, generalization, cause and consequence		**Data:** are facts, examples and statistics
Motivational evidence: is based on beliefs, convictions, circumstances or contexts		**Qualifier:** Represents the validity of a plea and context or circumstance in which the plea is "true"
Authoritative evidence: is based on references or experts' views		**Support:** refers to a source of authority for the warrant

The evidence-based dialogue mapping uses a set of icons to classify each sentence of a discussion to identify its components. The classification through icons helps participants visualize the argumentation and evidence or lack of evidence. In the *ENGAGE* project, the icons of the evidence-based dialogue map were used to represent key inquiry skills for RRI.

Table 2. *ENGAGE* rubrics to assess inquiry skills for RRI developed by Okada (2016)

Icons	RUBRIC	ATTRIBUTES to be checked	SCORE
(?)	Devise questions	refers to a socio-scientific issue	+1
(!)	Communicate Ideas	presents (informed) ideas related to the issue	+1
(-)	Critique claims	highlights counter-argument that refutes an idea	+1
(+)	Justify opinions	explains opinions linked to knowledge, facts or data	+1
(+/-)	Examine consequences	shows benefits or risks for society or environment	+1
(●)	Interrogate Sources	shows details about reliable evidence	+1

Although LiteMap and the system of rubrics (Table 2) was introduced through the *ENGAGE* MOOC for teachers, the majority of examples and practices using these approaches were developed by knowledge mapping practitioners.

To examine the potential of LiteMap and rubrics used by teachers to facilitate assessment, this study consider three challenges described by previous studies of the *ENGAGE* project:

1. Teachers who are not used to inquiry-based learning need resources and pedagogical strategies to move from science content to knowledge and skills for RRI (Okada and Bayram Jacobs 2016).
2. Although teachers are open to RRI materials, they lack pedagogical tools and training for teaching and assessing evidence-based discussions on topical socio-scientific issues (Kiki-Papadakis and Chaimala 2016).
3. LiteMap can be used to map discussions on RRI collaboratively by academic communities (Okada 2016) or evidence-based practices for RRI by educator-researchers, however it has not been used by teachers nor students for assessment (Okada et al. 2015);

The key contribution for the literature about Knowledge Cartography (Okada 2006) is to provide new ways to scaffold the process of evidence-based dialogue mapping for teachers and students who are not mapping practitioners through rubrics and annotation.

3 Methodological Approach

This study was developed at the Territorial Center of Professional Education - CETEP, in the municipality of Irecê, state of Bahia-Brazil, from October to December 2016. Irecê is located in the state of Bahia in the northeast of Brazil, which has been widely affected by the ZIKA virus.

It was based on the *ENGAGE* Exterminate project, which was introduced to the school as a non-compulsory activity, for a professional high school. All participants – teachers and students – were informed about the purpose of the study as well as how the lessons would be recorded and the method for the study: participatory-action research. Everyone joined the project and signed a consent form for video and audio recording including photos of the groups' discussions and their activities.

3.1 Research Questions

Based on the challenges highlighted in the previous section, this study examines whether the LiteMap application tool can be used by teachers to assess evidence-based dialogue on socio-scientific issues and provide feedback for students on inquiry skills for RRI. The specific questions in this study are: (1) How useful are rubrics to annotate and map students' evidence-based discussion? (2) In what ways can LiteMap be used by teachers to assess inquiry skills for RRI? (3) How helpful are rubrics and LiteMap visualizations for providing feedback for students?

3.2 Participants

Participants were 24 teachers, 08 coordinators and 21 classes. A total of 478 students of technical level courses participated in the *ENGAGE* project from the following courses: agricultural, administration, clinical analysis, commerce, nursing, environment, nutrition, advertising and occupational safety. Students were from 15 to 18 years old, 60.2% were female and 39.8% male. This qualitative study analyses the dialogue of 35 students (21 girls and 14 boys) in their third and fourth years randomly selected who participated in the final activity: a 1-h debate about the *ENGAGE* dilemma after completing the all procedures described in the following section.

3.3 Procedures

Initially the meetings were held with the school community to present the project proposal and reflect on how to best develop the project including all members of CETEP. Teachers and students received information about the project and activities organized in three phases: 1- set up the project (teacher-led), 2- analyze and solve (student-led) and 3- communicate (student-led with a teacher intro).

The first phase was "setting up the project". Teachers presented the socio-scientific dilemma "Should we exterminate the *Aedes Aegypti* mosquito?" The activities consisted of discussions through a game about the food chain in the ecosystem and the construction of a table where students recorded what they already knew about the subject, what they would like to investigate, where to find data and what they learned about the topic. The group discussions were recorded in a logbook. The teachers also took pictures and the group facilitators also captured video clips of the project's key discussions in school.

The second phase was "analysis and solution of the dilemma". The teachers proposed to students to read and discuss about the articles on genetically modified (GM) mosquitoes, released in Brazil by the British company Oxitec. Students used their mobile devices to search for information. They discussed about opinions related to the risks and benefits of using GM mosquitoes. They assessed research sources and were challenged to build evidence-based arguments to justify their answers about the dilemma. The systematization was mapped and recorded in the logbook.

The third final phase was communication. Teachers guided group of students to construct argumentative maps based on the LiteMap mapping software tool, including the rubrics icons: devise questions, communicate ideas, justify opinions, critique claims, examine consequences and interrogate sources, in order to systematize their evidence based opinions about the dilemma. However, due to problems with internet connection, it was not possible to use LiteMap. However, the groups used the same icons on paper to create maps, similar to LiteMap. The mapping activity was used to support students to develop their arguments and explanations based on evidence.

Students prepared slides in PowerPoint about their argumentative views on exterminating ZIKA virus with a variety of information from their portfolio of activities during the *ENGAGE* project, which included:

- Glossary about new concepts and definitions.
- Game of Life: what would happen with the ecosystem without mosquitoes
- Food web including the *Aedes Aegypti* mosquito.
- Discussion on scientific paper about GM mosquitoes produced by OXITEC.
- Press release developed by Students.
- Risks and benefits analysis of different solutions to reduce Zika virus.
- Analysis of risks and consequences.
- Dilemma discussion about exterminating or not the *Aedes Aegypti* mosquito
- Conclusions of their groups' projects with justifications.
- Photos and videos produced during the process.

After groups presenting their slides in the auditorium of the CETEP School, 35 students debated about the *ENGAGE* dilemma. This event was facilitated by the teacher mediator, two different subject teachers and the course coordinator teacher, whose reflections about the process was also shared using notes. This debate was filmed, annotated and mapped in LiteMap using the same rubrics for performance assessment. Data analyzed for this paper with participants' consent refer to this debate. The outcomes of the analysis were discussed and reviewed by the students, teachers and researcher authors. This qualitative study is based on participatory action research using various instruments to gather and analyze various types of data: photos, video, maps in LiteMap.

LiteMap application tool was used by the teacher-facilitator to analyze audio and video recording of group discussions, which was transcribed in Portuguese and saved in HTML for annotation. Various visualizations supported by LiteMap were used to reflect and review the analyses by the student-author and researcher-coordinator-author with an interpretive approach based on the studies of Becker et al. (2006); Stauss and Corbin (2008).

4 Findings

How Useful Are Rubrics to Annotate and Map Students' Evidence-Based Discussion?

The teacher facilitator who used LiteMap observed that the use of rubrics enabled the development and systematization of criteria and served as an indicator of analysis and evaluation, reducing the subjectivity of the process. The subject teachers mentioned that the rubric system helped to construct more transparent and coherent criteria in relation to learning objectives. Students also noticed that the annotations of their discussion using the LiteMap toolbar was helpful in highlighting more easily the marks referring to RRI skills (see extract 1). The teacher-facilitator observed that with the annotations, it was possible to visualize the sequence of the discussion, highlighting key points of emphasis of rubrics. All the participants could access the text with the annotations and reflect with the pre-defined rubrics. Thus, through the annotation of the students' discussion, subject teachers perceived that the definition of a system of headings connected to the rubrics facilitated the annotation and mapping of questions, ideas and arguments; in addition to developing the capacity of classification, categorization, clarity and prioritization of opinions facilitating the process of conclusion and evaluation (Fig. 1).

Student 3: " I read about the Zika virus in the newspaper, but there are not many cases in my area". When we discussed this topic deeper we realized that "it was something that would certainly hurt us" and our group came to the conclusion of non-extermination because of the food chain, and ? There is the question whether genetically modified mosquitoes should be used or not ; we are in favor of; but also, we are against it from the moment that many mosquitoes are released there might be overcrowding of the species in a certain area affecting the environment; overpopulation and extermination damages the ecosystem.

Fig. 1. First extract of the group discussion annotated with LiteMap

However, the teacher-facilitator who used LiteMap found out that the attributions of the rubric in classifying some arguments are not so simple and direct. Some questions can be classified as questions that reflect consequences (e.g. Does Brazil has the infrastructure to support so many sick people?). Moreover, there are many doubts about what to annotate or not. This requires time and many re- readings and also, recalling the context of the discussion, for instance through the video of the debate (Fig. 2).

Student 2: many groups advocate the genetically modified mosquito, but if the genetically modified mosquito can mate with all the wild females and all, reproduce the mosquito, and the mosquito is born weak and in the same way die, it will not eradicate many species of mosquito? I know it is wrong it is not ethical to exterminate the mosquito, because it is something that is already before us in the environment, but we must also think about the human being, if in Brazil today the health is already in this decadence, imagine with overcrowding, these mosquitoes only transmitting disease, every year that passes is a new disease, will Brazil have the infrastructure to support so many sick people?

Fig. 2. Second extract of the group discussion annotated with LiteMap

In What Ways LiteMap Can Be Used by Teachers to Assess Inquiry Skills for RRI?

The teacher who facilitated and annotated the discussion using rubrics observed that LiteMap was very useful to visualize and assess how the students used the knowledge, facts and data as evidence to support or refute the arguments (Fig. 3).

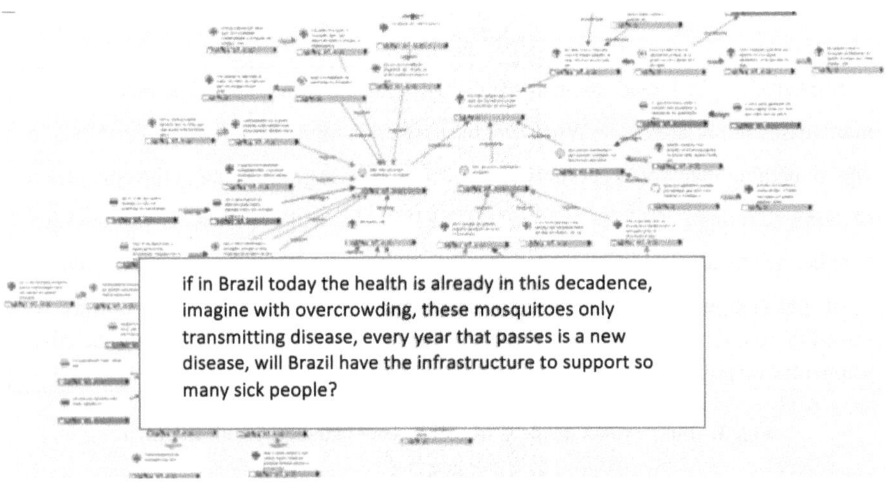

Fig. 3. Group discussion map created with LiteMap tool. There are zoom and orientation controls available and the mouse can be used to zoom in and out.

The process of annotating and mapping in LiteMap was useful to identify the components of argumentation which were neither explicit nor structured as they emerged in different moments during the chronological linear dialogue. With the map was possible to establish the multiple connections of the arguments used to support or refute the ideas. This multilinear view, enabled teachers and students to visualize the connections between arguments and also between arguments and evidence presented in the discussion. The evidence-based dialogue map provided a clear understanding of the argumentation based on knowledge, data or facts that were shared by students during the process.

Each annotated text, which includes a clickable icon representing the rubrics, provided a direct access to the map by its URL. Each sentence annotated from the text and represented by the icon was included as a node in an evidence-based dialogue map. These nodes enabled students to return to the annotated text, therefore, it was possible to visualize the rubrics in the original text from the map. LiteMap also enabled participants to add images, videos, photographs which complemented the evidence-based argumentation with concepts, facts and references.

Through LiteMap, it was possible for participants and research authors to navigate on the dialogue following multiple connections. It was also possible to visualise the most connected ideas with various connections or the most popular arguments with various nodes. Zoom-in and Zoom-out were used to explore the multi-linear visualisation and access specific ideas of the dialogue. LiteMap helped teachers, participants and collaborators to become aware of multiple connections of the components of evidence-based thinking which are also related to the skills for RRI. LiteMap enabled participants to identify weak arguments, checking whether there was more evidence across the whole discussion, identify relevant ideas that were not argued at all and identify strong arguments in order to support them to assess and review their conclusions and the evidence-based thinking process.

How Helpful Are Rubrics and LiteMap Visualizations for Providing Feedback for Students?

The rubrics of the ENGAGE project with LiteMap facilitated the process of mapping evidence-based argumentation. The LiteMap maps (e.g. Figure 3) and graphs (e.g. Figure 4) enabled teacher and students to access the visualization to identify strong and weak argumentation (with and without evidence - grey colour) between data and students' knowledge and opinions.

One of the LiteMap visualizations used to identify the most popular informed views was the "conversation nesting graph" that represents the assignment of rubrics in different colors (purple), questions (pink), arguments (green), counter-arguments (red), sources (grey), consequences/risks (blue).

The nested circles enabled participants to observe the most reflective ideas according to the level of depth through several concentric circles; and the broadest ideas based on diversity of arguments through larger circles with more elements. The various ways to gather feedback from LiteMap through the visualization of both annotated linear texts, maps with multiple arguments and the conversation nesting allowed the teachers and students to review their evidenced-based dialogue, observe how their thought was constructed and what influenced in a confirmatory or challenging way, The feedback for collaborative assessment enabled the group to examine evidence-based views presented by the group in the end of the discussion. In addition, it was possible to identify emerging ideas without any connection or nodes (smaller circles) to be substantiated future discussions.

Through this work, students were able to visualize graphically, perceive relationships more easily, and increase their understanding and comprehension of their evidence-based argumentation. The graphs and maps offered more visibility of students' thinking by making it more visible and accessible.

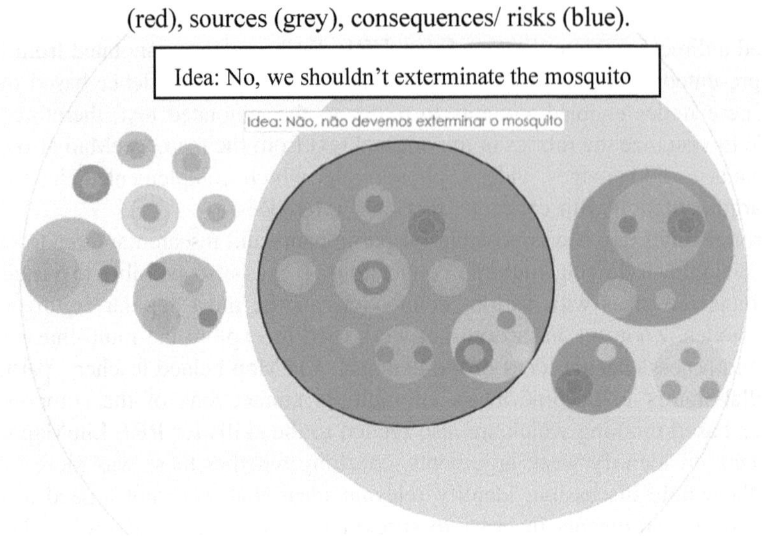

Fig. 4. Conversation nesting of the final group discussion generated by LiteMap (Color figure online)

Other useful LiteMap visualizations for providing feedback to students and teachers were quick overview and activity analysis.

The activity analysis visualization (Fig. 5) helped teachers and research collaborators identify that the map was accessed and viewed more than 100 times in the first week by participants during various days after the debate. It also revealed that the process of annotating and mapping a discussion requires time and feedback from participants. In terms of content categorized by rubrics, the quick overview visualization, for example, shows that the students' discussion included: 28 Supporting Argument, 12 Counter-Argument, 12 Notes/comments, 4 Idea and 7 Issues. In addition, this dialogue had approximately 101 words minimum as the average contribution, 836 words as the maximum, 2 logged-in participants viewed this Conversation 13 times between 6 and 14 days ago e 1 logged in person viewed this Conversation 1 time in the last 5 days while the teacher and authors were analyzing data.

Other collaborators who contributed to this project also accessed the dialogue mapping and graphs in LiteMap. Teachers who accessed the map observed that it was created during the first day and completed during the following two days. Any member of this community could add more information after the debate as well as make comments and provide score (+1) like and (−1) dislike in LiteMap based on the rubrics' system. The use of rubrics was reviewed by the three authors and participants who accessed the map. The content of the map was improved and edited after students' feedback.

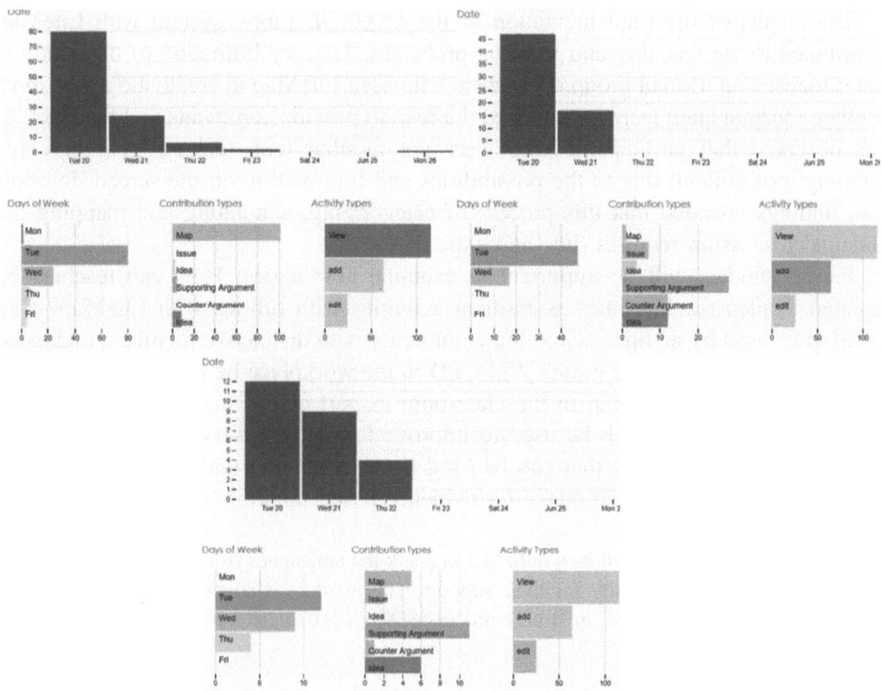

Fig. 5. Activity analysis visualization (view – add – edit)

5 Discussion and Conclusion

Findings of this study show that the *ENGAGE* project rubric system facilitated the annotation and mapping of questions, claims, arguments and evidence with LiteMap.

During this process, various preliminary activities were important to prepare students to use their knowledge and skills for evidence-based dialogue. Knowledge and skills highlighted by rubrics become more explicit when it is enhanced visually through icons, colors, connections and votes. The visualizations of the rubrics in the annotated discussion, the evidence-base dialogue map and the conversation nesting graph provided different perspectives, which can be used to support inquiry based learning of socio-scientific issues and formative assessment for RRI.

This study revealed that LiteMap was useful for representing students' evidence-based dialogue graphically and providing feedback for students to identify strong and weak opinions and conclusions. This occurred when educators and learners visualized and assessed components and connections of the scientific argumentation. According to Okada (2006) evidence-based dialogue maps can be used as a methodological tool to plan participatory action research (2008a); develop knowledge and inquiry skills (2008), assess argumentative discussions, scientific writing (2008), and improve pedagogical practices.

The results of the implementation of the *ENGAGE* rubric system with LiteMap contributed to the teaching and learning processes. The key limitation of this study is that it focused on a small group of teachers who used LiteMap to create the maps, most of other educators and learners accessed the map to provide comments and feedback. It was observed that participants who were not familiar with technology found this mapping tool difficult due to the possibilities and information on the screen. In addition, findings revealed that this process of categorizing, annotating and mapping the students' discussion requires time and experience.

Further studies will be important to examine new issues: How can teachers be engaged to plan teaching and assessment activities with rubrics with LiteMap? Can LiteMap be used by an open schooling community with distinctive members interested in the same socio-scientific issue? Will CPD in the workplace be relevant for teachers to learn how to use LiteMap in the classroom as part of the students' activities and projects? Can this approach be used to improve formative assessment with common and transparent procedures that can be used by teachers and understood by students through a common visual language for evidence based thinking?

Acknowledgements. The authors would like to thank the colleagues from the *ENGAGE* project and the COLEARN community for their support. This work was supported by the European Commission and CAPES/MEC in Brazil, process 88881.131870/2016-01, public notice PDSE, nº. 19/2016.

References

Okada, A.: Responsible research and innovation in science education report. In: Keynes, M. (ed.) The Open University – UK (2016)

Okada, A. (ed.): Engaging Science: Innovative Teaching for Responsible Citizenship. The Open University UK - Knowledge Media Institute, Milton Keynes (2016). http://oro.open.ac.uk/46455/1/Policy%20final%202016%20April.pdf

Okada, A., Young, G., Sherborne, T.: Innovative teaching of responsible research and innovation in science education. E-Leaning Papers. Open Educ. Europa J. **44**(1) (2015)

Reddy, Y.M., Andrade, H.: A review of rubric use in higher education. Assess. Eval. High. Educ. **35**(4), 435–448 (2010). https://doi.org/10.1080/02602930902862859

Simon, M., Forgette-Giroux, R.: A rubric for scoring postsecondary academic skills. Pract. Assess. Res. Eval. **7**(18) (2001). http://PAREonline.net/getvn.asp?v=7&n=18

Reddy, Y.M.: Effects of rubrics on enhancement of student learning. Educate **7**(1), 3–17 (2007)

Black, P., Wiliam, D.: Developing the theory of formative assessment. Educ. Assess. Eval. Accountability **21**, 5–31 (2009)

Wiliam, D.: What is assessment for learning? Stud. Educ. Eval. **37**, 2–14 (2011)

Okada, A., Buckingham Shum, S., Sherborne, T.: Knowledge Cartography: Software Tools and Mapping Techniques. Springer, London (2008). http://kmi.open.ac.uk/books/knowledge-cartography

Novak, J.D., Canas, A.J.: The theory underlying concept maps and how to construct them. Technical report IHMC Cmap Tools 2006-01 (2006). http://cmap.ihmcus/Publications/ResearchPapers/TheoryUnderlyingConceptMaps.pdf

Nesbit, J.C., Adesope, O.O.: Learning with concept and knowledge maps: a meta-analysis. Rev. Educ. Res. **76**, 413–448 (2006)

Rider, Y., Thomason, N.: Cognitive and pedagogical benefits of argument mapping: L.A.M. P. guides the way to better thinking. In: Okada, A.L.P., Buckingham Shum, S., Sherborne, T. (eds.) Knowledge Cartography: Software Tools and Mapping Techniques. AI&KP, pp. 113–134. Springer, London (2006). https://doi.org/10.1007/978-1-4471-6470-8_6

Okada, A.: Scaffolding school pupils scientific argumentation with evidence-based dialogue maps. In: Okada, A., Buckingham Shum, S., Sherborne, T. (eds.) Knowledge Cartography: software tools and mapping techniques. Springer, London (2008). https://doi.org/10.1007/978-1-84800-149-7_7

Hilbert, T.S., Renkl, A.: Learning how to use a computer-based concept-mapping tool: self-explaining examples helps. Comput. Hum. Behav. **25**(2), 267–274 (2009). https://doi.org/10.1016/j.chb.2008.12.006

Besterfield-Sacre, M., Gerchak, J., Lyons, M., Shuman, L.J., Wolfe, H.: Scoring concept maps: an integrated rubric for assessing engineering education. J. Eng. Educ. **93**, 105–116 (2004)

Okada, A.: Cartografia Investigativa – Interfaces epistemológicas comunicacionais para mapear conhecimento em projetos de pesquisa. Doctoral thesis. São Paulo: Programa de Pós-graduação em Educação: Currículo. Pontifícia Universidade Católica de São Paulo (2006)

Okada, A., Bayram-Jacobs, D.: Opportunities and challenges for equipping the next generation for responsible citizenship through the ENGAGE HUB. In: International Conference on Responsible Research in Education and Management and its Impact, London (2016). https://lsme.ac.uk/files/Research-Book-Jan-2016.pdf#page=42, http://www.engagingscience.eu/en/?wpdmdl=1759

Kiki-Papadakis, K., Chaimala, F.: The embedment of responsible research and innovation aspects in European science curricula. Revista Romaneasca pentru Educatie Multidimensionala **8**(2), 71–87 (2016). https://doi.org/10.18662/rrem/2016.0802.06, http://www.revistaromaneasca.ro/wp-content/uploads/2016/12/REV_december2016_71-87.pdf

Okada, A., Young, G., Sanders, J.: Fostering communities of practices for teachers' professional development integrating OER and MOOC, EC-TEL. In: The 10th European Conference on Technology Enhanced Learning (2015). http://www.engagingscience.eu/en/?wpdmdl=1078

Becker, S., Bryman, A., Sempik, J.: Defining 'Quality' in Social Policy Research: Views, Perceptions and a Framework for Discussion. Social Policy Association, Suffolk, Lavenham (2006)

Strauss, A., Corbin, J.: Basics of Qualitative Research: Techniques and Procedures for Developing Grounded Theory, 3rd edn. Sage Publications Inc., Thousand Oaks (2008)

Okada, A.: Cartography for inquiry: epistemological and communicational interfaces to map knowledge in academic projects. Doctoral's thesis. São Paulo PUC-SP University & The Open University – Knowledge Media Institute OU-UK (2006)

Okada, A.: Evidence-based dialogue maps as a research tool to evaluate the quality of school pupils' scientific argumentation. Int. J. Res. Method Educ. **31**(3), 291–315 (2008a). Okada, Alexandra and Buckingham Shum, Simon (2008)

Okada, A., Scaffolding school students' scientific argumentation in inquiry-based learning with evidence maps. In: Okada, A., Buckingham Shum, S. J., Sherborne, T. (eds.) Knowledge Cartography: Software Tools and Mapping Techniques. Advanced Information and Knowledge Processing, pp. 135–172. Springer, London (2014). https://doi.org/10.1007/978-1-4471-6470-8_7

Assessment of Engagement: Using Microlevel Student Engagement as a Form of Continuous Assessment

Isuru Balasooriya(✉), M. Elena Rodríguez, and Enric Mor

Universitat Oberta de Catalunya, Barcelona, Spain
{ibalasooriya, mrodriguezgo, emor}@uoc.edu

Abstract. Student assessment is a challenging topic where methods are still being developed to embed active learning, deeper understanding, fairness and appropriateness to the learning process. As a candidate assessment factor, student engagement is a known contributor to student success, although the lack of student engagement and success, particularly in online environments are both challenging and ongoing issues. Student engagement is typically measured in retrospective data collection to understand how engagement has affected student learning. However in online learning environments we have access to data in a timely manner from resource access to assessment tasks, where they can be captured seamlessly and used in analytics to understand student behaviours and learning patterns. By combining a microlevel student engagement measurement we have implemented, with the goal of assessing engagement, we present initial results in this paper from a study we have carried out at Universitat Oberta de Catalunya in Spain, which shows promise in student engagement measurement as a form of continuous assessment. By measuring microlevel engagement, we have observed we can collect a variety of missing subjective dataset to complement the system-level data, and it can also be an opportunity for students to reflect on their own engagement as well as have a method to record their microlevel state. In several courses teachers rewarded points based on engagement, leading to continued engagement of students and a stream of actionable information to understand where students have challenges of engagement in their learning and revision of course content.

Keywords: Student engagement · Continuous assessment · Online education

1 Introduction

Online learning has been gaining momentum in recent years (Bonk and Kim 2006; Ni 2013; Allen and Seaman 2015) with traditional universities opting for online degree programs, Massive Open Online Courses (MOOCs), online distance learning programs, self-paced online courses and blended classroom settings. However challenges persist in online learning environments such as psychological risks that affect the students who have less experience (Braunsberger et al. 2016) and higher dropout rates than traditional classrooms, as high as 80% (Carr 2000). Furthermore online learning has a more student-centric environment compared to a traditional classroom

E. Ras and A. E. Guerrero Roldán (Eds.): TEA 2017, CCIS 829, pp. 150–162, 2018.
https://doi.org/10.1007/978-3-319-97807-9_12

environment (Smith and Hardaker 2000; Ni 2013), which could lead the students to success or to failure depending on the level of support given particularly in challenging areas such as Science, Technology, Engineering and Mathematics (STEM).

In a discussion about learning, assessment has an equal importance as it has been defined as the measurement of the learner's achievement and progress in the learning process (Keeves 1994; Hettiarachchi et al. 2016) and particularly continuous assessment as the assessment intended to enhance teaching and learning (Cowie and Bell 1999). Studies have identified lower grades in online learning compared to traditional face-to-face courses (Cavanaugh and Jacquemin 2015), therefore assessment should be further investigated and strengthened to resolve these disparities.

Student engagement also has a critical value in learning since it is a known contributor and predictor of student success (Carini et al. 2006; Shernoff and Schmidt 2008; Ladd and Dinella 2009). Student engagement data has the potential to provide a highly detailed index of the students' learning process and timely data in particular could be used to diagnostically fine-tune learning (Coates 2005). Student engagement is often considered as an aggregate of three dimensions of behavioural, cognitive and emotional engagements (Connell and Wellborn 1991; Skinner et al. 2009) and considered to be dynamically interrelated within an individual and cannot be separated from the environment in which it occurs (Fredricks and McColskey 2012). Taking these factors together into consideration, it becomes clear that microlevel student engagement has the potential to diagnose student learning and to act as a detailed map of what the students are actually doing and as a by-product measuring microlevel student engagement also becomes a process of engaging students. This is especially important at a time when it is claimed that students perceive school education as boring or as performing as little as possible to receive passable grades (Burkett 2002; Pope 2002; Fredricks et al. 2004).

Considering the challenges that online learning environments and conventional student engagement measurement have imposed, a microlevel student engagement (MSE) measurement can act as an underlying system to monitor and assist students in online learning environments (Balasooriya et al. 2017) as well as become an integral part of the assessment process of learning in general. This paper is aimed at proposing how a MSE measurement can become an alternative form of continuous assessment, as well as an accessory to the ongoing continuous assessment processes by introducing assessment of engagement. This can be an enabler for reflection on students' own engagement and thereby receive richer data that can describe student learning in a detailed subjective angle, which is also an important component of learner data (Appleton et al. 2006), but with the possibility of placing them in the already captured objective data. Section 2 of this paper presents a literature overview on student assessment methods used in online higher education and Sect. 3 presents our proposal for assessment of engagement as a form of continuous assessment. Section 4 presents a pilot study that we have carried out in order to explore potential MSE data and Sect. 5 discusses the implications of our approach on real-life educational contexts and future improvements that we hope to achieve.

2 Assessment and Engagement in Online Education

E-assessment in particular has become a topic of interest in online learning, as it automates some aspects of feedback where possible and can increase the frequency of assessment and feedback resulting in improved student motivation (Gibbs and Simpson 2004; Hettiarachchi et al. 2016). Research suggests that the most valid form of assessment comes from breaking down the assessment into components such as the knowledge content, problem solving skills, communication skills and assess the outcomes separately rather than from a single measure (Fairweather 2008). Therefore continuous assessment should ideally break down into a series of assessment components measured throughout the study period. Summative assessment on the other hand is generally administered as an examination at the end of the study period which assesses the overall knowledge and skill acquisition and to provide a certification (Crisp 2011).

Formal continuous assessment which is offered at particular points throughout the semester is a more discrete process. However informal methods of continuous assessment can shed more light on the ongoing learning of students. Skill assessment is more formative than knowledge assessment, since skills generally acquired through continued practice. In subject areas such as STEM, practice is a larger component which leads to higher engagements than a typical knowledge acquisition in a passive manner. Active learning, which particularly appeals to STEM characteristics such as group problem solving, in-class task completion, use of personal response systems for feedback, has shown an increase in student performance and final grades in contrast to traditional lecture-based learning (Freeman et al. 2014). Active learning also would be particularly useful and easy to implement in online learning environments where technology enhanced tools and resources are readily available. With the same tools it would also present an opportunity to capture the activeness of students based on engagement data.

Student Engagement has been defined as an aggregate of three dimensions of behavioural, cognitive and emotional (Connell and Wellborn 1991). The behavioural dimension relates to observable actions of students from classroom attendance to extracurricular activities, whereas cognitive engagement refers to invested effort to understand concepts and apply them and finally the emotional engagement being the feelings towards the learning and the environment. Research on student engagement has built on these dimensions in order to develop instruments of measurement to conceptual models.

2.1 Assessment of Engagement

Reflection is a well-established aspect of learning, known to enhance learning (Ash and Clayton 2004), that allows understanding gained through experience enabling better choices in the future (Rogers 2001) and requires a connection between the course material to the act of reflecting (Welch 1999). Nicols and Macfarlane-Dick (2006), state that students already monitor and assess their own engagement and generate internal feedback, and that higher education should utilize and build on this ability. Therefore it can be seen that a continuous reflection can enhance the learning process and it can be done ideally in context timely with a connection to the learning resources. Timeliness is especially important in the case of reflection since retrospective judgments differ strongly and systematically from real-time experiences (Goetz et al. 2013).

By using the four basic types of assessment, (1) Diagnostic (2) Integrative (3) Formative (4) Summative (Crisp 2011), we then move towards a conceptual model where a microlevel assessment of student engagement can become a form of continuous assessment and can be embedded within the other assessment types as illustrated in Fig. 1 and also used within the other types.

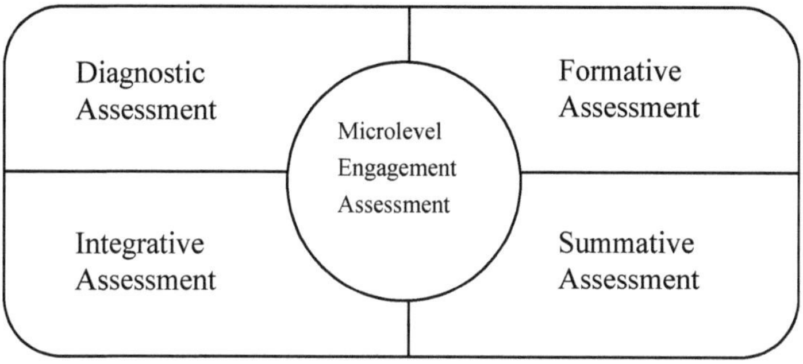

Fig. 1. Embedding microlevel assessment of engagement within assessment

The proposed approach is to focus more towards an ongoing assessment of student engagement, in order to learn more of student engagement in all three dimensions. We have explored the potential of MSE as an extended branch of Learning Analytics (LA) called Engagement Analytics (Balasooriya et al. 2017) or specifically *MSE Analytics*. However from a point of view of assessment, we have yet to establish a clear correlation of the goals of MSE measurement with that of assessment. Based on the importance of self-reflection, the task here is to make the student reflect their own engagement immediately afterwards an activity in order to have a clear indication whether the engagement was successful or not. At this granularity level, the data is timely and useful for both the student and the teacher to make a decision about the student's trajectory. As an example, a student watching an instructional video is a visible act of engagement, usually captured at the system level by establishing whether the student has played the video or not. The more intangible dimensions of engagement, i.e. cognitive and emotional are not captured in traditional modes of LA. In our model of MSE data capture we also focus on self-reported data about cognition and emotions (Balasooriya et al. 2017) which visualizes that specific act of engagement both timely and in a more comprehensive way. While in our initial design of the instrument, we intended the data capture process as separate and optional, we observed severe limitations in feedback from the students. In order to answer this drawback of our approach, we integrate it with the assessment component of course subjects.

As mentioned in Sect. 2, continuous assessment is a tool intended to enhance teaching and learning. The measurement of MSE as a continuous assessment is intended to integrate the reflection aspect to the learning process when it happens rather than in retrospect. In this format, we consider the student engagement in a virtual learning environment (VLE) as an ongoing/continuous assessment and therefore measure it and use its assessment for final student grades. A VLE hosts a variety of learning resources, that includes multimedia learning materials, tools, forums, practice tasks, assignments etc. In order to measure the engagement with these different learning resources, we have chosen to define the cognitive and emotional aspect of each engagement, whereas behaviour is reflected through the student actions in the VLE. We define engagement questions for each resource based on an instrument we have created that splits the traditional engagement survey model into a series of micro-surveys placed at microlevel learning resources. Single item or such shorter measures have been known to provide empirically valid data particularly in academic affective (emotional) and academic motivations research (Gogol et al. 2014). Cognitive data refers to whether learning resources are comprehensible, easy to complete; relevant to the current activity, whether the instructions or resources are helpful or the number of resources adequate etc. Emotional data is based on what the student feels during engaging with a particular learning resource, whether the learning resources are interesting, the instructor's involvement satisfactory, the lesson is valuable to the overall goals etc. By identifying the cognitive and emotional data counterparts to each resource we define a data template for each resource, making sure the behavioural data is also captured at a system-level.

As examples, Figs. 2 and 3 present two such micro-survey templates created for two types of learning resources.

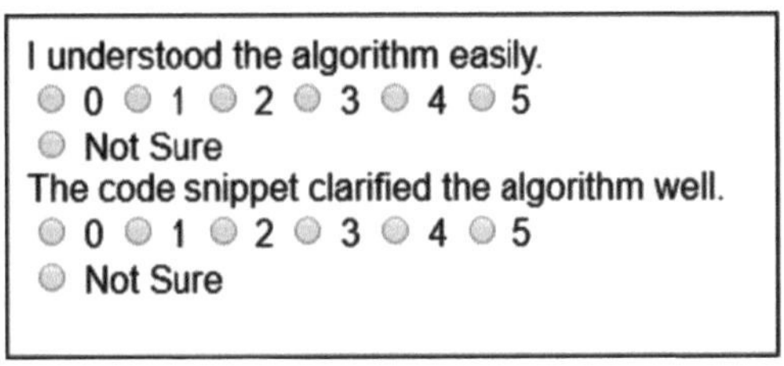
I understood the algorithm easily.
0 1 2 3 4 5
Not Sure
The code snippet clarified the algorithm well.
0 1 2 3 4 5
Not Sure

Fig. 2. A micro-survey template for an algorithm resource

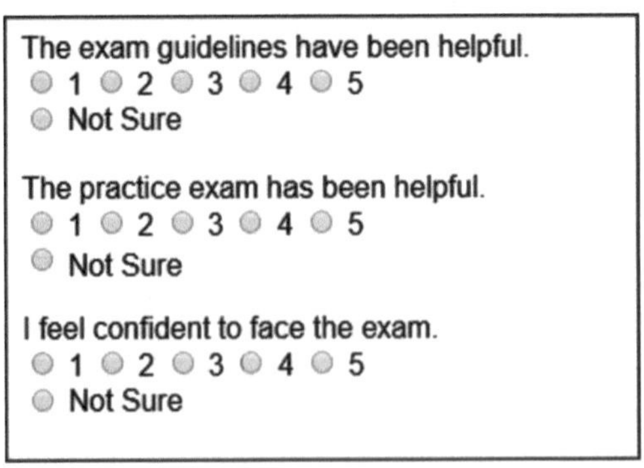
The exam guidelines have been helpful.
1 2 3 4 5
Not Sure

The practice exam has been helpful.
1 2 3 4 5
Not Sure

I feel confident to face the exam.
1 2 3 4 5
Not Sure

Fig. 3. A micro-survey template at the end of the course prior to the examination

Our goal here is to represent student engagement in its theoretical form alongside cognitive and emotional aspects of engagement which are especially critical since there is an overemphasis on behavioural engagement in practice (Appleton et al. 2006). A 1–5 Likert scale is used in these micro-surveys that contain at most 3 items, and contains a mixed variety of cognitive and emotional engagement based questions. These micro-surveys are then prompted at various locations of the learning resources which are ideally answered at the end of the activity. The data captured through this process is self-reported, meaning that the students' subjective perception is captured as a part of their engagement, which is as important as capturing their physical behaviour within the VLE (Appleton et al. 2006).

In addition, micro-surveys were also designed for each assignment, to incorporate all engagement dimensions, and were specifically aimed at the assignment task, such as the student's perception of how easy it was to complete, how much the learning materials helped, how hard the student worked on it, how happy he/she is about the performance in the assignment and the amount of time it took to complete.

3 Data from an Empirical Study

Our study is based at the Open University in Barcelona Universitat Oberta de Catalunya (UOC), Spain where all student learning and assessment is done online and a large body of students exist. Using an action research methodology (Susman and Evered 1978), we tested our design in an actual learning environment and iteratively improve the design based on the results. The UOC currently utilizes a data-mart system in which all the system-level data (behavioural) is recorded and archived. In a pilot study conducted at UOC to test our design on MSE data to develop Engagement Analytics (Balasooriya et al. 2017) we collected student data from Fundamentals of Programming, a mandatory 6 ECTS credit course offered to both the Telecommunication Engineering and Computing Engineering degrees. This was an optional task to the students and there was no reward system in place for students who left engagement data as feedback. From a total of around 150 students we received data from around 50 students during the semester. Also this data analysis was done after a user anonymization process conducted by the e-Learn Centre at UOC therefore no special permissions were required from the students regarding the data collection. In the second iteration of the study, teachers from several courses offered to adopt our approach of assessment of engagement, and students who submitted assignment related micro-surveys were offered points. We observed higher submission rates of surveys with this approach and extracted richer information which were not possible before.

The assignment micro-surveys enabled us a look at microlevel changes between different types of assignments, in our case study, CATs (Continuous Assessment Tasks) as well as practicals (projects which are larger in scope). Multiple CATs and practicals are given in a single semester in a given subject. Figure 4 illustrates a comparison between these assessment tasks during the semester based on the answers submitted by the students.

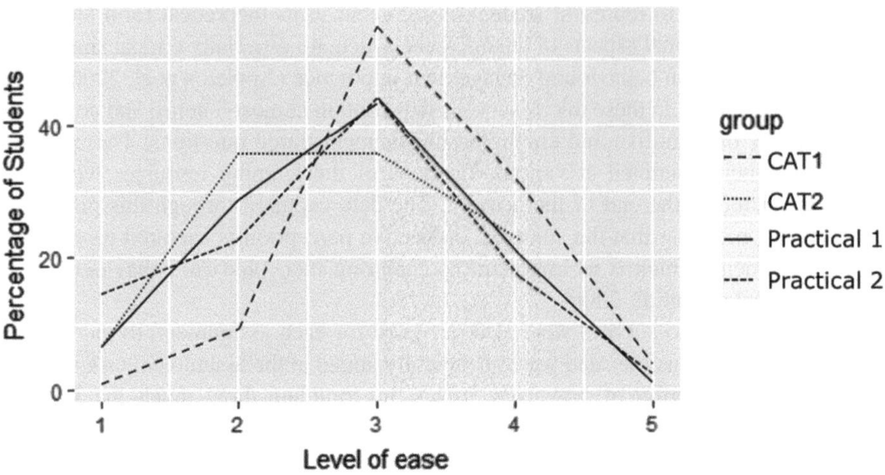

Fig. 4. Comparison of the student reported level of ease of the assessment task

The data shows the student answers more biased towards '*not easy*' after the first CAT. To explore each of the lines above, by combining the other factors such as invested time for the task and the grade received we can further shed light on the engagement and success as shown in Fig. 5.

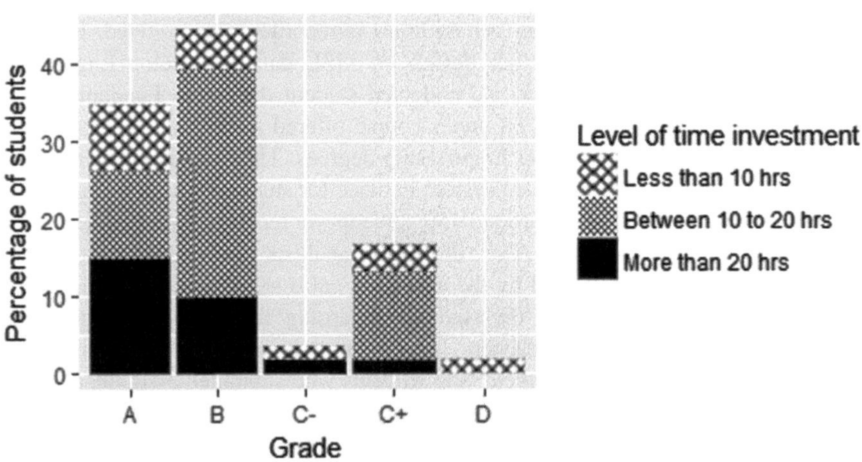

Fig. 5. Comparison of the time investment to the assessment task and the grade received

To explore the CAT 2 line in Fig. 4, which shows a notable deviation from the level of ease reported, we can compare it with Fig. 5, which illustrates the percentages of students who invested an amount of time as indicated, and the grades they received. The results show the highest percentages of students who worked on it for more than 20 h were able to receive the best grades.

Furthermore, we can also visualize the student happiness on their own performance before they receive grades, simply by recording their subjective opinion. This data shows an interesting pattern as illustrated in Fig. 6.

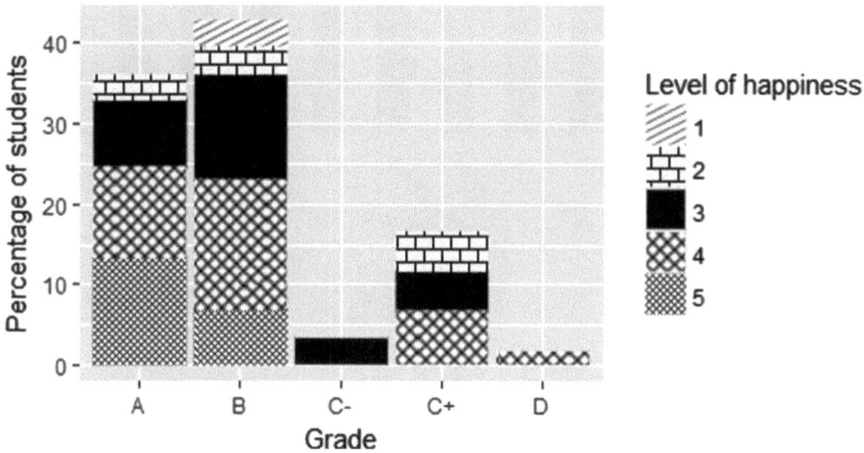

Fig. 6. Average student interest levels in lessons

Students who only reported '*very happy*' levels have later received the top grades. While statistical correlations are further required to demonstrate the validity of these comparisons, we believe as initial results they are promising.

Apart from assignment based surveys, the base approach was integrating the microlevel data capture module in the online learning environments. In the wiki platform of one of the courses which holds the learning resources, one aspect we measured were the interest levels in the lessons as part of their emotional engagement. Figure 7 illustrates the average values for the self-reported student interest levels.

It can be seen that the results show an ongoing and varying levels of interest which can be useful for the students as a scale of which lessons to pay more attention to, and for the teachers to re-think the teaching approach for them to be more interesting. While our initial pilot study was aimed towards the implementation of Engagement Analytics, it has informed us of its validity as a data collection design for using it as a continuous assessment plan based on engagement and reflection.

Furthermore we could derive average levels of the cognitive ease of using different resource components in the learning environments through the microlevel data capture approach. Figure 8 illustrates the student feedback answered in a scale from 1 to 5, 1 being very hard to understand and 5 being very easy to understand. The results show algorithms, examples and videos being better enablers of understanding programming concepts (easy to understand), and that students have difficulty understanding tables and code snippets.

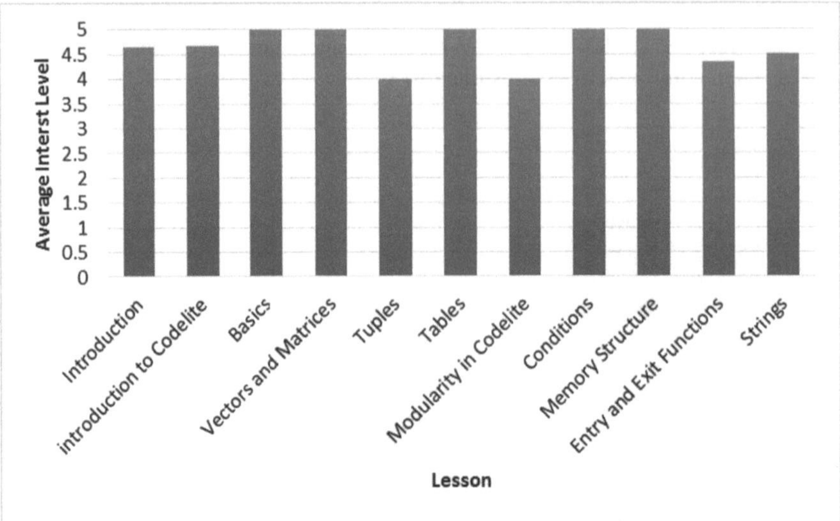

Fig. 7. Average student interest levels in lessons

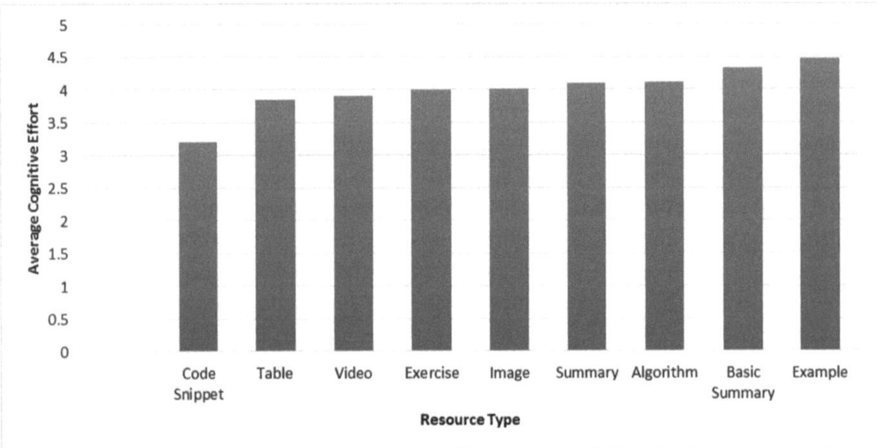

Fig. 8. Average cognitive engagement effort by resource type

4 Discussion, Limitations and Future Work

One of the requirements of using MSE measurement in continuous assessment is that it becomes a form of assessment of engagement of a student. Therefore it is necessary to have clear guidelines by the teachers about the assessment of engagement. In formal assessment, it should be part of the official grading system. These guidelines should also be made clear to the students. As an informal assessment it can still be invaluable to understand how students engage with the activities. In both of these variations, it can be seen that engagement is a worthy aspect of assessment.

The strength of our approach is based on its ability to invoke student engagement as it tries to measure the engagement itself. As illustrated in Figs. 1 and 2, the time the student takes to answer meta-questions about their own engagement is a time taken to reflect on their engagement. Their ability to confidently answer questions about engagement is also reflected in their confidence in their accomplishment of the learning task. This idea can be clearly seen in Fig. 6, with the students' happiness levels about their own performances later relate to top grades.

A limitation of our approach comes from the intrusiveness of self-report instrument. While the well-known student engagement surveys such as NSSE, MSLQ reply on the self-reported data from students, they are administered only once at the end of a semester or an academic year. Adapting a self-report instrument throughout the semester even with a minimal number of items present challenges in order to not intrude on the actual learning of students. There are strong reasons why self-report measures cannot be replaced, particularly when it comes to internal dimensions of engagement such as cognitive and emotional. What a person thinks or feels cannot be confirmed only by the externally manifested behaviours and artefacts (Shum and Crick 2012) and data collected otherwise becomes highly inferential (Appleton et al. 2006). In addition, in order to minimize the intrusiveness of the instrument and to keep it relevant, we have also had to limit the inclusion emotional engagement based questions in certain occasions.

The motivation behind this paper is based on the successful implementation of a MSE data collection design for Engagement Analytics in our previous study (Balasooriya et al. 2017). However as an assessment component, the applicability of measuring student engagement is very promising based on our results. With our micro-surveys embedded in the learning environments, and the micro-surveys sent out after each continuous assessment tasks, the MSE data obtained could visualize a zoomed-in view of student engagement, which would be a richer representation of a continuous assessment in an informal sense, rather than mere grades acquired through continuous assessment tests. Therefore the proposed approach would be beneficial for the students to reflect on their learning and make that engagement part of their self-assessment and learning management as well as for the teachers to gain a better understanding of the students' learning and engagement in the classroom while providing them an incentive to engage more.

5 Conclusions

The central theme of this research has been the combination of the concepts of continuous assessment and student engagement in the form of: how can we assess engagement, preferably at a microlevel where the data is relevant and timely. The need for richer data on student engagement has stemmed from the transition from face-to-face classroom model to a virtual one where much of the student engagement is obscure. In challenging subject areas, especially such as STEM where high number of dropout and low grades persist, it has become critical to ensure the students engage with their learning. In order to achieve this, we have proposed to bridge our design a microlevel student engagement measurement approach with continuous assessment. Assessment of engagement presents an opportunity to the teacher to engage the students more, and informs about the overall dimensions of engagement in the classroom, and works as a self-reflection task for the student as well. It includes the cognitive and emotional aspects of engagement in addition to the behavioural engagement usually captured system-logs. From a pilot study we have carried out in order to test this data capture design, we have successfully obtained self-reported data from students about their continuous engagement. In this paper we have tried to present our second iteration of how we incorporated this data to be part of the continuous assessment process. While further validations are necessary, even at a first glance our data suggest that microlevel engagement data has the potential to inform about enhanced learning and higher academic achievement, and therefore worthy of being included in the assessment process.

Acknowledgments. This work has been funded by the project Open Data for All: an API-based infrastructure for exploiting online data sources given by the Spanish Ministerio de Economía, Industria y Competitividad (ref. TIN2016-75944-R) and a doctoral grant from the Universitat Oberta de Catalunya (UOC).

References

Allen, I.E., Seaman, J.: Grade Level: Tracking Online Education in the United States. Babson Survey Research Group and Quahog Research Group, LLC. (2015). http://www.onlinelearningsurvey.com/reports/gradelevel.pdf

Appleton, J.J., Christenson, S.L., Kim, D., Reschly, A.L.: Measuring cognitive and psychological engagement: validation of the student engagement instrument. J. Sch. Psychol. **44**(5), 427–445 (2006)

Ash, S.L., Clayton, P.H.: The articulated learning: an approach to guided reflection and assessment. Innov. High. Educ. **29**(2), 137–154 (2004)

Balasooriya, I., Mor, E., Rodríguez, M.E.: Extending learning analytics with microlevel student engagement data. In: Proceedings of EduLearn 2017 (2017)

Bonk, C.J., Kim, K.J.: The future of online teaching and learning in higher education: the survey says. EDUCAUSE Q. Mag. **29**(4), 22–30 (2006)

Braunsberger, K., McCuiston, V., Patterson, G., Watkins, A.: Perceived risks and psychological well-being in online education: implications for grade expectations and future enrollment. In: Groza, M., Ragland, C. (eds.) Marketing Challenges in a Turbulent Business Environment. Developments in Marketing Science: Proceedings of the Academy of Marketing Science, pp. 487–488. Springer, Cham (2016). https://doi.org/10.1007/978-3-319-19428-8_123

Burkett, E.: Another Planet: A Year in the Life of a Suburban High School. Harper Collins, New York (2002)

Carini, R.M., Kuh, G.D., Klein, S.P.: Student engagement and student learning: testing the linkages. Res. High. Educ. **47**(1), 1–32 (2006)

Carr, S.: As distance education comes of age, the challenge is keeping the students. In: Chronicle of Higher Education, Information Technology Section (2000). http://chronicle.com/free/v46/i23/23a00101.htm

Cavanaugh, J., Jacquemin, S.J.: A large sample comparison of grade based student learning outcomes in online vs. face-to-face courses. In: Online Learning, vol. 19, no. 2 (2015)
Coates, H.: The value of student engagement for higher education quality assurance. Qual. High. Educ. **11**(1), 25–36 (2005)
Connell, J., Wellborn, J.G.: Competence, autonomy, and relatedness: a motivational analysis of self-system process. In: Gunnar, M.R., Sroufe, L.A. (eds.) Self Process in Development: Minnesota Symposium on Child Psychology, vol. 2, pp. 167–216. Lawrence Erlbaum, Hillsdale (1991)
Cowie, B., Bell, B.: A model of formative assessment in science education. Assess. Educ.: Principles Policy Pract. **6**(1), 101–116 (1999)
Crisp, G.: Teacher's Handbook on e-Assessment. Transforming Assessment-An ALTC Fellowship Activity, vol. 18 (2011)
Fairweather, J.: Linking evidence and promising practices in science, technology, engineering, and mathematics (STEM) undergraduate education. Board of Science Education, National Research Council, The National Academies, Washington, DC. (2008)
Fredricks, J.A., Blumenfeld, P.C., Paris, A.H.: School engagement: potential of the concept, state of the evidence. Rev. Educ. Res. **74**(1), 59–109 (2004)
Freeman, S., Eddy, S.L., McDonough, M., Smith, M.K., Okoroafor, N., Jordt, H., Wenderoth, M. P.: Active learning increases student performance in science, engineering, and mathematics. Proc. Natl. Acad. Sci. **111**(23), 8410–8415 (2014)
Fredricks, J.A., McColskey, W.: The measurement of student engagement: a comparative analysis of various methods and student self-report instruments. In: Christenson, S., Reschly, A., Wylie, C. (eds.) Handbook of Research on Student Engagement, pp. 763–782. Springer, Boston (2012). https://doi.org/10.1007/978-1-4614-2018-7_37
Gibbs, G., Simpson, C.: Conditions under which assessment supports students' learning. Learn. Teach. High. Educ. **1**(1), 3–31 (2004)
Goetz, T., Bieg, M., Lüdtke, O., Pekrun, R., Hall, N.C.: Do girls really experience more anxiety in mathematics? Psychol. Sci. **24**(10), 2079–2087 (2013)
Gogol, K., et al.: "My questionnaire is too long!" the assessments of motivational-affective constructs with three-item and single-item measures. Contemp. Educ. Psychol. **39**(3), 188–205 (2014)
Hettiarachchi, E., Balasooriya, I., Mor, E., Huertas, M.A.: E-assessment for skill acquisition in online engineering education: challenges and opportunities. In: Caballé, S., Clarisó, R. (eds.) Formative Assessment, Learning Data Analytics and Gamification in ICT Education, pp. 49–64 (2016)
Keeves, J.P.: Methods of assessment in schools. In: International Encyclopedia of Education, pp. 362–370 (1994)
Ladd, G.W., Dinella, L.M.: Continuity and change in early school engagement: predictive of children's achievement trajectories from first to eighth grade? J. Educ. Psychol. **101**(1), 190–206 (2009)
Ni, A.Y.: Comparing the effectiveness of classroom and online learning: teaching research methods. J. Public Affairs Educ. **19**(2), 199–215 (2013)
Nicol, D.J., Macfarlane-Dick, D.: Formative assessment and self-regulated learning: a model and seven principles of good feedback practice. Stud. High. Educ. **31**(2), 199–218 (2006)
Pope, D.: Doing school: how we are creating a generation of stressed-out, materialistic, and miseducated students. Yale University Press, New Haven (2002)
Rogers, R.: Reflection in higher education: a concept analysis. Innov. High. Educ. **26**, 37–57 (2001)
Shernoff, D.J., Schmidt, J.A.: Further evidence of an engagement–achievement paradox among US high school students. J. Youth Adolesc. **37**(5), 564–580 (2008)

Shum, S.B., Crick, R.D.: Learning dispositions and transferable competencies: pedagogy, modelling and learning analytics. In: Proceedings of the 2nd International Conference on Learning Analytics and Knowledge, pp. 92–101. ACM (2012)

Skinner, E.A., Kindermann, T.A., Connell, J.P., Wellborn, J.G.: Engagement and disaffection as organizational constructs in the dynamics of motivational development. In: Handbook of Motivation at School, pp. 223–245 (2009)

Smith, D., Hardaker, G.: e-Learning innovation through the implementation of an internet supported learning environment. Educ. Technol. Soc. **3**, 1–16 (2000)

Susman, G.I., Evered, R.D.: An assessment of the scientific merits of action research. Adm. Sci. Q. 582–603 (1978)

Welch, M.: The ABCs of reflection: a template for students and instructors to implement written reflection in service-learning. NSEE Q. **25**, 22–25 (1999)

Assessment of Relations Between Communications and Visual Focus in Dynamic Positioning Operations

Yushan Pan(✉), Guoyuan Li, Thiago Gabriel Monteiro, Hans Petter Hildre, and Steinar Nistad

Norwegian University of Science and Technology, 6025 Ålesund, Norway
Yushan.pan@ntnu.no

Abstract. Assessment of maritime training has been a growth in collaborations between nautical instructors and researchers in marine operations. Through a qualitative study and using eye tracking data, this paper presents a case study wherein the relations between communications and visual focus in dynamic positioning (DP) operations in maritime operations are examined. We investigated how communication and visual focus are related to DP operations in a team of marine operators. The results show that communications and visual focus do affect marine operations in the consistency, conciseness and maximum effect of communication skills through two rules—(1) the effectiveness of communications and visual information from eyes, (2) the goldfish memory skills for communications.

Keywords: Assessment · Maritime simulation · Communication
Human factor

1 Practical Background

Researchers have drawn attention on assessment of dynamic positioning operation since it is a key part of the subsea installation. Dynamic positioning (DP) operation, as defined in maritime technology, is a computer-controlled operation (see Fig. 1) to maintain a vessel's position and heading by using its propellers and thrusters [1]. Although automation engineers believe that DP operation could be done automatically [2], an operation of DP systems requires cooperation among maritime operators [3]. Thus, it is worthy to assess how marine operators work with DP systems. In this manner, we focus on work practices of marine operators in the DP workplace rather than the technical aspects of DP systems. Thus, assessment of DP systems becomes an investigation process of how maritime operators work with DP systems and how they communicate with each other regarding cooperation and safety issues during the DP operation. This paper mainly addresses on this topic.

There are a few studies addressing the evaluation of maritime training and using the DP systems as a technical platform. The contributions of these studies are twofold – (1) technical evaluation of vessels' automation abilities and (2) Assessment of work procedures of maritime training.

E. Ras and A. E. Guerrero Roldán (Eds.): TEA 2017, CCIS 829, pp. 163–175, 2018.
https://doi.org/10.1007/978-3-319-97807-9_13

Fig. 1. Dynamic positioning operational systems (white circle) and communication systems (red circle) in Ocean Training & Competence AS (OTC) simulator (Color figure online)

For example, researchers assess the frequency of position loss, establish vessel speed, and distance profile involved in position loss. Based on these assessments, the completion of DP operation is concluded based on the estimating probability of successful intervention in the case of position loss [4]. The study mainly focus on the assessment of the abilities of automated maritime types of machinery. The cooperation with maritime operators and their work practices in the DP workplace are dismissed.

Other examples address the human aspects of assessment of DP systems. There is a study focusing on how DP operators should be trained and be able to perform when DP systems have to be operated manually. In such case, scholar uses eye tracker as an assistive tool for the training procedure on DP operation [5]. Josson and Holmström [6] conduct the qualitative research to investigate how accommodation specific DP operation could be developed. The purpose is to minimize risk and contribute to safer marine operations via analysis of communication, human factors, and other sensors.

1.1 Research Question

As mentioned above, these twofold contributions have their merit from a technical aspect and human factor aspect on assessment of DP operation. It is important to note that DP operation may have many faces when addressing on a deeper investigation. For example, the cooperation with maritime operators is a core element in DP operation. As discussed by researchers in workplaces studies, computer technology may not be able to support cooperative work of maritime operators, in general, cooperative work [7–9]. In addition, training on work procedures may be insufficient to enable maritime operators because it may not support duplication of safe work practice in a "lab-based" environment within a fixed training scenario [10]. All these factors result that it is difficult to assess marine operations with a larger focus overall workplace and work practices of all maritime operations. Thus, *the research question of this paper is about how to use qualitative research and eye tracking data to interpret cooperative work in a team of marine operators when operating DP systems*. We investigate cooperative work in a team within the DP workplace, focusing on work practices of maritime operators. Thus, a mixed research method is used in this research. With qualitative research, we did observation and interview. The purpose is to make sense of the work practices of maritime operators regarding their behaviors, such as visual focus and communication in their work practices. With quantitative research, we used eye tracker to identify how maritime operators behave during their DP operations. The aim is to make sense of the relations between their communications and visual focus in the DP operation.

The paper is structured as follows: Sect. 2 presents existing studies in communications and eye tracking in the maritime domain. Section 3 presents the methods that we use to collect data and our empirical setting and experiment design. Findings and discussion are presented in Sect. 4. Section 5 concludes the paper.

2 Literature Review

2.1 Communication in and Outside of Maritime Domain

Communication training refers to various types of training to develop necessary skills for communication in different domains. Effective communication is vital for the success in various situations, such as business and transportation fields in airline cockpit [11–15], maritime navigation [16–18], and emergency services [19, 20]. The concentrated points of communications are different from domains such as listening, negotiation, and report writing skills in communication, speaking and interacting skills in network working environment. For example, researchers use a micro-analytical approach to identify the work practices that speakers display in pre-scripted user-device interaction, such as airline operation center and air traffic control [21]. Whalen and Zimmerman argue that the organization of citizen calls to emergency services reveals how the sequential machinery of conversation is adapted by speaker-hearers to organize, coordinate and exhibit to one another their knowledge and purposes on particular occasions [22]. The study proposes that the following organization of communication is a fundamental resource for social activities directed to matters outside of, but addressable through talk, and for achieving regular, recurrent patterns of action in the face of varying details and circumstances [19]. They point out the importance of communication that should involve what events are occurring, and who is reporting them, and what their importance is, given who it is that is calling [23]. Tracy and Tracy [20] critique assumptions made in past emotion labor and organizational burnout studies through the case of 911 call-takers. Through examining the different ways of human feelings, the study presents that in 911 emergency situation, a call-taker can be verbally helpful and sympathetic to a caller while displaying irritation, amusement or disgust to fellow call-takers through nonverbal expressions such as tone of the voice and gestures.

In the maritime domain, studies on communication are few. Those studies can be divided into mainly two categories – (1) social studies on maritime language use and (2) communication in interactive work between human operators and digital devices. For example, Pritchard and colleagues [16, 17] investigate the status of Maritime English regarding the minimum International Maritime Organization's requirements (IMO STCW Convention 1978/1995). They suggest that Maritime English Syllabus should be further developed in its context with collaboration from an interdisciplinary environment such as general & theoretical linguistics, cognitive science, information science and teaching theory. Such efforts could offer a standard requirement of Maritime English from the development of digital computer systems to the training of seafarers. Bailey et al. [18] examine how 'bridge teams' utilize a range of practical communication approaches and devices in carrying out the days work within a context where temporal and spatial considerations are paramount. The studies explore empirical examples of interaction and identify the way that an interactional accomplishment is a confirmatory form of talk that is utilized to avoid confusion and maritime disaster. They suggest that bridge teamwork is accomplished, organized, and sustained by inquiry and modify training practice of articulation work. In a recent study, the researchers used the method of conversation analysis to check whether marine operators have done "read back" during their communications [24]. In a readback loop in a communication process, everyone repeat themselves while receiving and sending messages. All those studies mainly address on how social orders of work practice are conducted. Another study on communication investigated the interactive relations between human operators and researchers assert that design of communication channels should focus on those interactional work [25]. Also, those studies also address on how such orders of work practices can shed light on a technology use and design.

It is nothing new in maritime domain to focus on communications studies; however, it seems new that evaluation of maritime communications due to safety concerns in cooperative work situations. As abovementioned, studies in social orders of work practice do not point out a direction where should we focus on maritime training. Even though a study suggests, the vital point is the interactive relations in communications with a focus on 'what-you-see-is-what-I-see' between cooperative human operators; no study focuses on an assessment of how communications effectively relate to other perceived sight information to help human operators to accomplish their works in a safety-critical environment. Hence, below it is important to introduce how visual focus are used for training purposes.

2.2 Eye Tracker Use in and Outside the Maritime Domain

Visual information is an essential factor in human interactive applications. It has been observed for years that detecting visual focus is beneficial to understand human behavior [26]. In particular, two primary eye movements—eye fixation and saccades, provide information of location and shift of visual attention. In addition, tracking gaze points, improvements in eye-tracking technology, such as deploying high-speed cameras together with versatile eye tracking solutions by using either wearable glasses or desktop mounted system enable measurement of statistical eye metrics, e.g., defining regions in the stimulus that are of interest, applying heat maps to show the general distribution of fixations, and finding out the scan pattern for individuals. Differences of the metrics have been proposed as markers of ability for identifying varying skill levels [27].

As a method of assessment, eye tracking has been applied as a training tool in various fields, ranging from surgery [28] and aviation [29] to sports [30]. A concept known as "quiet eye" defines how people perform precise motor-like skill like driving a car [31]. It is a way to examine visuomotor planning and control regarding coordination and reflex for human physical and cognitive performance. Eye trackers, in this case, are considered a useful intervention to enhance attentional control. Comparative studies between experienced and novice participants such as the difference of search pattern can provide valuable information for teaching [32]. Also, analysis of eye-tracking data is a valid mechanism in the debriefing process, which not only improves training by objective evaluative feedback of eye tracking but also makes the most effective use of time [33].

Although eye tracking as a training tool in maritime domain is applicable, maritime eye tracking is just used as a measuring means rather than investigation tool. That means the data extracted from eye movement does not point out how visual information is used by operators with other means such as communications, regarding different work situation and context. Thus, we position our study in this field to fulfill such concerns with aims to unpack opportunities which might be useful to effectively use visual focus with communication in an assessment of marine operations.

3 Theoretical Background and Methods

3.1 Qualitative and Quantitative Ethnography

Ethnomethodology is originally a perspective within sociology which focuses on the way people make sense of their everyday world. People are seen as rational actors, but employ practical reasoning rather than formal logic to make sense of and function in society. Ethnomethodology leads to the findings of conversation analysis, which has found its place as an accepted discipline. However, our account of the ethnomethodologically alternative to mainstream social science has thus far been piecemeal, with parts being surfaced for particular purposes. We, as engineers, are not social scientists and we may not find it an important matter to follow the twists and turns of social science thinking about how to study social world. Instead, we seek how engineers could buy into the importance of understanding the social for assessment purposes, and ethnomethodology itself may support such understanding on how to utilize knowledge from social sciences to serve the engineering studies.

Ethnomethodology's core concerns are to do with how society is understood and with specifying what it considers to be erroneous formulations of what it is and how it can be studied [34].

Such efforts have proved to be of value to design research, enabling designers, evaluators, and other experts to appreciate the things that people actually do in some setting or domain and how they do them in practice, which in turn enables designers, evaluators, and other experts' to build knowledge around these understanding [35]. In line with this, we conducted video and audio recording with the purpose to understand how human operators cooperate to finish their tasks in safety-critical situations. We mainly focus on the conversations during the designed scenario of DP operations.

3.2 Eye Tracking and Questionnaires

Taking advantages of the eye tracking device, the gaze data in time series was collected. The data includes the timestamp, the gaze position and direction, the eye movement type and so on. By selecting interested recording, the heat map and the scan path were obtained. If needed, AOI can be customized, and the corresponding hits statistics can then be calculated. Besides, the data from the onboard sensors such as the gyroscope and the accelerometer was collected and synchronized by default.

Also, pre- and post- questionnaires were developed. The pre-questionnaire mainly focuses on the background information, such as the participants use DP simulators and report their experiences on maritime training. Moreover, we are particularly interested in their experience on maritime communication training. In the post-questionnaire, a Likert-scale [36] is used. The questions mainly address on their perceptions of the relations between communications and visual focus, also; we asked a question regarding work practices in a team.

3.3 Empirical Setting and Experiment Design

To assess the role of both communication and vision during DP operations, we designed the following experiment to be conducted in a maritime simulator located at the Norwegian University of Science and Technology (NTNU) - campus Ålesund. The experiment consists on simulating the operation of transferring cargo from the deck of a platform supply vessel (PSV) A, to the deck of another PSV B. The cargo transfer will be performed using an oil rig crane, which should lift the cargo container from the deck of PSV A and land it safely on the deck of the PSV B. Due to a short weather window and tight schedules, the vessels need to move closer together under the rig crane so the operation can be finalized as soon as possible.

To position the vessels and keep them at the correct location, the PSVs pilots make use of DP systems while communicating with the other PSV pilot and with the crane operator to be aware of the current state of each actor involved in the operation and let other actors be aware of his/her intended actions.

Aiming to make the communication process even more relevant, when the two PSVs are close to their final position, a system failure in the propulsion system of one vessel will be triggered, disabling that vessel's DP system. This mechanical failure together with the wave and current directions defined in the simulated scenario will require a fast response from the PSVs pilots to avoid an imminent collision.

The empirical setting is located in the Ocean Training & Competence AS (OTC) facilities at NTNU in Ålesund. It consists of a maritime simulator, which is a system capable of realistically simulating maritime equipment, ships, oil rigs and maritime environment for teaching, training, research and other purposes.

Figure 1 shows a reproduction of a typical ship bridge from a PSV, located on the OTC facilities. This installation will be used in our experiment to accommodate the operators controlling one of the PSVs. The red circle in Fig. 1 indicates the DP system, which will be used by an operator for the position keeping operation. The green circle highlights the communication system, which will be used by a second operator in the bridge to communicate with the crane operator and with the other vessel, which can be seen on the simulator screen, circled in blue. This other vessel is operated by another pair of operators in another room like this one.

In Fig. 2, the control console of the OTC maritime simulator is shown. In the picture, the simulator staff members can be seen coordinating the simulation. From this main console, it is possible to define all the parameters for the desired operation, including number and types of vessels and oil rigs, weather condition, waves and current direction and intensity and so on. For the current experiment, no crane simulator was used, since the goal was to evaluate the communication and vision regarding the use of DP system on the vessels. Instead, the OTC staff used the main control console to mimic the presence of a real crane operator, providing communication between crane and vessels. It was from this control console that the propulsion system failure was triggered during the experiment.

Fig. 2. OTC simulator main control console.

3.4 Experiment Procedure

The designed experiment was performed six times. In each case the experiment was run, the environmental conditions were defined as calm, with small wave heights, but with enough current speed to make the vessels drift in case the DP systems are not activated.

During each one of the scenarios, the operators from one of the vessels were tracked. To track the communication and vision of the operators, two different approaches were used. For tracking the communication, audio and video recording equipment were used. For tracking the vision of the DP system operator, a Tobii® eyes tracker was used.

At the beginning of each scenario, the PSVs were positioned around 50 to 70 m away from the desired position, and the experiment starts with the crane operator requiring the PSVs operators to position the vessels closer to the required location, under the oil rig crane. The approximation process is gradual and should be conducted in several small steps to avoid a collision. When the vessels are close to the final position, a propulsion system failure is triggered in one of the vessels, requiring an emergency maneuver from both PSVs.

4 Finding and Discussion

4.1 Communication and Visual Focus

Like most studies in communications [16, 24, 37, 38], we also found 'readback' is a rule of thumb for the DP operations, especially for teamwork tasks. Differently from these previous studies; our focus was not about the social concerns regarding communications. Moreover, we consider how communications are conducted in a particular working context where maritime technologies are present (e.g., maritime simulators).

For example, in the airline cockpit studies, Nevile argues that the institutional talk and turn talk are important factors for evaluating of communications in safety-critical and high-pressure working environment, such as airplanes [11]. In most cases, pilots know who will say what to whom, and when, because they are legally required to use scripted procedural wording [13]. By following such scripted procedural wordings, checklists should be completed [15]. However, we found this is a difference between airplane operation and DP operation on the vessel. For maritime operations, such as DP operation, there is no scripted procedural wording. Also, there is no institutional talk as the airline industry. However, there is turn talk in the maritime communications, such as readback [24]. From our experiment, readback is not always correctly used by all maritime operators. For example, we found that even though five groups of our participants are trained in the maritime simulators regarding operations, communications and emergency situation handling were not good as the maritime trainers expected. Only one group followed their way to make the communication effective by repeating their names and the questions/requests they heard once or twice before replying. For example,

[00:16:01] A: This is Sola. I will move 20 m, 2–0 m further.
[00:16:21] B: Sola, this is Haram. Yes, you move 20 m. I will hold my position.

According to our post questionnaire, all participants (100%) replied that 'readback' is important. Also, they self-reported that all numbers should be clarified in answering questions and making statements. Moreover, 'readback' should be standardized as they choose the answer: a formatted script for maritime operations is necessary.

4.2 Goldfish Memory Myth in Communication Analysis

Regarding their statement about standardized scripts in maritime communication, we examined all voice recording. Many fishes – such as minnows, sticklebacks, and guppies – are capable of the same intellectual feats as many mammals [39]. However, when the environmental, sounds and behavioral habits are regularized. If not, mistakes will raise up. For example, we found that the communication can be accurate when the duration of communication is short, and language use is concise. However, when the language use is complex regarding working context, some information could be misinterpreted. Below is a good example from our transcribed materials.

[00:24:33] A: Haram, This is Sola. I have [to move] 1–5 m closer to the platform.
[00:24:42] B: Moving 15 m closer to the platform.
[00:26:26] A: Haram. This is Sola. I will now move 10 m. 1–0 m

In this example, in roughly two minutes two marine operators could concisely express their idea. They repeat their ideas, such as numbers and names to make their communication effectively. However, this is the only group in our experiment which can express themselves even in our human-made situation. Most of the groups couldn't make their communication clear even during a simulated working context. For example, when one of the vessels lost power during the operation, we identify this communication:

[00:17:32] C: Haram. This is Crane. You are 3–0 m away from your final position.
[00:18:30] D: Crane, This is Haram. 2–0, 20 m to the final position? Sola, Sola. I will move 20 m.
[00:19:30] E: Haram, this is Sola. I will move 10 m.
[00:19:40] D: This is Haram. Will you move 10 m?
[00:19:42] D: Are you move[ing] 20 m?

It is interesting that even when the communication had roughly the same duration (2 min), not all participants could express themselves concisely and accurately. When we discussed with the maritime instructor regarding the communication training, the trainer stated that there are rules in communication training. However, there is a shortage of standardized format in detail for checking speaking language of maritime operators. However, a standardized format requests more efforts in the maritime domain. Maybe a detailed exploration of international telecommunication for maritime mobile and mobile-satellite is a platform [40].

4.3 The Relationships Between Communications and Visual Focus

Our participants also report that there are indirect relationships between communications and visual focus. For example, when asked whether they are using their visual focus to judge the distances between two vessels on DP displays, the participants replied in most times (higher than 75%) that look outside during DP operations. And when asked "do you look outside to monitor the distance between two vessels and the crane," participants replied that they only spend 50% of the time during the DP operation looking outside. However, they also reported that "it is important to have distance information on the DP systems (100%) and it is important to use such information in their communication (80% importance)". Well, DP systems do not function to measure distances. This is an interesting finding that may reveal current simulators request improvement regarding our assessment of DP operations.

However, although they report there are relationships between communications and visual focus, eye tracking data from one group might disagree with their statements. We chose the best performing group as a case and found out that looking outside is more important than information on DP systems (see Figs. 3 and 4). Two of the participants spent more time (heating maps, red color) looking outside and perform the experiments properly.

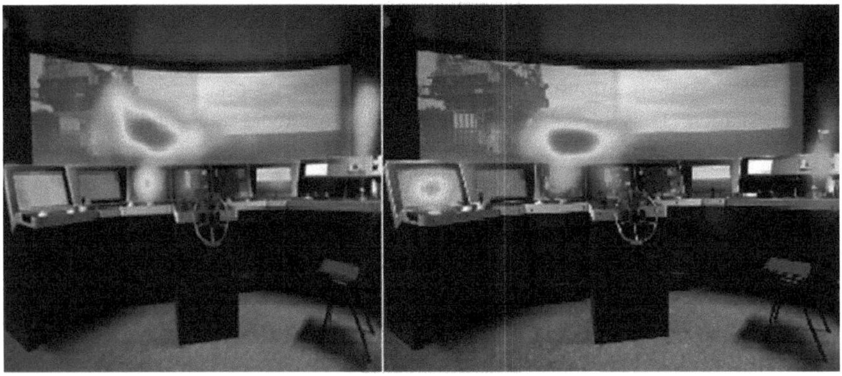

Fig. 3. A good example of DP operation. (Color figure online)

Fig. 4. Bad examples of DP operations (Color figure online)

The rest of the groups spent more time on DP systems. As advised by the maritime instructors, such behavior is insufficient. During the DP operation, the participants should spend more time to observe outside than the monitors inside the bridge. Through this experiment, we realized that the maritime operations training might need to teach trainees where to get useful information and how to present this information to who and in what way. This may contribute to the maritime training with more accuracy means in the maritime courses. For example, recorded heatmap could help to guide trainees to get useful information and to learn how to present it to the correct receivers.

5 Concluding Remarks

In this paper, we examined the relationship between communications and visual focus in the dynamic positioning operations in a team-based work. Through the study, we find that visual focus and communications together affect the quality of marine operations. However, due to lack of experience marine operators may be unable to properly combine their verbal and visual focus information for their work tasks. We find three important factors which affect the quality of marine operations. To increase the quality of maritime training, we assert that the communications and sight information should be used together. Also, the communications should be effectively and efficiently done within a short timescale. In doing so, a good training should educate marine operators where to grasp information on visual focus and how to express it properly.

Acknowledgement. We wish to thank all colleagues and students who made our study possible. In particular thank to maritime instructor Arnt Håkon Barmen for organizing and setting up the scenario and for sharing his knowledge of maritime operations. The project is funded by the Research Council of Norway, and the project number is 234007.

References

1. Wolden, G.: Dynamisk posisjonering for arktis: systemet skal muliggjøre kompliserte operasjoner i is og ekstremvær (2017). https://www.tu.no/artikler/forskning-systemet-skal-muliggjore-kompliserte-operasjoner-i-is-og-ekstremvaer/375918
2. Dynamic Positioning Committee: Guidelines on Testing of DP Systems (2015)
3. Pan, Y., Finken, S.: Visualising actor network for cooperative systems in marine technology. In: Kreps, D., Fletcher, G., Griffiths, M. (eds.) HCC 2016. IAICT, vol. 474, pp. 178–190. Springer, Cham (2016). https://doi.org/10.1007/978-3-319-44805-3_15
4. Chen, H., Nygärd, B.: Quantified Risk Analysis of DP Operations - Principles and Challenges (2016). http://www.onepetro.org/doi/10.2118/179452-MS
5. Zheng, S.: Impact of eye-trackers on maritime trainer-trainee experience (2014)
6. Josson, B., Christoffer, H.: A study of how accommodation vessel DP simulator training courses could be improved: an analysis of floatel international AB's DP-system training on critical elements during advanced marine operations (2015)
7. Schmidt, K.: The critical role of workplace studies in CSCW. In: Workplace Studies: Recovering Work Practice and Informing System Design, pp. 141–148. Cambridge University Press (2000)

8. Anderson, B.: Where the rubber hits the road: notes on the development problem in workplace studies. In: Workplace Studies: Recovering Work Practice and Informing System Design, pp. 215–229. Cambridge University Press (2000)
9. Baxter, G., Sommervile, I.: Socio-technical systems: from design methods to systems engineering. Interact. Comput. **23**, 4–17 (2011)
10. Rooksby, J.: Wild in the laboratory: a discussion of plans and situated actions. ACM Trans. Comput. Hum. Interact. **20**, 1–17 (2013)
11. Nevile, M.: Talking without overlap in the airline cockpit: precision timing at work. Text Talk **27**, 225–249 (2007)
12. Nevile, M.: Integrity in the airline cockpit: embodying claims about the progress for the conduct of an approach briefing. Res. Lang. Soc. Interact. **37**, 447–480 (2005)
13. Nevile, M.: Understanding who's who in the airplane cockpit: pilot's pronominal choices and cockpit roles. In: McHoul, A., Rapley, M. (eds.) How to Analyse Talk in Institutional Settings: A Case Book of Methods, pp. 57–71. Continuum, London (2001)
14. Nevile, M.: Making sequentiality salient: and-prefacing in the talk of airline pilots. Discouse Stud. **8**, 279–302 (2006)
15. Nevile, M.: Checklist complete. Or is it? Closing a task in the airline cockpit. Aust. Rev. Appl. Linguist. **28**, 60–76 (2005)
16. Pritchard, B., Kalogjera, D.: On some features of conversation in maritime VHF communication. In: Selected papers from the 7th IADA Conference, pp. 185–195 (1999)
17. Pritchard, B.: Maritime english syllabus for the modern seafarer: safety-related or comprehensive courses? MWU J. Marit. Aff. **2**, 149–166 (2003)
18. Bailey, N., Housley, W., Belcher, P.: Navigation, interaction and bridge team work. Sociol. Rev. **54**, 342–362 (2006)
19. Whalen, J., Zimmerman, D., Whalen, M.: When words fail: a single case analysis. Soc. Probl. **35**, 335–362 (1988)
20. Tracy, S., Tracy, K.: Emotion labour at 911: a case study and theoretical critique. J. Appl. Commun. **26**, 390–411 (1998)
21. Goodwin, G., Goodwin, M.H.: Seeing as a situated activity: formulating planes. In: Cognition and Communication at Work, pp. 61–95. Cambridge University Press (1996)
22. Whalen, M.R., Zimmerman, D.H.: Sequential and institutional contexts in calls for help. Soc. Psychol. Q. **50**, 172 (1987)
23. Whalen, M.R., Zimmerman, D.H.: Describing trouble: practical epistemology in citizen calls to the police. Lang. Soc. **19**, 465–492 (1990)
24. Froholdt, L.L.: "I see you on my radar": displays of the confirmatory form in maritime technologically mediated interaction. Sociol. Rev. **64**, 468–494 (2016)
25. Pan, Y.: Suggestions on communications systems for off- shore vessels. In: Selected Paper from Dilemmas for Human Services: Organizing, Designing and Managing, pp. 1–10 (2015)
26. Holmqvist, K., Nyström, M., Andersson, R., Dewhurst, R., Jarodzka, H., van de Weijer, J.: Eye Tracking: A Comprehensive Guide to Methods and Measures. Oxford University Press, Oxford (2011)
27. Tien, T., Pucher, P.H., Sodergren, M.H., Sriskandarajah, K., Yang, G.-Z., Darzi, A.: Eye tracking for skills assessment and training: a systematic review. J. Surg. Res. **191**, 169–178 (2014)
28. Law, B., Atkins, M.S., Lomax, A.J., Mackenzie, C.L.: Eye gaze patterns differentiate novice and experts in a virtual laparoscopic surgery training environment. In: ETRA 2004 Proceedings of the 2004 Symposium on Eye Tracking Research and Applications, vol. 1, pp. 41–48 (2004)
29. van de Merwe, K., van Dijk, H., Zon, R.: Eye movements as an indicator of situation awareness in a flight simulator experiment. Int. J. Aviat. Psychol. **22**, 78–95 (2012)

30. Wood, G., Wilson, M.R.: Quiet-eye training for soccer penalty kicks. Cogn. Process. **12**, 257–266 (2011)
31. Vickers, J.N.: Advances in coupling perception and action: the quiet eye as a bidirectional link between gaze, attention, and action (2009)
32. Dzeng, R.J., Lin, C.T., Fang, Y.C.: Using eye-tracker to compare search patterns between experienced and novice workers for site hazard identification. Saf. Sci. **82**, 56–67 (2016)
33. Henneman, E.A., et al.: Eye tracking as a debriefing mechanism in the simulated setting improves patient safety practices. Dimens. Crit. Care Nurs. **33**, 129–135 (2014)
34. Button, G., Crabtree, A., Rouncefield, M., Tolmie, P.: Deconstructing Ethnography: Towards a Social Methodology for Ubiquitous Computing and Interactive Systems Design. HCIS. Springer, Cham (2015). https://doi.org/10.1007/978-3-319-21954-7
35. Dourish, P., Button, G.: On "Technomethodology": foundational relationships between ethnomethodology and system design. Hum. Comput. Interact. **13**, 395–432 (1998)
36. Likert, R.: A technique for the measurement of attitudes (1932). http://psycnet.apa.org/psycinfo/1933-01885-001
37. Pyne, R., Koester, T.: Methods and means for analysis of crew communication in the maritime domain. Arch. Transp. **17**, 193–208 (2005)
38. Falzon, P.: Discourse segmentation and the management of multiple tasks in single episodes of air traffic controller-pilot spoken radio communication. Linearization Segm. Discourse **4**, 1–17 (2009)
39. Webster, M., Whalen, A., Laland, K.N.: Fish pool their experience to solve problems collectively. Nat. Ecol. Evol. **1**, 0135 (2017)
40. International Telecommunication Union: Manual for Use by the Maritime Mobile and Maritime Mobile-Satellite Services. International Telecommunication Union (2009)

On Improving Automated Self-assessment with Moodle Quizzes: Experiences from a Cryptography Course

Cristina Pérez-Solà[1,2], Jordi Herrera-Joancomartí[1,2(✉)], and Helena Rifà-Pous[2,3]

[1] Universitat Autònoma de Barcelona, Bellaterra, Catalonia
jordi.herrera@uab.cat
[2] CYBERCAT-Center for Cybersecurity Research of Catalonia, Tarragona, Catalonia
[3] Universitat Oberta de Catalunya, Barcelona, Catalonia

Abstract. Although Moodle quizzes are a wide used tool for e-assessment, they present some limitations regarding the possibility to provide randomized quizzes with different questions for each different student. In this paper, we present different approaches to incorporate variables with randomness in questions within Moodle, so that multiple versions of the same question can be generated automatically reducing the workload of the teacher when preparing the quizzes. Furthermore, we explain our experiences in the design and deployment of self-assessed questions, with randomness and feedback, to an online Cryptography course.

1 Introduction

The wide adoption of Internet worldwide has revolutionized higher education learning. From online-only universities, that award official university degrees to students that have followed their courses online, to MOOCs (Massive Open Online Courses), that focus on bringing quality high level education to the masses in an open way, Internet has led to the emergence of new ways of learning (and teaching) that were difficult to imagine just a few years ago.

Online learning has one obvious advantage: it provides flexibility by removing the need to physically attend a traditional class (with a fixed schedule, a specific location, and a limited capacity). But this is not the only benefit online learning offers. By putting Information and Communication Technologies (ICTs) in a central place, online learning is able to provide students and teachers with enhanced learning tools and experiences.

Within these enhanced learning tools appears the ability to create automated individualized self-assessed problems or quizzes, that can be used both during the learning process and for evaluation purposes. Whereas creating and reviewing one (or even multiple) different problems for each individual student is very time consuming in a traditional (analog) setting, ICTs provide ways of doing so with minimal effort.

Specifically, in this paper we deal with automatic self-assessed quizzes containing questions that include randomized variables. We create a new tool, MoodleRanQ, that

E. Ras and A. E. Guerrero Roldán (Eds.): TEA 2017, CCIS 829, pp. 176–189, 2018.
https://doi.org/10.1007/978-3-319-97807-9_14

automatically generates multiple versions of the same question by introducing randomness to a set of variables of the question. MoodleRanQ allows to create as many versions as needed of a single question, whereas retaining the automatic assessment capabilities. This tool enhances the standard functionality of the randomized Moodle quizzes since it provides a simple, fast and efficient method for the teacher to create as many questions as desired in an automated process, for its later use as input in a Moodle random quiz.

We make use of our tool for creating automated self-assessed quizzes (with randomized input questions) with two different goals. First, we intend to improve learners experience by allowing them to practice the resolution of problems related to the subject. By providing students with as many problems as they want, we ensure each student is able to obtain a number of practice problems that matches their learning needs. Moreover, by carefully designing the automated feedback the quizzes provide, we intend to guide the student through the learning process, either by providing clues on the errors that lead to wrong answers or by suggesting additional content to further explore a topic after a successful answer. Second, our tool is also used to generate self-assessed quizzes as an assessment tool: they can be used to evaluate to which extent a student has learned a given topic. With this regard, introducing randomness to questions ensures each student obtains an individualized quiz to solve that is different from the quizzes provided to fellow classmates. This may hinder cheating attempts, since students are no longer able to directly copy other students' answers. Note that, in our case, students solve the quizzes online over the Internet (without any kind of external supervision); they have about two hours to solve the quiz once they have visualized the questions; and they are given a time frame that may last from a few days to a few weeks to make the attempt. Therefore, introducing randomness to the questions obstructs any copying effort. Of course, being an automated tool, another direct benefit of using these quizzes for assessment is that they allow a teacher to evaluate a huge number of students with minimal effort.

Beyond these two main goals, we have found the usage of automated self-assessed quizzes to have other benefits. For instance, students tend to be very satisfied with the fact that they get feedback (and, if applicable, grades) immediately after they finish their attempt, in contrast with traditional activities graded manually by teachers, where feedback takes at least a few days to get back to the student.

This paper provides two main contributions. On the one hand, it describes three different technical approaches to incorporate variables with randomness in questions within Moodle's Virtual Learning Environment (VLE), so that multiple versions of the same question can be generated automatically. We expose the limitations and highlight the benefits of each of the approaches. This know-how can be used by other teachers when designing their online activities. On the other hand, the paper explains our experiences in the design and deployment of self-assessed questions, with randomness and feedback, to an online-only Cryptography course. We give an overview of the observations collected during five different editions of the course and using these questions within two different quizzes' models: giving students two attempts on a graded quiz or providing (ungraded) practice questions together with a one-attempt only graded quiz.

The rest of the paper is organized as follows. First, we provide a basic description of Moodle quizzes, the tool we used to deploy our quizzes, and describe past related works. Then, an overview of the kinds of problems into which we introduce randomization within our Cryptography course is presented. After that, we describe and evaluate the three technical approaches to introduce randomness to the inputs of Moodle questions. We next summarize the results of deploying automatic self-assessed quizzes with randomization during five different editions of the Cryptography course. Finally, the conclusions and lines for future research are highlighted.

2 Background on Moodle Quizzes and Related Work

Moodle is a widely used open source VLE with multiple functionalities, including e-assessment tools. One of these tools is the Quiz module that allows to build quizzes from a set of questions drawn from the Question bank. The Question bank stores all the existing questions. Questions can be classified in categories, which in turn may be nested within other categories, allowing to effectively organize the set of available questions.

Moodle supports different kinds of questions, from basic True/False or Multiple Choice questions, to Calculated ones (where answers are described as mathematical formulas that are evaluated at visualization time). Each type of question has its own set of configuration parameters, for instance, to describe how is the correct answer identified or how is grading computed. Moreover, questions may also include feedback to be given to students, either conditioned to specific answers or general to anyone who attempts the question.

Once the questions are created, they can be used in Quizzes. Quizzes are created by selecting a subset of questions from the bank, assigning a punctuation to each question inside the quiz, and configuring the behavior of the general quiz. Questions can be arranged in a predetermined order (or the order may be left to random). Additionally, one may also include randomly chosen questions in a quiz. In this case, a category of questions is selected, and the quiz will randomly pick one of the questions of that category to show during the attempt.

Multiple authors in the scientific literature point out the potential of Moodle quizzes as a self-assessment tool. Blanco and Guinovart [1] describe the use of Moodle quizzes as an assessment tool for undergraduate subjects in applied mathematics. Salas-Morera et al. [2] show that using online quizzes, in a subject related to project methodology, organization, and management, has a proven positive influence on students' academic performance. Furthermore, one of the problems associated with e-assessment is related with the risk of cheating and copying the answers. Randomized questions, like the approach discussed in this paper, is an interesting approach to reduce such a risk, as different authors has already pointed out in the literature [3, 4].

3 The Cryptography Course

"Cryptography" is a 6-ECTS credits course addressed mainly to computer science undergraduate students. Students enrolled into the course are expected to have already completed basic programming and mathematical courses.

The course is taught entirely online. Students are provided with a course manual that contains the theoretical content of the course, together with access to a virtual learning environment (VLE). The VLE used in this course is the virtual campus of Universitat Oberta de Catalunya (UOC) [www.uoc.edu]. This VLE has a modular architecture design that allows Moodle classrooms to be smoothly integrated, allowing us to use standard Moodle quizzes in the course.

The course is focused on modern cryptography with a short introduction including historical cryptography. Among many other concepts, the subject teaches different kinds of cryptographic schemes. The cryptographic schemes themselves (or, at least, parts of them) can be seen as functions that compute an output from a set of input variables.

For instance, one of the most basic cryptographic schemes, the Caesar system [5], works by substituting each letter of an input plaintext with the letter that is found three positions afterwards in the alphabet. For example, the input plaintext ATTACK-ATDAWN is transformed to DWWDFNDWGDZQ when ciphered using Caesar.

Although this is just a trivial example, there are many interesting problems within the subject which follow this very same structure: the goal is to compute an output of a certain function given a set of inputs. Following with the previous example, the goal would be to compute the ciphertext (output) of a given plaintext (input) applying the Caesar cipher (function). The particularity of these kinds of problems is that the same exact problem (function), with different input variables, gives totally different results.

We were interested in generating automated self-assessed questions that followed this pattern, that is, questions where the input variables were selected randomly from the set of valid inputs and answers were computed on execution time, by applying a function or algorithm to the set of generated inputs.

4 Technical Approaches to Random Question Generation

Although Moodle's Calculated questions already provide a way to generate questions with dynamic parameters, the set of functions that can be implemented with this type of questions is very reduced. Because of the complexity of the functions that compute outputs for a cryptography course (e.g., they may include processing large integers, performing finite field arithmetic operations, or implementing complex algorithms), Moodle's Calculated questions are far away from fulfilling the needs for our course.

In order to overcome these limitations, we have been following three different approaches: (1) using the WIRIS[1] quizzes plugin to dynamically compute the answers, (2) computing the answers with external tools and embedding them in a WIRIS question, and (3) generating multiple individual questions with MoodleRanQ, our tool for random Moodle questions generation.

In the next sections we describe the three alternatives. As an example to illustrate the three approaches, we use a Multiple choice question that asks for ciphering a given plaintext using a generalization of the Caesar cipher explained in Sect. 2. Instead of

[1] WIRIS - http://www.wiris.com.

looking for the letter three positions ahead, the number of positions is arbitrary and represents the key of the cipher. Figure 1 shows a specific example of the question. In this case, the input variables to which randomness is applied are two different ones: the plaintext and the key. The plaintext can be any sentence without spaces (in the attempt shown in Fig. 1 the plaintext was chosen randomly to be "`TREATISEONENIGMA`") and the key can be any possible integer from 1 to 25 (in Fig. 1 attempt the key was chosen randomly to be 3). In order to build the question, the correct answer must be computed from the input parameters, as well as four additional (wrong) answers that will be shown as the other possible choices.

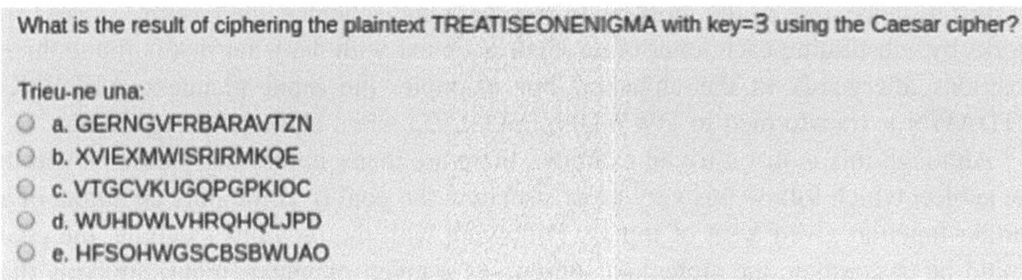

Fig. 1. An attempt on the Caesar cipher question

4.1 WIRIS Questions

The first approach we followed is to use WIRIS quizzes [6], a Moodle plugin that provides an additional set of Moodle question types replicating the standard Moodle types but incorporating advanced scripting features.

With these new question types, one is able to specify a set of variables within the question and compute the answer programmatically, by applying a predefined algorithm to the input variables. Then, when the student attempts the question, the variables are instantiated, and the answer computed at that moment by applying the algorithm as defined when creating the question. In contrast with Moodle's calculated questions, WIRIS allows to implement not only basic functions but also algorithms, with control flow instructions, so WIRIS effectively increases the set of functions that can be implemented with respect to basic Moodle Calculated questions. Moreover, the plugin provides a graphical interface, the WIRIS quizzes studio, from which the teacher can create this kind of questions.

Figure 2 shows an example of the Caesar question algorithm implemented using WIRIS CAS, the mathematical editor for formulas and algorithms integrated within WIRIS quizzes studio. Inside the libraries box the algorithm for ciphering with Caesar is defined. Then, in the variables box, the key and plaintext are chosen randomly and the `CaesarCipher` algorithm is used to cipher the chosen plaintext. The variables defined in this box can then be used in the text of the question. Note that, following this approach, both the algorithm and the randomization procedure are implemented with WIRIS.

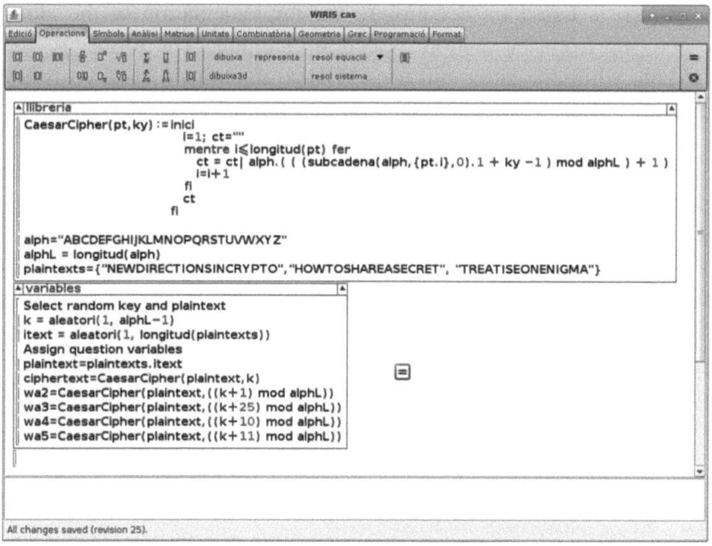

Fig. 2. Code to implement the Caesar question with the WIRIS plugin

However, this approach has some limitations. First, algorithms have to be described using the own WIRIS syntax [7], for which there is a small amount of documentation, community support, and debugging tools. Note, for instance, that the keywords used by the code in Fig. 2 are Catalan words (e.g. `inici`, `mentre`, `fer`, `fi`), since the WIRIS instance running in our server is configured to use that language (currently WIRIS is available in Catalan, Spanish, English, and Danish). Second, depending on the deployment and in order to create the questions, the teacher needs to execute a Java applet in their browser, or download and execute a (.jnlp) file in their own computer file to be able to introduce the code that implements the desired function. This is often a source of technical problems that complicate the procedure. Finally, in contrast to the Moodle open source approach, WIRIS is a license-based software.

4.2 WIRIS Questions Combined with SageMath

The second alternative we deployed is to combine the potential of WIRIS question types together with an external tool. In our case, the external tool was SageMath [8] (previously known as sage), an open-source software for mathematics that uses a Python-like syntax. Python [9] is currently one of the most used programming languages [10], and there exists huge amounts of documentation, debugging tools, and editors for programmers, as well as a very active community. SageMath provides a complete programming language with many libraries that are designed to deal with number theory, algebra, cryptography, etc. Therefore, implementing the cryptographic algorithms needed for our course with SageMath is a much easier task than doing so with WIRIS.

This approach is based on decoupling the implementation of the algorithm that solves the question from the random selection of inputs. The former is implemented using SageMath, while the latter still uses WIRIS functionalities. As a result, we take advantage of SageMath when implementing cryptographic schemes together with the flexibility of WIRIS to introduce randomness into Moodle's questions.

Specifically, the procedure of creating a question with this approach is as follows. First, we implement the cryptographic algorithm within SageMath. Then, we use the implementation to generate multiple different tuples of values, with each tuple containing all the information needed for a single question (input parameters and answers). Finally, we create a WIRIS question that randomly choses one of the tuples. From a technical standpoint, *n* dimensional tuples are exported from SageMath and imported to WIRIS using *n* different lists, that is, a list is exported/imported for each single variable of the question.

```
num_questions = 10

# Caesar cipher
caesar = AffineCryptosystem(AlphabeticStrings())
alph_len = len(AlphabeticStrings().alphabet())
plaintexts = ["NEWDIRECTIONSINCRYPTO", "HOWTOSHAREASECRET", "TREATISEONENIGMA"]

# Generate random variables and answers
for _ in range(num_questions):

    # Select random key and plaintext
    k = randint(1, alph_len-1)
    plaintext = caesar.encoding(random.sample(plaintexts, 1)[0])

    # Generate question variables
    ciphertext = caesar.enciphering(1, k, plaintext)
    wa2 = caesar.enciphering(1, int(mod(k+1, alph_len)), plaintext)
    wa3 = caesar.enciphering(1, int(mod(k+25, alph_len)), plaintext)
    wa4 = caesar.enciphering(1, int(mod(k+10, alph_len)), plaintext)
    wa5 = caesar.enciphering(1, int(mod(k+11, alph_len)), plaintext)

    # Store data to export to wiris
    wiris_data = store_to_wiris(wiris_data, plaintext, k, ciphertext, wa2, wa3, wa4, wa5)
```

Fig. 3. SageMath code to generate variables for the Caesar question

Figure 3 shows the SageMath code to generate the Caesar question. Note that the gains in code conciseness and readability can already be appreciated in a question as simple as this one. The code generates `num_questions` tuples of values, with each tuple containing: plaintext, key, ciphertext, and 4 wrong answers.

The values generated by SageMath can then be imported in a WIRIS question (see Fig. 4). Then, the WIRIS algorithm only needs to select a random integer that defines which of the tuples is selected for the current attempt. Again, from an implementation point of view, the random integer is used as the index of each of the lists.

The main drawback of this approach comes from using two different tools for a single task: question authors need to be have access to both software and must manually copy the results from one to the other. However, the potential of SageMath allows to construct questions based on complex algorithms without much effort.

```
llibreria
corr_answ = ["NUCZUYNGXKGYKIXKZ", "CANJCRBNXWNWRPVJ", ... ]
keys = [6, 9, 25, 14, 2, 20, 25, 16, 2, 14]
plaintexts = ["HOWTOSHAREASECRET", "TREATISEONENIGMA", ... ]
was2 = ["OVDAVZOHYLHZLJYLA", "DBOKDSCOYXOXSQWK", ...]
was3 = ["NUCZUYNGXKGYKIXKZ", "CANJCRBNXWNWRPVJ", ...]
was4 = ["XEMJEIXQHUQIUSHUJ", "MKXTMBLXHGXGBZFT", ...]
was5 = ["YFNKFJYRIVRJVTIVK", "NLYUNCMYIHYHCAGU", ...]
variables
Select random index
i = aleatori(1, longitud(plaintexts))
Assign question variables
k = keys.i
plaintext=plaintexts.i
ciphertext=corr_answ.i
wa2=was2.i
wa3=was3.i
wa4=was4.i
wa5=was4.i
wa5=was4.i
```

Fig. 4. WIRIS code to randomly select variables computed in SageMath

4.3 MoodleRanQ

Our third alternative consisted in developing our own tool, MoodleRanQ, that allowed us to generate random Moodle questions, using the potential of SageMath/Python but removing the need to interact with the WIRIS plugin.

MoodleRanQ is a Python application with a web interface implemented with flask [11], a microframework for web development. Therefore, MoodleRanQ interface can be accessed with any standard web browser. MoodleRanQ can be deployed as a standalone app (using flask built in minimal web server) or in combination with a proper web server (e.g. Apache, nginx or lighttpd).

In order to create a new question, the author selects the type of question to create and then introduces the title, category, text, and answers. The special character # is used to include variables within the question (in a similar way than the WIRIS plugin). Additionally, the authors also determine the total number of versions of the question to generate and the function that will be called to create the answers.

Figure 5 shows an example of creating the Caesar function with MoodleRanQ. Checkboxes are used to indicate the correct answer.

The function that generates the tuples must be a SageMath/Python function with a specific template: it receives a single parameter (the number of versions of the question to generate) and returns a dictionary with as many keys as variables introduced in the question. For each key, the dictionary contains a list with as many elements as versions of the question to generate. MoodleRanQ then combines the information given by the user with the results of the function and generates the questions. Different versions of the same question are grouped into a single category, so that they can be afterwards properly included in a quiz.

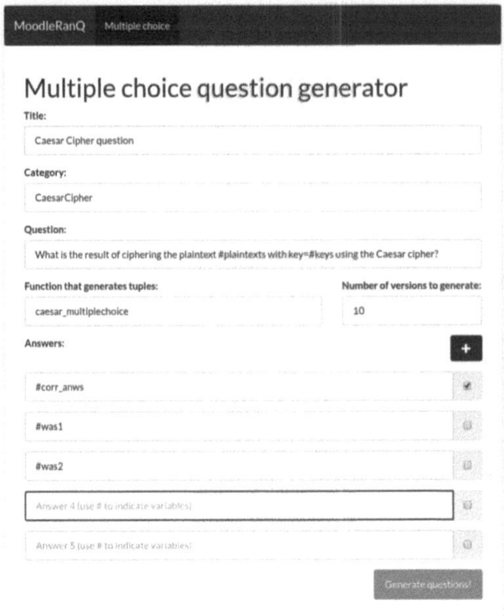

Fig. 5. Caesar question generation via MoodleRanQ web interface

Importing the questions into Moodle requires minimal interaction from the authors. MoodleRanQ generates a file using the Moodle XML format [12] (a Moodle-specific format designed specifically for importing and exporting questions for the Quiz module). This file can be directly uploaded into Moodle.

Figure 6 shows a minimal example of a Moodle XML file for the Caesar question. First, a dummy question with the category type is used to define the category for the questions. Then, multiple questions of type multichoice are created (the image, for brevity, shows only the first of the questions). For each question, the answers together with details such as the numbering type or whether to shuffle answers within the question are specified.

With the previous two alternatives, described in Sects. 4.1 and 4.2, each individual problem is implemented as a single Moodle question that uses the WIRIS potential to generate multiple versions of the same question, resulting in different numbers for each attempt. On the contrary, this third alternative is based on generating multiple Moodle questions for each individual problem and then resorting to standard Moodle's random question selection. Therefore, in order to include a question generated by MoodleRanQ to a quiz, the author indicates that a random question from that category must be included in the quiz (instead of directly including the single question). Since different versions of the same question are grouped into categories, by selecting a random question from the category we are effectively selecting a random version of the question.

```
<quiz>
    <question type="category">
        <category>
            <text>$course$/ MoodleRanQ / CaesarCipher </text>
        </category>
    </question>
    <question type="multichoice">
        <name>
            <text>Caesar Cipher question</text>
        </name>
        <questiontext format="html">
            <text><![CDATA[<p> What is the result of ciphering the
                plaintext TREATISEONENIGMA with key=14 using the Caesar
                cipher?</p>]]>
            </text>
        </questiontext>
        <shuffleanswers>true</shuffleanswers>
        <single>false</single>
        <answernumbering>abc</answernumbering>
        <answer fraction="100.0" format="html">
            <text><![CDATA[<p> HFSOHWGSCBSBWUAO </p>]]></text>
        </answer>
        <answer fraction="0" format="html">
            <text><![CDATA[<p> IGTPIXHTDCTCXVBP </p>]]></text>
        </answer>
        <answer fraction="0" format="html">
            <text><![CDATA[<p> GERNGVFRBARAVTZN </p>]]></text>
        </answer>
        <answer fraction="0" format="html">
            <text><![CDATA[<p> RPCYRGQCMLCLGEKY </p>]]></text>
        </answer>
        <answer fraction="0" format="html">
            <text><![CDATA[<p> SQDZSHRDNMDMHFLZ </p>]]></text>
        </answer>
    </question>
...
</quiz>
```

Fig. 6. Moodle XML file with a Caesar question

As the previous approach, MoodleRanQ has the benefit of using all the potential of SageMath/Python for implementing the algorithms that solve the questions, a major advantage when questions involve complex computations. Additionally, it removes the burden of using two different tools and having to manually copy information from one to the other: questions can be directly imported to Moodle from the xml files generated by MoodleRanQ. The disadvantage this approach poses in front of the other two is an overhead on storage: since multiple Moodle questions are created for each real question (one for each version), text and question structure is replicated multiple times. However, given the size of each question, this should not be a problem for any modern computer.

5 Experiences of Randomized Moodle Questions in the Cryptography Course

In this section, we provide the results obtained by using randomized Moodle questions in a cryptography course. The course is divided in eight units and has five automatically graded self-assessment activities (A1 ··· A5) implemented using Moodle's quizzes, as depicted in Table 1.

Table 1. Overview of the quizzes in the course

	Num. of questions	Max. attempts	Time (minutes)	Num. practice questions	Units
A1	7	2	90	0	1 and 2
A2	4	1	90	2	3
A3	7	1	90	5	4
A4	10	1	90	4	5 and 6
A5	9	2	90	0	7 and 8

Two of the activities in the course (activities A1 and A5) are quizzes with two possible attempts. The grade of the activity is computed as the highest grade obtained in any of the two attempts (and the lowest grade is discarded).

The other three activities (A2 to A4) are quizzes that allow just one attempt (with the final grade of the activity being the grade on that unique attempt). However, for those quizzes, we also have a set of (ungraded) practice questions, which the students may attempt as many times as they want, with the only limitation being the elapsed time between attempts, which must be of at least 30 min. This restriction is included to avoid indiscriminate attempts with bruteforcing intentions.

Data analyzed in this section includes results on 5 different editions of the course, deployed during 3 different academic years (2014–15, 2015–16, and 2016–17). Table 2 summarizes the overall number of students per edition, detailing how many of them where active. We consider a student to be active if she has participated in at least one of the activities of the course.

Table 2. Number of students per edition

Edition	Number of students	Number of active students
E1	55	54
E2	12	12
E3	30	26
E4	60	60
E5	20	18
Total	177	170

5.1 Two Attempts per Graded Quiz

As would be expected, when two attempts on a quiz are allowed, most of the times the majority of the students do use both attempts.

Figure 7 shows the percentage of students that use either 1 or 2 attempts. The horizontal axis of the figure shows the five editions of the course, labeled from E1 to E5. Notice that for each edition two bars are depicted, one for activity A1 and another one for activity A5. The first bar of each edition (blue bar) represents activity A1 and the second bar (green bar) represents activity A2. The vertical axis shows the percentage of students that perform one. To this regards, bars for each activity are divided between the percentage of students that have used one attempt only (darker zone) and students that used both attempts (lighter zone). The 50% value is depicted as a dash line. Notice that, the only activity where there were more students that used one attempt than students that used both of them was A1 in edition E4. However, it is also interesting to note that even the final grade of the activity was set as the maximum grade of two attempts, the percentage of students that use only a single attempt is maintained above 16% in all editions for both activities.

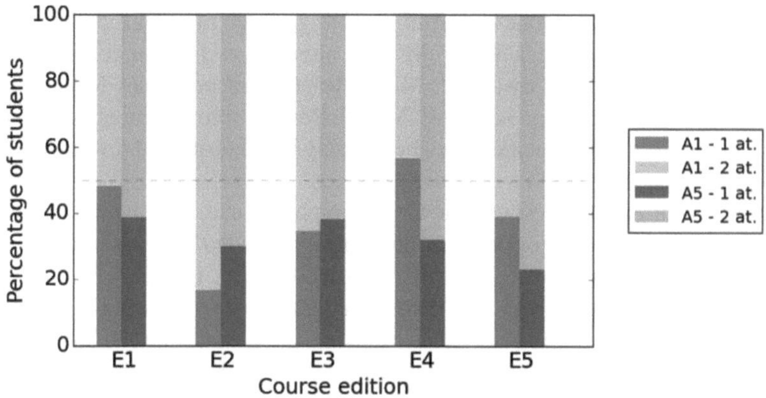

Fig. 7. Percentage of students with 1 or 2 attempts (per activity and edition) (Color figure online)

5.2 Practice Questions and One Unique Graded Attempt

Regarding the graded activities that offer a set of practice questions, we have found a positive correlation between the number of practice questions a student solves and her mark at the graded quiz. For all the analyzed activities, the average mark of students that hadn't solved any practice question was below five (the pass mark for the course).

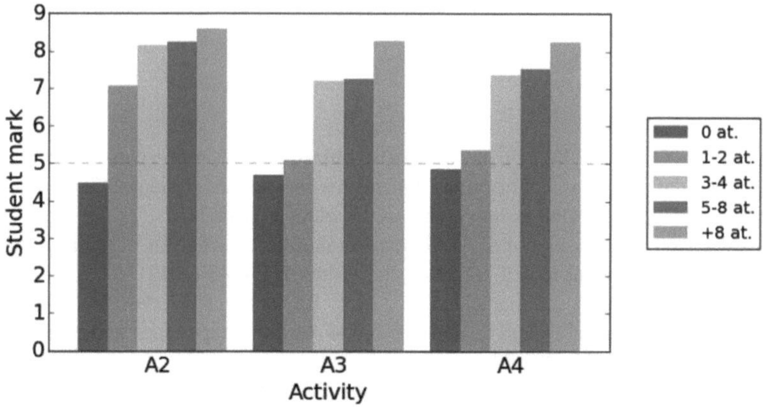

Fig. 8. Average mark given the number of practice questions solved

Moreover, the average mark increased with the number of practice questions the student attempted. Figure 8 shows the average marks for students given the number of attempts on practice questions for activities A2, A3 and A4 (the results are aggregated over different editions).

6 Conclusion and Future Work

We have found Moodle quizzes a very useful tool for online learning and assessment. However, Moodle quizzes alone are insufficient to generate randomized questions with complex algorithms. After evaluating different alternatives for overcoming this limitation, we implemented our own tool, MoodleRanQ, that combines Moodle quizzes functionality with Python/sage scripting. MoodleRanQ improves the question creation process, easing the authors' work both when coding the algorithm and when adding the question into Moodle.

Regarding our experiences with the Cryptography course, we have found that most students indeed make use of various attempts on graded quizzes when they are available. Apart from improving their mark on the activity, this has consequences on the learning process, as it may entail that students do learn during the evaluation process. Moreover, we have detected a positive correlation between the number of practice questions a student performs and the mark she obtains in the graded test.

We intend to follow two different lines of work in order to expand this paper. First, we expect to further develop MoodleRanQ, to convert it from a prototype to a fully functional application. We think that a complete product allowing to build randomized Moodle questions powered up by Python's algorithmic features would serve the entire online teaching community (especially regarding math and computer science related learning). Second, we intend to further analyze Moodle quizzes student data with more advanced statistics techniques, in the interest of extracting knowledge that can be used both to enhance future editions of our courses and to design new online courses.

Acknowledgements. This work is partially supported by the Spanish ministry under grants number 785 TIN2014-55243-P, TIN2014-57364-C2-2-R and TIN2015-70054-REDC, and the Catalan AGAUR grant 2014SGR-691.

References

1. Blanco, M., Ginovart, M.: On how Moodle quizzes can contribute to the formative e-Assessment of first-year engineering students in mathematics courses. Rev. Univ. Soc. Conoc. **9**, 354 (2012). Universitat Oberta de Catalunya, Barcelona
2. Salas-Morera, L., Arauzo-Azofra, A., García-Hernández, L.: Analysis of online quizzes as a teaching and assessment tool. J. Technol. Sci. Educ. **2**, 39–45 (2012)
3. Guerrero-Roldán, A.-E., Hettiarachchi, E., Mor, E., Antonia Huertas, M.: Introducing a formative e-Assessment system to improve online learning experience and performance. J-JUCS 21(8) 1001–1021 (2015)
4. Clariana, R., Wallace, P.: Paper–based versus computer–based assessment: key factors associated with the test mode effect. Br. J. Educ. Technol. **33**, 593–602 (2002)

5. Caesar Cipher. Wikipedia. https://en.wikipedia.org/wiki/Caesar_cipher. Accessed 10 Feb 2017
6. WIRIS. WIRIS Quizzes. http://www.wiris.com/en/quizzes. Accessed 10 Feb 2017
7. WIRIS Language Manual. http://www.wiris.net/demo/wiris/manual/en/html/abc/index.html. Accessed 10 Feb 2017
8. SageMath. http://www.sagemath.org/. Accessed 10 Feb 2017
9. Python. https://www.python.org/. Accessed 10 Feb 2017
10. Carbonnelle, P.: PYPL PopularitY of Programming Language (2016). http://pypl.github.io/PYPL.html
11. Flask, web development, one drop at a time. http://flask.pocoo.org/. Accessed 10 Feb 2017
12. Moodle XML format. https://docs.moodle.org/24/en/Moodle_XML_format. Accessed 10 Feb 2017

Pathways to Successful Online Testing: eExams with the "Secure Exam Environment" (SEE)

Gabriele Frankl(✉), Sebastian Napetschnig, and Peter Schartner

Alpen-Adria-Universität Klagenfurt, Klagenfurt, Austria
{gabriele.frankl, sebastian.napetschnig, peter.schartner}@aau.at

Abstract. eExams can potentially improve didactics, efficiency, objectivity, flexibility, accessibility, and even sustainability compared to written exams. However, they also present great challenges such as security, reliability, integrity, as well as the availability of computer rooms of sufficient size. To conduct large-scale online exams, we implemented the "Secure Exam Environment" (SEE) in 2011. The SEE enables online testing in any lecture hall using students' own devices – and loan devices if needed – while blocking access to unauthorized files or internet pages. After booting the SEE, assessment is conducted via Moodle and additional software (e.g. GeoGebra, Excel or Eclipse) can be used as well. To maintain quality of service, we developed a monitoring solution to control the technical infrastructure of the SEE. As of July 2018, we have conducted 1,605 such online exams with 57,607 students. Moreover, the SEE offers the possibility for slotted exams where students can choose freely the time of their exam within a week. Since technical solutions cannot solve all problems, the organization of eExams is vital to guarantee smooth operations as well as integrity. This paper offers a technical solution for the implementation of a secure and highly available exam environment with the various benefits of eExams, and provides organizational recommendations for the successful roll out of online exams as well as for overcoming technical challenges.

Keywords: Secure online testing · Secure Exam Environment Benefits of eExams · Organization of eExams · Security · High availability Monitoring

1 Introduction

Assessment methods have a profound influence on how students learn [1, 2]. Assessment generates students' activities and engagement, heavily influences student behaviour, shapes students' experiences, and generates feedback and thus opportunities for improving students' knowledge as well as reflection and removing misunderstanding [3–5]. Unfortunately, current assessment approaches have proved to be unsuitable for measuring complex learning [6]. In spite of the considerable importance of assessment and the increasing availability of alternative methods for assessing

E. Ras and A. E. Guerrero Roldán (Eds.): TEA 2017, CCIS 829, pp. 190–209, 2018.
https://doi.org/10.1007/978-3-319-97807-9_15

students' knowledge and competencies like dynamic question types, training software, videos, or games, paper-and-pencil exams and written summative assessments continue to be the dominant method of assessment. This leads, among other things, to learning processes being directed towards the acquisition of factual knowledge and towards rote learning at schools, at universities as well as in organizational training. Even though the didactical opportunities of paper-and-pencil exams are quite limited, their management costs various resources, visible mainly as increased workload for academic staff. While technology has proven its potential for enhancing learning processes [7–10], it offers opportunities for improving assessment methods as well. However, we found a lack of technical solutions for conducting secure online exams for larger audiences. The problems we encountered were twofold: first, classical computer rooms were simply too small for large-scale exams. Second, like in all other electronic "business scenarios", confidentiality, integrity, authenticity, accountability, privacy, and reliability (and thus availability) are also mandatory in the context of electronic exams. Especially, if they come with the property "secure". The first five aspects are commonly addressed by the use of cryptography (e.g. encryption of transmitted and stored data, network-based security mechanisms like firewalls, and authentication of messages and users) as well as organizational measures to compensate for the limits of technical solutions. The last one may be overcome with physical and logical redundancy and continuous monitoring of the IT system [11]. This includes the continuous monitoring of the infrastructure (hardware, software and network) as a preventive measure to help detect issues before they cause any major problems.

To overcome these shortcomings, we implemented the Secure Exam Environment (SEE). This paper demonstrates how the technical implementation of the SEE can make eExams "*secure*", and provides recommendations for extending Moodle as a learning platform for conducting "*exams*", as well as expertise for the organization and design of an "*environment*" for successful eExams.

2 Benefits Offered by eExams

Online testing has great potential as a tool for conducting exams. Next to didactical benefits, they improve the efficiency and objectivity of exams, offer increased flexibility for lecturers as well as students, are sustainable if the personal devices of the students are used and offer students with disabilities increased accessibility.

2.1 Didactical Benefits

From a didactic point of view, eExams improve the execution of traditional question types like free text answers or multiple choice questions, and expand the range and variety of assessment methods by offering a number of new question types. Thus, online exams provide didactical benefits and have the potential to assess higher order thinking skills and different kinds of knowledge, e.g. procedural knowledge.

Free text questions remain invaluable even in the digital era when it is crucial to let learners explain something in their own words and thus to check if they understand more complex concepts adequately. With online exams, students can structure their answers in a clear and concise manner while making as many revisions and corrections as necessary. This provides students and teachers with increased clarity about the basis of the evaluation.

Multiple-choice or -response questions are appropriate if the recognition of the correct information within a set of selection options, the analysis of situations or scenarios, or the evaluation of adequate options is of interest. For didactical reasons, multiple-response questions should be preferred as this reduces the likelihood of students simply guessing the right answers. Cloze is suitable if the context of the learning content is essential, and particularly for short answers and terms that should be used correctly. The electronic delivery of cloze allows various forms of gaps to be filled via selection options, as short answers or drag-and-drop operations.

In addition to optimizing traditional question types, online exams also expand the repertoire of questions. While paper-and-pencil question types remain static, online testing offers variety, e.g. calculations with ranges of validity, and even dynamic types of questions, like drag-and-drop questions, the integration of variables into the question text or into items of multiple-choice questions, or the integration of videos or games (if sound is necessary for these questions, headphones should be available to not disturb colleagues during exams). Drag-and-drop questions within online testing include dragging of texts and/or images, for example, dragging several texts into an image and thus marking special areas of this image. Consequently, this question type is well suited when learners need to assign related elements, prioritize or organize elements. Videos and games may include procedural and complex information in questions, offering a new dimension in the assessment of situations, procedures, and dynamic content. Thus, analysis and evaluations of social dynamics, e.g. the communication between doctors and patients, technical procedures or meteorological processes, to name a few, are quite easily assessable. To sum up, question types should be selected based on the content being assessed.

Another and outstanding advantage of online testing is the opportunity to push the boundaries of static question types by including additional software in exams, making software, which is available for teaching and learning, also available for testing. More complicated problems can be solved in this way. According to Biggs and Tang [1] and their concept of "constructive alignment", coherence between all phases and elements of the learning process is essential for high quality education. Intended learning outcomes, teaching/learning activities, assessment tasks as well as grading should support one another [1, 12]. Thus, the software tools used for teaching and learning - e.g. mathematical or statistical calculations and analysis, programming, literature essays - should be used during the examination process as well. Being able to use specific software and multimedia in electronic exam environments paves the way to promising (hands-on) performance assessments too.

Beyond this, eExams can extend general feedback to each question and thus to all students without additional work for lecturers, leading to more valuable feedback for students about their level of knowledge [13]. Moreover, individual feedback may be made available to every student. We have observed that while students do not necessarily come to personal feedback talks they always want to see online feedback for an eExam.

In addition, opportunities for statistical analysis of questions may be utilized to improve the quality of questions over time.

2.2 Efficiency

Online exams result in a noticeable reduction of academic workload and thus result in significant savings [14] due to the improved readability, structure and clarity of typed open-text answers, along with automatic delivery, storage and (semi-)automated correction of (semi-)standardized question types. Handwritings in paper-and-pencil exams are often difficult to decipher and answers are quite often supplemented and extended using any blank regions on the paper sheet. Thus, the correction of free text answers takes a lot of time without any benefit for teachers or students. With online exams, the answers to free text questions are effortlessly readable. Additionally, eExams bring further advantages such as improved correction possibilities. The sorting of all students' answers to one question is done by the machine, which means an ease of correction. For exams conducted by several lecturers, e.g. for qualifying subject examinations, the correction can be done by several colleagues simultaneously. In addition, correction work can be done more easily while traveling since all exams are available online, eExams do not get lost, and – compared to paper-and-pencil exams - they may be copied effortlessly. The question pool may be improved over time through the adaptation, modification or extension of questions, thus simplifying the creation of new exams. Finally, as technical support staff may take over the supervision of the exams, lecturer may concentrate on other activities.

The greater efficiency of eExams provides students with instant grading and - if supported by lecturers - feedback [15]. Moreover, since today's students are more used to typing than to extensive handwriting [16], online exams prevent hand pains and bad handwriting related to paper-and-pencil exams.

2.3 Objectivity

eExams restrict the halo-effect which occurs when different handwriting styles influence the lecturer when grading [4, 17–19]. Online exams enable each question to be evaluated on its merits without being influenced by other answers provided by the student and thus subjective construction processes. Furthermore, online exams facilitate blind grading in many learning management systems, e.g. in Moodle, increasing objectivity.

Importantly, cheating may be minimised through the shuffling of questions and test-items and thus the avoidance of simultaneously displayed questions and test-items, the automatic selection of random questions out of a sufficiently large question pool as well as the opportunity to create questions including variables which are assigned different values for each student. Additionally, technical security concepts go far beyond the security possibilities of paper-and-pencil exams.

2.4 Flexibility

Furthermore, online exams provide greater flexibility compared to traditional testing methods [14]. Next to the extended correction possibilities mentioned above (simultaneous correction, correction on mobile devices whilst traveling) candidates are able to use their own familiar devices for an exam which helps to reduce stress as well as costs. In addition, implementing our secure exam environment (SEE) enabled us to offer so-called "slot-exam-weeks" where students can freely choose their examination date within one week (see Sect. 3.8).

2.5 Sustainability

Students usually have their own computers. Using these existing devices of the students (bring your own device – BYOD) minimizes institutional asset requirements to a few loan devices for students without portable computer or in case of a computer failure during the exam. Thus, the acquisition of new computers, which are mainly used for auditing purposes, is minimized. Additionally, eExams save paper and consequently contribute to the environmental protection.

2.6 Accessibility

Display magnifiers (screen loupes), screen readers, Braille input and output devices, mouth sticks or other devices allow students with disabilities to take an exam in a way quite similar to their colleagues. Thus, easy access to exams for people with disabilities is much more convenient with online exams. eExams are therefore also in compliance with the Austrian law which grants students with disabilities unrestricted accessibility to exams. In particular this means that students have the right "to be examined according to an alternative method if they suffer from a permanent disability which makes it impossible for them to take an examination in the prescribed manner and the other method does not limit the content and standards of the examination" [20].

3 The Secure Exam Environment (SEE)

Our efforts to take advantage of the above mentioned benefits together with an unsuccessful search for a satisfactory technical solution for eExams led to the development of the Secure Exam Environment (SEE) for online testing at the Alpen-Adria-Universität Klagenfurt (AAU) in 2011 [21]. The aim to make use of modern teaching and testing strategies next to the need to support large class sizes while working within budgetary and organizational constraints required a flexible and thin development. By making use of the students' existing personal computers (laptops), the SEE increases efficiency since ordinary lecture halls can be used for large scale online testing as well as effectiveness since the students are presumably familiar with their own devices. The SEE disables access to students' own files, data, and external hardware as well as to unwanted internet sites. Loan devices are offered for those who do not own a laptop or whose laptop is not compatible with the SEE. As a result, institutional asset requirements as well as the associated maintenance costs are minimized. We are currently able to test up to 220 students simultaneously with a stock of 80 loan devices [22].

3.1 Integration with Moodle

The actual exams are presented as quizzes, a key component of the Moodle learning management system (LMS) utilized by the AAU. Moodle offers various types of questions:

1. Questions which require manual grading like free text answers (called "essays" in Moodle).
2. Questions which are graded semi-automatically such as short answers. For these, examiners define a set of answers which allow the question to be evaluated automatically. Since students' responses might be correct but not included in this set, markers should manually check answers where students did not receive the maximum points available.
3. Question types which are evaluated automatically, including true/false questions, multiple choice and -response questions, numerical as well as calculated questions and calculated multichoice, matching, embedded answers (cloze), select missing words as well as drag-and-drop into text, onto image or drag-and-drop markers.

In the context of testing, archiving exams is another important aspect. According to Austrian legislation [23], documents related to written exams have to be archived for at least six months. Moodle, however, offers a practical solution as it automatically archives exams, which dramatically reduces the physical storage requirements and, as a positive environmental side-effect, the amount of paper needed (especially in the case of no-shows).

Furthermore, Moodle settings allow additional security measures to be defined such as the IP-range within which eExams can be taken.

3.2 Additional Software and Resources

The SEE facilitates the integration of different software tools and programmes, which are increasingly used for teaching and learning into the exam environment, fostering pedagogical coherence [1]. At the moment we support GeoGebra, Eclipse, Office-products like Excel or Word, calculators, PSPP, as well as any combination of these tools.

Furthermore, PDF-documents or websites which are allowed and could be used during an exam can be provided.

3.3 Security and Bring Your Own Device – BYOD

In contrast to other electronic exam environments (e.g. [24]), we avoid the use of special equipment and encourage students to use their own device. However, accessing the Moodle server directly via a common web browser running on the student's operating system (OS) is an insecure approach. In this case, blocking connections to Wikipedia or other online resources may be simple, but cheating by using materials stored on the local hard drive is rather easy. Since we do not want to force students to install additional software (such as lockdown modules) on their personal laptops, we have to use our own OS in order to restrict the access to the local resources and programmes that are prohibited during the exam. We decided to boot this OS via the Preboot eXecution Environment (PXE) protocol over a local area network (LAN), since the handling of USB sticks or DVDs is very error-prone, time-consuming and inflexible, especially when additional software is needed [22]. Using wireless LANs (WLANs) would be an alternative solution, but with technical limitations to guarantee security since WLANs are very interference-prone. Each student with an easily obtainable jammer could interfere the WLAN. Nonetheless, we developed organizational security concepts for the SEE via WLAN, but are still focusing on LAN as it is sufficient for our current requirements and technically more secure.

Clearly, booting our own OS requires that the client is able to boot via the network. In order to support a very broad range of (private) laptops, our solution is designed as a minimal Linux system. At the moment, this OS is realized using Fedora and Knoppix, which enables us to boot Legacy and UEFI devices. To support Apple hardware we boot a minimal macOS image. In order to restrict the access to external resources, we implemented corresponding firewall rules. Since Moodle as an LMS not only provides exam features but also chatting capabilities and course related material, a solution was needed to prevent access to such resources and activities during exams. Running an ordinary web browser – even when restricted with firewall rules – would not have completely solved the cheating problem. Fortunately, the Safe Exam Browser (SEB – [25]) is fully supported by Moodle-core. The SEB is far more than an ordinary browser. Beside it's common browser functionality it offers a complete lockdown of all OS interface functions as opening, switching and closing applications other than the SEB itself. Furthermore, together with a SEB moodle plugin it also guarantees (when set up appropriately) that a moodle quiz can only be accessed by the SEB and all moodle graphical user interface (GUI) functions which would allow interaction outside the quiz are suppressed. However, the SEB is only available for Windows and macOS. Therefore, we boot a minimized Windows 7 as a virtual machine on the minimized Linux system via VirtualBox [26] (see Fig. 1). Despite the availability of online tools and platforms, proprietary software which only runs on Windows remains widespread in the educational sector. On the one hand, the reliance on a virtual machine and Windows 7 is a drawback in terms of performance, on the other hand, it adds flexibility regarding the management of the virtual machine image. Furthermore, hardware driver management is done completely in Linux, which is known for its broad, out of the box hardware support especially for older devices. The selection of the allowed programmes during the exam (in addition to the SEB) is set via a configuration file, which is retrieved from an intranet service. In the GUI of this service, administrators are able to configure different combinations of GeoGebra, Excel, Word, Calculator, Eclipse, and PDFs for the exam.

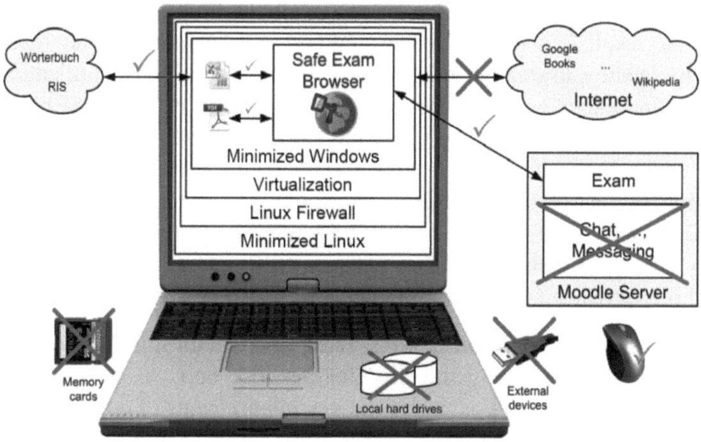

Fig. 1. The operating principle of the Secure Exam Environment (SEE)

Starting an online exam using the SEE begins by booting a minimized Linux from the LAN, then the minimized Linux automatically starts the Windows 7 virtual machine (VM), Window 7 automatically starts the SEB, the SEB automatically connects to the homepage of the AAU's learning management system Moodle, and finally users have to log in to Moodle with their own account and enter the Moodle course in order to select the exam they want to take [22].

3.4 Maximizing the Availability of the SEE

The availability of an exam environment is an issue of critical importance. Even a short downtime of the SEE could prevent hundreds of students from taking exams which might be urgently needed to get marks or certificates, take new courses, finish modules, classes or studies, get financial aid for higher education studies, or even get a new job. Furthermore, students tend to be quite nervous before an exam and a technical glitch would undoubtedly increase stress and erode trust in the exam environment. Thus, perception of the SEE's reliability (from both for examiner's and examinees' viewpoint) depends on the availability of the (information) technology during the exam [5].

During the SEE boot process, the SEE-servers (and the personal computers with which the exams are written) have to operate properly as well as the network including the switches in the lecture halls. At the time of writing an eExam, the SEE depends on the online connection between the SEB and the Moodle-server. Consequently, the availability of the SEE can be affected by hardware failure, network drop-outs or service outages. Analyzing and identifying failures when a breakdown occurs usually costs a lot of time, which is at a premium while conducting an eExam. Thus, a continuous monitoring solution of the various IT components involved - e.g. servers and computer networking technologies – to prevent failures and optimize the availability of the SEE is mandatory, particularly considering the SEE is based on various hardware components which are administered by different departments of the university.

Drop-outs of components or services or deviations from thresholds within defined time intervals result in alerts, allowing support staff to react to and resolve issues immediately, leading to crucial time-savings within the failure identification process. Monitored components and services include the availability of the SEE-servers (implemented with centOS) including CPU and storage, as well as DHCP, NFS, TFTP, and HTTP services; the availability of the administration backend of the SEE including the corresponding HTTP service; the availability of Moodle including HTTP-access as well as end-to-end-tests in the lecture halls with minimal computers (Raspberry Pi); the availability of the network (connection between SEE-server, clients and Moodle), and end-to-end performance tests within the network with low-cost probes (Raspberry Pi).

Monitoring the High-Availability SEE-Host and Including Services. The availability of the server, providing the SEE for network boot, as well as services like DHCP, NFS, HTTP and TFTP is one of the key requirements of online testing with the SEE.

We operate the SEE-server as a high-availability and stable system by running multiple redundant SEE-servers. Using DRBD/Heartbeat or Pacemaker/Corosync in a failover setup (to define one server as the master server and the other one as slave) enables us to switch from one server to the other automatically in case of a failure or manually in case of scheduled maintenance. Thus, a new update can be safely implemented within the system by installing it on one server and, after careful testing, on the other and thus the production system.

While monitoring the services mentioned above, we log CPU utilization, RAM and hard disc usage, and the status as well as the utilization of the network interface. Additionally, we periodically check for pending updates, especially security updates, to eliminate failures or prevent hack-attacks on the system and improve performance. Controlling upcoming updates enables us to schedule maintenance periods efficiently around exams.

Measuring Network Performance. Measuring the run-time of the network including the connection between the SEE-server, clients and Moodle during an eExam in real time generates significant data about the latency and utilization of the network. The open source software SmokePing is a suitable tool for measuring and visualising the round-trip-time (RTT) of Linux-based systems by defining the specific hosts as well as relevant external hosts which are reachable via ICMP. By default, every five minutes twenty ICMP-packages are transmitted to each specified host and used to calculate RTTs. Package loss is a signal for capacity overload of the main host or related hosts, or for a failure or an erroneous configuration of a network device. Black 'smoke' at an interval of measurement shows the range of fluctuation of the RTT. Increased smoke indicates a high variation of the RTT per ping and thus capacity overload of the network. The combination of SmokePing and probes (Raspberry Pi's) placed in the SEE-network enables us to monitor all servers and network devices and thus to recognise network bottlenecks and failures at an early stage.

Maximizing Availability of the Network Connection. In order to maximise network availability, we only use wired LAN connections at this point of time. Despite recent developments, WLAN remains too error-prone and, additionally, a malicious user could easily perform a denial-of-service (DoS) attack on the WLAN access points and hence prevent all users from taking the exam. To achieve such an attack, a battery-powered pocket-sized WiFi jammer could be placed close to or in the room where the eExams take place.

To ensure the maximum stability of the network system, the network department of our university provides high redundancy within the network-core, distribution-switches, firewalls, and the border-router, as well as load sharing via the Border Gateway Protocol (BGP) in a multihomed environment and redundant cables. In addition, the equipment used in the core and distribution layer are high-end components.

Infrastructure. The availability of our Secure Exam Environment (SEE) is affected by the infrastructure in which the SEE components are embedded. One critical issue is an Uninterruptible Power Supply (UPS) for the SEE-server as well as for the network to protect the system from power failures. The UPS also guards against over- and undervoltage and is backed by means of batteries (short-term power failures) and a diesel generator (long-term power failures).

Another important topic is the geographical distribution of the (redundant) hardware components. The two SEE-servers are located in different areas of the university and thus, in the case of an extended power failure, fire or flooding, it is unlikely that both servers will be affected.

Backups. One indirect approach to guarantee the availability of the SEE-servers, and thus the SEE, is frequent, well organized backups. In case of an outage like hardware failure, the SEE-server must be restored to the most recent valid state. An up-to-date, functioning backup reduces the mean time to repair (MTTR). A well-organized backup-strategy includes the evaluation of functionality of the frequently executed backups as well as the documentation and frequent testing of the backups and training of the responsible staff. Furthermore, it should be guaranteed that spare hardware (like hot-standby harddisks, power supplies and spare network components) is immediately available in case of serious hardware failure.

Monitoring the Availability of the Administration Backend of the SEE Including the Corresponding HTTP Service. The administration backend is another key component of the SEE, offered via web interface and used by the supporting staff to activate any additional software (e.g. a calculator or Eclipse) for an exam. The administration backend is accessible only via a URL https://backend.spu.aau.at. A periodical check of the HTTP server's reachability is performed monitoring the HTTP status code. If the wrong status code is returned from the backend, an alarm is sent to the service team. Additionally, it is possible to check the server's response times. Longer response times could be an indicator of network outages or a server problem.

Centralized Monitoring of all SEE-Components and Services. Deviations from threshold values of all components and services of the SEE are reported at regular intervals. Every outage triggers an alarm (via e-mail or SMS) which, together with centralized monitoring, helps the service team to rapidly identify the cause of a failure, saving additional time.

Optimizing the SEE Based on Monitoring Data. The constant monitoring of all components and services of the SEE offers the opportunity for (trend) analysis (also see Sect. 5.1 "Further developments") as a basis for the continuous optimization of the systems' performance.

3.5 Reliability

Reliability for examiner and examinee is a critical issue and depends on the availability of (information) technology - e.g. computers and computer networking technologies - during the exam [5, 11]. At the time of writing, the SEE depends on the online connection between the SEB and the Moodle-server. As a result, users cannot save current results or proceed to the next question during a network failure. Thus, the temporary storage of the answers (during network failures) remains a problem. Fortunately, Moodle saves the last answer received and the progress of each examinee. Therefore, the examinee is allowed to continue the exam from the point where the error occurred after potential network problems are solved. In the worst case scenario, the last answer of the examinee is lost. Similarly, laptop failure is not a severe problem because all answers provided up to the failure would have been stored on the server and the student can simply continue his or her exam on one of our loan devices.

3.6 Loan Devices

Loan devices serve two purposes within the SEE: Firstly, it cannot be assumed that all students have a portable device, and secondly, they may substitute a student's personal device in the case of technical problems or breakdowns during the exam. The AAU currently has approximately 80 laptops serving as loan devices for students.

3.7 Secure Exams for Students with Disabilities

Impaired students have very different needs. Thus, one single standard solution for students with disabilities would not meet the requirements. Therefore, we provide for each student with specific needs a unique solution for eExams using different tools (see Sect. 2.6). Since the integration of these tools would pose severe security problems for the SEE, we conduct eExams for students with disabilities on their own, familiar device but with local restrictions or, if required, on loan devices.

3.8 Offering Flexibility with Slot-Exams

One service for students, which followed from the development of the SEE, are so-called slotted eExams. For the execution of eExams with the SEE, we developed an online-process to register for an eExam some time before the test takes place as well as an online-registration process right before the exam in the lecture hall. Thus, exams, registration data as well as access rights are available online. These processes enabled us to offer several time-slots for an eExam within a week, from which students can freely choose when they want or are able to take an exam. Especially for students who are employed next to their studies, who need to foster children or relatives or whose mobility is restricted, this service is very helpful.

The decision as to whether an eExam is conducted in a traditional way on a fixed examination date or as a slotted eExam is made by the lecturer: slotted eExams can only work if a suitably large question pool is available, such that on different days randomly generated questions and/or exams are sufficiently dissimilar from each other [11].

4 Organizational Issues of eExams

Careful planning and organization are crucial for the smooth, secure and reliable operation of eExams. Organization is vital not only for the preparation of eExams but also to close security gaps. As a result, many aspects have to be considered before, during and after exams.

4.1 Organizational Measures Beforehand

In addition to informing teachers and students about the basics of eExams before an exam, support staff must be trained and available, rooms must be booked and tests must be created correctly.

Provide Information. Some lecturers, particularly if they have only recently taken up their position at the university or are external teachers, are not aware of the possibilities of online testing and especially not of the SEE as a specific solution at the AAU. Hence, we offer videos introducing the SEE, clearly arranged checklists for the preparation of casual eExams or slotted eExams with the SEE, a Moodle-course with information and a ‘playground’ to try online-tests and get familiar with eExams as well as advanced training courses and personal trainings.

The eLearning-hotline is available 24/7 to support lecturers as well as students in case of open questions, e.g. if a personal device fails immediately before an exam and a loan device is needed.

Support Students with the Preparation of their Devices. Since students have to change the boot-order of their devices to start the SEE, we offer special information days once or twice a week to support them with this task. Over a six hour period, students are offered the opportunity to change the boot order of their device and test if it is compatible with the SEE. In addition, first time students learn something about the eExam process. The type of device, the key combination to enter the boot-menu or the need for a loan device are stored in a database to improve preparations for future eExams.

Training of a Flexible Support-Team and Team-Building. Successful written exams require the cooperation of multiple staff members. As the Alpen-Adria Universität Klagenfurt conducts online exams from 8 a.m. to 10 p.m., five days a week, we supplement our core team of four employees which are responsible for the entire eLearning services of the university, with students trained as e-tutors. At the moment our team includes 12 e-tutors working between two and 12 h a week to successfully deliver a growing number of tests.

The team has received significant coaching and teambuilding to manage the technical, organizational as well as personal challenges related to online exams. For example, the support staff must remain calm in the event of failures, errors or problems, particularly as students are already under stress due to the examination situation and should not be subjected to further strain. Students who start as e-tutors initially perform simple tasks like the transport of loan and registration devices into the lecture hall, setting up loan devices for replacement in the lecture hall or supervision of the exam. Once they have gained experience with the handling of eExams, they receive further training as 'lead-e-tutors', taking over contact with lecturers before the exam, the final check of the test-setting and questions in Moodle, and the activation of the correct exam-version (e.g. unlocking additional software).

To schedule availability of the support staff for each eExam, we use a shared spreadsheet (ev. Screenshot) where each team-member fills out his or her (non-) availability for each exam-slot. The core-team then decides who will be the lead of an eExam and who will be in the support team.

Organizing Lecture Halls for eExams. The room for an eExam is booked mainly by the lecturers in coordination with our eLearning-team and the room administration of the university. Obviously, it is important to ensure that not too many eExams take place simultaneously, overstraining support staff and loan device capacities. Furthermore, enough time must be allocated for test-settings (e.g. additional software or websites allowed) before and after an exam and for setting up registration and loan devices in the lecture hall as well as the registration process itself.

Organizing Tests and Questions. Many lecturers need support with didactical and technical issues surrounding the creation of test questions and tests when starting out with eExams. Moreover, the general conditions must be set for each exam: Will subject-specific supervision be available? Are written materials allowed during the exam? Should websites and/or additional software be available and, if yes, which ones?

As Moodle's test settings are crucial for successfully conducting secure eExams with the SEE, the settings for each eExam are checked along with the questions themselves by the support team.

Registration of Students Before an Exam. Students have to register for any exam. During the registration process for an eExams students must confirm that they attended an information day for eExams and that they have had their device checked for compatibility with the SEE and they will bring it to the eExam, or that they will use a loan device. In addition, students can indicate if they require a barrier-free exam environment, in which case communication with the support staff follows to clarify the conditions for the accessibility of the exam.

If the number of registered students exceeds the capacity of the lecture hall, a second exam slot is typically organized. Students who cannot prebook a loan device due to unforeseen demand are placed on a waiting list.

4.2 Organizational Measures at the Time of the eExam

eTutors ensure that the exam venue is open and that the required registration and loan devices are available. The support team receives instructions from the lead-e-tutor about the specific exam requirements then (e.g. permitted software, websites, -documents, notes or materials).

Additional loan-devices are set up as backups for any computers that fail during the exam. The number of the replacement devices depends on the number of registered students. Experience shows that one backup device for every 10 to 20 students is sufficient.

The identities of students are verified upon arrival in the lecture hall by scanning their student card using a card reader. Following processing via our university's examination administration system, eLearning staff are informed if the student registered for the specific eExam, if s/he needs a barrier-free examination environment and if s/he will use his or her personal device or a loan device.

After checking in, students receive a LAN-cable and a loan device if needed and are seated appropriately in the lecture hall. In the meantime, the specific exam is made visible in the Moodle-course, the proper version of the SEE is activated (with a correct selection of additional software, websites as well as documents) and the network switches are activated.

Powerpoint slides are presented in the lecture hall with detailed step-by-step instructions for the installation of the LAN-cable, the booting-process and as well as for navigating through and eventually submitting the test. Afterwards, the students boot the SEE. During the booting process, and a video is played to inform students about the examination modalities in a comprehensible and traceable way, e.g. about how to start the eExam, how to navigate between test questions, how to submit the eExam, which actions are considered cheating and the corresponding consequences.

Fig. 2. Instructions for students in the lecture hall before an eExam

Finally, once the support staff has informed the students about any special features of the exam, the exam starts.

During the exam, the support staff verifies if each student has logged into Moodle with his or her proper account by matching their physical student identity card with the login data. Furthermore, the e-tutors supervise the exam and support in case of technical failures or problems.

After submitting the exam, the students return the LAN-cable, the loan devices (where applicable) and check out by replacing their student identity card on the card reader.

4.3 Organizational Measures After the eExam

After all, students have submitted the exam or the examination period has expired, the exam-slot is closed, the test is made invisible for students in the Moodle-course and a backup of the exam is created.

5 Experiences with eExams at the AAU and Further Developments

In June 2011 we began offering online exams with the SEE. Table 1 shows the growth of eExams conducted with the SEE at the AAU over the last six years.

Table 1. The progression of eExams with the Secure Exam Environment (SEE), * in progress

	2011	2012	2013	2014	2015	2016	2017	2018*	Total
eExams	10	59	159	208	234	286	373	276	1,605
Examinees	288	2,717	7,475	7,082	8,954	10,352	12,252	8,487	57,607

5.1 Experiences with Supporting Students' Own Devices

The aim of supporting all student laptops is quite challenging because the dedicated installation of drivers would be too time consuming and risky. Nonetheless, we try to support as many devices as possible [27]. Figure 2 shows the proportion of supported devices over time (Fig. 3).

As shown in the figure, in 2012 the SEE system supported 65% of the hardware provided by the students. As hardware evolved and, in particular with the introduction of UEFI in newer laptops, the percentage of supported devices decreased until 2016. In response to this, in 2016 we began to work on a second OS image (based on Fedora) and as a result, the number of supported laptops has begun to increase.

Most of the remaining compatibility problems stem from exotic hardware (Linux integrates the most common and widespread hardware components), which mainly appear in low budget and top end laptops as well as sub notebooks. For example, gaming laptops with GeForce graphic cards are often unsupported since NVIDIA only provides proprietary drivers and the open source drivers lack support for mobile gaming graphic cards.

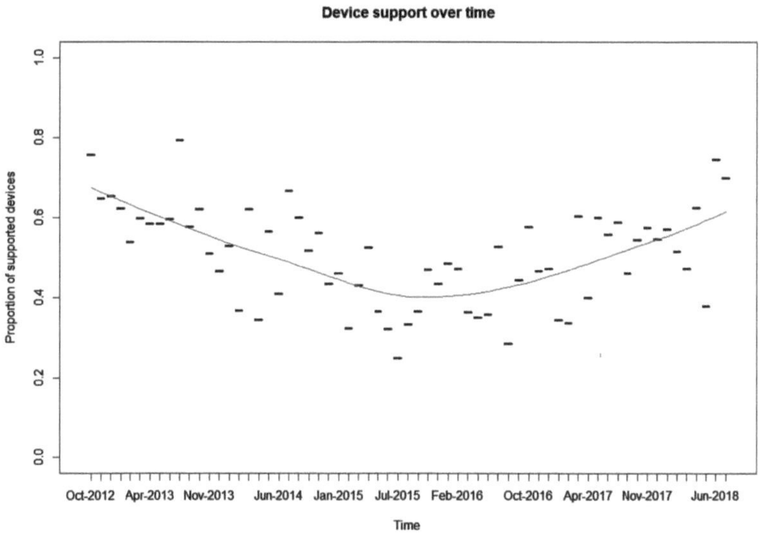

Fig. 3. Supported student laptops from 2012 to (ongoing) 2018

Unfortunately, device support data from 2012 until the beginning 2016 is somewhat incomplete, as during the early stages of the implementation of the SEE we focused on the technical solution. Data was collected to find out which devices were bootable with the SEE and which devices not, thus, where effort should be invested, i.e. which devices were popular enough to require a technical solution. As testing procedures were not standardized the data does not distinguish between when the tester could not get a device to work and when it was not supported, and how this information was recorded was not standardized. Over time, we have standardized the procedure for testing students' devices as well as the documentation of device support.

Since every supported laptop currently needs to be fully functionable without the installation of additional drivers or custom configurations for specific hardware combinations, we consider a support rate of over 70% as a success. In combination with our 80 loan devices we have been able to offer eExams as required and conduct online assessment of up to 300 students.

5.2 Further Developments

Didactical Improvements. Although online testing has the potential to extend the variety of question types as well as software and multimedia available for an exam, the question types offered by LMS are nevertheless rather limited and the software available restricted to licensing agreements. Hence, examination has improved with eExams, but has not reached a new level yet. Consequently, we are continuing our work to improve the ways in which knowledge is tested and adapt it to current knowledge requirements.

Stable and Flexible Network Connection. One of the current challenges of online exams is the necessity of a stable and preferably flexible network connection. As WLAN is still prone to failure, LAN is the best option for stability, especially for larger groups of students. This results in another challenging aspect, namely that lecture halls require LAN and power sockets near at least every second seat. Unfortunately, not all lecture halls fulfill these requirements and retrofitting is extremely expensive, resulting in a lack of flexibility. The obstacle with the LAN sockets could be overcome with access points. Thus, we are evaluating solutions to provide eExams for devices without ethernet port via WLAN or a hybrid boot (usb/ethernet) solution. To compensate technical weaknesses, we defined organizational measurements to increase the availability of WLANs. However, running laptops purely on battery power is risky.

New Generations of Hardware. New generations of laptops, requiring continuous adaptation of the SEE, remain a persistent challenge. For example, we had to invest significant effort to support UEFI as a new interface between the hardware and the OS. As laptops become slimmer, more devices come without dedicated ethernet ports, forcing us to support adapters within the SEE. Unfortunately, some manufacturers do not support even PXE boot with USB ethernet adapters, leading to the need to find workarounds.

Improved Monitoring. Further developments in monitoring will include the integration of the students' devices and the loan devices into the monitoring concept and predictive maintenance (for details refer to [28–30]). In more detail, we will pursue the following ideas:

- By gathering and analyzing the devices' log-files, whenever they are connected to the SEE, *students' devices* and the *loan devices* may be directly integrated into the monitoring system. This will help to keep the loan devices up-to-date, because a problem detected on a single device (currently in use) can (automatically) be fixed on all other instances of the same model. A similar process can be applied for the students' devices: a problem detected with one device can either trigger an update of the SEE (e.g. with respect to drivers) or a warning for other students using the same model. In the long-term, the log-data may be included in a predictive model.
- The goal of *Predictive Maintenance* is to determine the condition of equipment (servers, laptops, and network-infrastructure such as switches and cabling) in order to predict when maintenance should be performed in order to avoid failures. This is contrary to the classical approach, where maintenance is either triggered by a concrete failure (aka the break-fix model [31]) or an interval-based approach, which often causes unnecessary costs. In short, predictive maintenance promises time and cost savings and a higher level of availability.

Different Versions of Simultaneous eExams. Currently, we are only able to execute one eExam with specific settings, e.g. additional software, at the same time. Therefore, we are developing a boot environment that supports multiple eExams with different additional software simultaneously by recognizing the identity of the lecture hall and subsequently by recognizing the identity of the student and transmitting the proper exam environment.

Identity Verification. Checking the identity of an examinee by verifying the picture on his/her (student) identity card is a quite common process at the beginning of exams. However, when it comes to large scale exams (say 200 or more examinees), this process in total gets quite time consuming. In order to enhance the efficiency of the identity verification process we plan to integrate authentication by use of biometric features. These features might include a picture of the face (available on the identity card and in the students' record) or even a fingerprint. If the (students) hardware provides the according sensor, the identity checking could take place at his/her seat. In case of a camera needed to verify an image of the face, this is quite likely with modern laptops. Since fingerprint readers are most commonly only available to the operating system (or special) applications, a fingerprint reader could be placed next to the RFID-reader that reads the students identity card.

General Data Protection Regulation (GDPR). Of course, the processing of personal data calls for compliance to the GDPR [32], especially when biometric data (Art. 9 GDPR: special categories of personal data) is processed. When conducting electronic exams, besides of identity verification, there are several processes that have to be concerned. Some of them are already compliant with the GDPR (e.g. notification of the outcome/grade, or right of access to the exam), but some are not or have to be implemented yet (e.g. right for a copy of the exam, or automatic compliance to deadlines for storage or deletion). So another open topic is to adapt the SEE concept and Moodle for GDPR-compliance.

6 Conclusion

eExams extend the possibilities for assessment in many ways, especially in terms of quality (e.g. didactics and objectivity) and efficiency. However, the transition from paper-based to electronic exams raises "new" security-related problems. Traditional paper-based exams handled requirements like confidentiality, privacy, integrity, authenticity, accountability and availability in a straight-forward manner: simply preventing access before and after the exam guarantees their confidentiality, the paper and well established organizational and personnel processes do the rest (privacy, integrity, authenticity, accountability, and availability). The security gaps in paper exams have not always been sufficiently taken into account, especially due to the lack of an alternative. For eExams, all the aforementioned aspects have to be addressed by complex, often technical mechanisms.

One solution to overcome these challenges is the Secure Exam Environment (SEE) used at the Alpen-Adria-Universität Klagenfurt (AAU) as presented in this paper. The SEE provides didactical benefits of online testing by extending the questions types offered by the LMS Moodle with additional software, multimedia and online resources, all within a secure environment. The system's BYOD-approach, utilizes students' familiarity with their devices to provide efficiency and sustainability while restricting access to local resources and to the Internet. Furthermore, this paper contains a description of our low-cost monitoring system that helps us achieve a high quality of service level with respect to the availability of the SEE. Finally, this paper considers the underlying organizational measurements supporting pathways to successful online testing.

References

1. Biggs, J., Tang, C.: Teaching for Quality Learning at University. McGraw Hill, Berkshire (2011)
2. UK Quality Code for Higher Education: Part B: Assuring and Enhancing Academic Quality. Quality Assurance Agency of Higher Education (2001). http://www.qaa.ac.uk//en/quality-code/the-existing-uk-quality-code/part-b-assuring-and-enhancing-academic-quality. Accessed 13 July 2018
3. Marriott, P.: Students' evaluation of the use of online summative assessment on an undergraduate financial accounting module. Br. J. Edu. Technol. **40**(2), 237–254 (2009)
4. Müller, F.H., Bayer, C.: Prüfungen: Vorbereitung - Durchführung - Bewertung. In: Hawelka, B., Hammerl, M., Gruber, H. (eds.) Förderung von Kompetenzen in der Hochschullehre, pp. 223–237. Asanger, Kröning (2007)
5. Sharpe, R., Oliver, M.: Designing courses for e-learning. In: Beetham, H., Sharpe, R. (eds.) Rethinking Pedagogy for a Digital Age. Designing and Delivering e-Learning. Routledge, London (2007)
6. Clarke-Midura, J., Code, J., Mayrath, M.C., Dede, C., Zap, N.: Thinking outside the bubble: virtual performance assessments for measuring complex learning. In: Technology-Based Assessments for 21st Century Skills, pp. 125–146 (2012)
7. Benkada, C., Moccozet, L.: Enriched interactive videos for teaching and learning. In: 8th International Workshop on Interactive Environments and Emerging Technologies for eLearning (IEETeL2017) and 21st International Conference on Information Visualisation, London (2017)
8. Põldoja, H., Väljataga, T., Laanpere, M., Tammets, K.: Web-based self- and peer assessment of teachers' digital competencies. World Wide Web **17**(2), 255–269 (2012)
9. Howell, D.D., Tseng, D.C.Y., Colorado-Resa, J.T.: Fast assessments with digital tools using multiple-choice questions. Coll. Teach. **65**(3), 145–147 (2017)
10. Ardito, C., et al.: Usability of e-learning tools. In: AVI 2004 Proceedings of the Working Conferences Interfaces, pp. 80–84 (2004)
11. Frankl, G., Schartner, P., Jost, D.: The "Secure Exam Environment": e-testing with students' own devices. In: Tatnall, A., Webb, M. (eds.) WCCE 2017. IFIP AICT, vol. 515, pp. 179–188. Springer, Cham (2017). https://doi.org/10.1007/978-3-319-74310-3_20
12. Müller, A., Schmidt, B.: Prüfungen als Lernchance: Sinn, Ziele und Formen von Hochschulprüfungen. Zeitschrift für Hochschulentwicklung, vol. 4, no.1, pp. 23–45 (2009)
13. Price, M., Handley, K., Millar, J., O'Donovan, B.: Feedback: all that effort, but what is the effect? Assess. Eval. High. Educ. **35**(3), 277–289 (2010)
14. Anakwe, B.: Comparison of student performance in paper-based versus computer-based testing. J. Educ. Bus. **84**(1), 13–18 (2008)
15. Hewson, C.: Can online course-based assessment methods be fair and equitable? Relationships between students' preferences and performance within online and offline assessments. J. Comput. Assist. Learn. **28**(5), 488–498 (2012)

16. Fluck, A.: eExaminations Strategic Project Final Report for Academic Senate, University of Tasmania (2011). (Meeting 1/2011, cited in Fluck, A., Hillier, M.: Innovative assessment with eExams. Paper presented at the Australian Council for Computers in Education (ACCE) conference, 29 September–2 October, Brisbane, Queensland (2016))
17. Fleming, N.D.: Biases in marking students' written work: quality? In: Brown, S., Glaser, A. (eds.) Assessment Matters in Higher Education: Choosing and Using Diverse Approaches, pp. 83–92. McGraw-Hill Education, London (1999)
18. Sweedler-Brown, C.O.: Computers and assessment: the effect of typing versus handwriting on the holistic scoring of essays. Res. Teach. Dev. Educ. **8**(1), 5–14 (1991)
19. Brown, S., Glaser, A.: Assessment Matters in Higher Education: Choosing and Using Diverse Approaches. McGraw-Hill Education, London (2003)
20. Bundeskanzleramt Österreich, Universitätsgesetz 2002, § 59 Abs. 1. Z 12. https://www.ris.bka.gv.at/Dokumente/Erv/ERV_2002_1_120/ERV_2002_1_120.pdf. Accessed 13 July 2018
21. Frankl, G., Schartner, P., Zebeding, G.: The "Secure Exam Environment" for online testing at the Alpen-Adria-Universität Klagenfurt/Austria. In: World Conference on E-Learning in Corporate, Government, Healthcare, and Higher Education. Association for the Advancement of Computing in Education (AACE), Hawaii (2011)
22. Frankl, G., Schartner, P., Jost, D.: Guaranteeing high availability of the "Secure Exam Environment" (SEE). In: Proceedings of the 10th International Conference on Computer Supported Education, vol. 2, pp. 130–136 (2018)
23. Bundeskanzleramt Österreich, Universitätsgesetz 2002, §79 Abs. 3 and 4 and § 84 Abs. 1. https://www.ris.bka.gv.at/Dokumente/Erv/ERV_2002_1_120/ERV_2002_1_120.pdf. Accessed 13 July 2018
24. SoftwareSecure. http://www.softwaresecure.com/. Accessed 16 Aug 2017
25. Safe Exam Browser (SEB). http://www.safeexambrowser.org/news_en.html. Accessed 13 July 2018
26. Virtual Box. http://www.virtualbox.org. Accessed 13 July 2018
27. Frankl, G., Napetschnig, S.: Bring your own device to secure online exams. In: Technology Enhanced Assessment (in press)
28. Sasisekharan. R., Seshadri, V., Weiss, S.M.: Proactive network maintenance using machine learning. In: Workshop on Knowledge Discovery in Databases (KDD94), pp. 453–462 (1994)
29. Susto, G.A., Schirru, A., Pampuri, S., McLoone, S., Beghi, A.: Machine learning for predictive maintenance: a multiple classifier approach. IEEE Trans. Ind. Inform. **11**(3), 812–820 (2015)
30. Hashemian, H.M., Bean, W.C.: State-of-the-art predictive maintenance techniques. IEEE Trans. Instrum. Meas. **60**(10), 3480–3492 (2011)
31. General Electric Company: Beyond the break-fix model: predictive services to leverage GE's record $229 billion backlog. GE Reports, 18 October 2003. http://www.gereports.com/beyond-the-break-fix-model. Accessed 17 Aug 2017
32. Regulation (EU) 2016/679 of the European Parliament and of the Council of 27 April 2016 on the protection of natural persons with regard to the processing of personal data and on the free movement of such data, and repealing Directive 95/46/EC (General Data Protection Regulation - GDPR). https://publications.europa.eu/en/publication-detail/-/publication/3e485e15-11bd-11e6-ba9a-01aa75ed71a1/language-en. Accessed 13 July 2018

Calculating the Random Guess Score of Multiple-Response and Matching Test Items

Silvester Draaijer[1(✉)], Sally Jordan[2], and Helen Ogden[3]

[1] Faculty of Behaviourals and Movement Sciences,
Department of Research and Theory in Education, VU University Amsterdam,
De Boelelaan 1105, 1081 HV Amsterdam, The Netherlands
s.draaijer@vu.nl

[2] School of Physical Sciences, The Open University, Robert Hooke Building,
Walton Hall, Milton Keynes MK7 6AA, UK
sally.jordan@open.ac.uk

[3] Formerly Open University Consultant and at the University of Southampton,
Southampton, UK
h.e.ogden@soton.ac.uk

Abstract. For achievement tests, the guess score is often used as a baseline for the lowest possible grade for score to grade transformations and setting the cut scores. For test item types such as multiple-response, matching and drag-and-drop, determining the guess score requires more elaborate calculations than the more straightforward calculation of the guess score for True-False and multiple-choice test item formats. For various variants of multiple-response and matching types with respect to dichotomous and polytomous scoring, methods for determining the guess score are presented and illustrated with practical applications. The implications for theory and practice are discussed.

Keywords: Item-writing · Question development · Test development
Cut score · Standard setting · Selected response test items
Selected response questions · Multiple-choice questions · MCQs

1 Background

An essential step in test construction are the rules for setting cut score and score-to-grades. An important consideration in this step is determining the lower bound of the score range that students can achieve on the basis of random guessing. In this paper, methods and tables for calculating or looking up guess values for multiple-response and matching test items are presented and discussed.

First of all, there is not one 'optimal' method for establishing cut score [1–4]. A suitable method depends on the goal of the test and available resources. The main methods for standard setting can be classified as criterion referenced methods (setting a cut score on the basis of the content of the test and considerations of minimum levels of achievement needed related to that content), norm referenced methods (setting a cut score in relation to the score distribution of the population that took the test), and combining these methods somehow (setting a cut score based on a combination of both

E. Ras and A. E. Guerrero Roldán (Eds.): TEA 2017, CCIS 829, pp. 210–222, 2018.
https://doi.org/10.1007/978-3-319-97807-9_16

approaches). In many situations in higher education in the Netherlands and the UK, the random guess score for a test with selected response test items is taken into account [5–9] for both types of standard setting. The random guess score provides a criterion for the lowest score that can be awarded the lowest possible grade for a student. The assumption is that this is the score that is obtained by simply filling in answers randomly[1] but according to instructions for filling in (e.g. the instructions regarding the number of options to select for a test item).

With the advent and increased use of e-assessment [12–14], teachers in higher education can more easily than ever use test items types other than True-False or multiple-choice. In particular, multiple-response, matching and drag-and-drop test items can be deployed easily. The question therefore becomes more pressing how the guess score must be calculated for such items [15]. Mackenzie and O'Hare [16] discussed the problems associated with establishing such a base guess factor for complex test item formats such as multiple-response and drag-and-drop questions. They argued that in the random response mode for such questions, nodes appear for groups of test-takers that achieve a certain score based on specific settings of question answering and that the guess factor is often more prominent than one would expect. They reported these findings on the basis of simulations they performed using a Marking Simulator. Unfortunately, since the publication of MacKenzie and O'Hare, no progress has been reported concerning the development of the Marking Simulator application. Further Jordan [17] presented a general approach to establishing guess values for multiple-response items, multiple attempt multiple-response items and drag-and-drop items. Her approach was very principled from a mathematical viewpoint and a stand-alone program was developed for use by experts. This leaves teachers in higher education and less mathematically proficient test item authors on their own in dealing with this problem.

In this article, we will put forward some methods and tables that allow testing experts and teachers in higher education to calculate or find the random guess score for multiple-response and matching type questions based on various set-ups of these items.

2 Basic Principles for Calculating the Random Guess Score

In principle, the random guess score of a test item S_{guess}, equals the sum of the probability for each possible outcome for a question $p(O_i)$, multiplied by the score for that outcome O_i: S_{O_i}. This can be written:

$$S_{guess} = \sum p(O_i) * S_{O_i} \tag{1}$$

For True-False test-items, a dichotomous item, there are two combinations of choices possible. One combination leads to score 0 and one combination to the maximum score. The probability p of scoring 0 points is the number of occurrences of

[1] Some other methods try to incorporate student's knowledge level in estimating guessing level using formula scoring [10] but this is abandoned because of validity problems [11].

0 points, divided by the total number of combinations. This is expressed as a probability $p = \frac{1}{2}$. Given a maximum score of 1 point, this random guess score is $S_{guess} = p(O_0) * 0 + p(O_1) * 1 = \frac{1}{2} * 0 + \frac{1}{2} * 1 = 0.5$ points.

For a four choice multiple-choice item, four combinations are possible of which three options lead to a score of 0 points and one leads to a score of 1 point. The random guess score now equals $S_{guess} = p(O_0) * 0 + p(O_1) * 1 = \frac{3}{4} * 0 + \frac{1}{4} * 1 = 0.25$ points.

3 Multiple-Response Test Items

A multiple-response test item is similar to a multiple-choice test item, but there is more than one correct answer. Multiple True-False test items are similar to multiple-response test item with regard to random guess score. For the random guess score of multiple response test item two characteristics are of importance.

1. Is the scoring of the test items dichotomous (correct or incorrect) or polytomous (multiple points can be acquired by specific selection of options)?
2. Is the examinee informed what the number of correct alternatives is?

3.1 Dichotomous Scoring

For example, let us take a 5 alternative multiple-response test items of which three alternatives are correct. The student is instructed to select the three correct alternatives (out of five possible alternatives). Suppose we use a dichotomous scoring model in which the student receives 1 point if the answer is completely correct and 0 points for all other situations. For this test item we can calculate the number of combinations of possible choices as being $\binom{n}{m} = \frac{n!}{m!(m-n)!}$ which yields for this example $\binom{5}{3} = \frac{5!}{3!(5-3)!} = 10$.

Only 1 of those combinations leads to a score of 1 point, the rest leads to a score of 0 points. We can represent a specific combinations of choices as CO_i. Now, the random guess score can be calculated as follows: $S_{guess} = p(CO_{0pt}) * 0 + p(CO_{1pt}) * 1 = \frac{9}{10} * 0 + \frac{1}{10} * 1 = 0.1$ points.

3.2 Polytomous Scoring

A different situation occurs if we use a polytomous scoring model for the test items in which the student receives 1 point for each correctly chosen alternative and the student is also *instructed* to select the three correct alternatives. For this test item, 10 combinations of selections are possible. By tabulating all possible options and assigning scores to each option, the random guess score can be calculated.

S_{guess} now follows from: $S_{guess} = p(CO_{0pt}) * 0 + p(CO_{1pt}) * 1 + p(CO_{2pt}) * 2 + p(CO_{3pt}) * 3 = 0 * 0 + \frac{3}{10} * 1 + \frac{6}{10} * 2 + \frac{1}{10} * 3 = 1.80$ points.

A more elegant approach to this calculation is given by Jordan [17] and a simpler form of that follows now. For the situation above, where the student is told in advance how many correct alternatives there are, we can find S_{guess} using a simple formula, which may be derived as follows: think of all the responses as balls in a bag. There are n "correct" balls in the bag, with labels $C_1, \ldots, C_n$ on them, and m balls in total. The student is told to select n balls from the bag. Any one of the m balls is equally likely to be in the students' selection (therefore it can be regarded a random variable), with probability $\frac{n}{m}$, since there are m balls in total, and we pick n of them. So, the probability the first correct ball, C_1, is selected is $\frac{n}{m}$, the probability C_2, is selected is $\frac{n}{m}$, and so on.

A theorem in probability theory is that the expected value of the sum equals the sum of the expected values of the accompanying random variables, whether they are dependent or not. So we can write $S_{guess} = \sum p(O_i) * S_{O_i} = \sum \frac{n}{m} * S_{O_i}$.

If we have the simple scoring rule where each correct response scores 1 point, then:

$$S_{guess} = \sum \frac{n}{m} * S_{O_i} = \frac{n^2}{m} \tag{2}$$

Or, we can write this as a percentage of the total possible achievable score of n points as $100 * \frac{n}{m}\%$. If we apply this formula to the example above, where we are told that there are $n = 3$ correct answers of the are $m = 5$ total answers, $S_{guess} = \frac{n^2}{m} = \frac{9}{5} = 1.8$ points. So we arrive at the same result as we did by counting the possible combinations. If the students are told the number of correct responses, then we can extend the argument above to give:

$$S_{guess} = \sum \frac{n}{m} * S_{O_i} \tag{3}$$

where the sum is over all m possible choices, and where the "score" given for selecting an incorrect response may be actually be negative, to give a penalty for incorrect responses.

3.3 Giving the Number of Correct Responses

It seems that in the case where we are given the number of correct responses, the random guess score should be fairly easy to find. However, if we are not given the number of correct responses, we could compute the random guess score by assuming that each possible selection of options is equally likely to be chosen. We will assume a random selection of options in the section below. Given this method, Table 1 is constructed. The table contains the random guess score for commonly encountered multiple-response test items. For multiple-response test items with different scoring rules, different tables should be constructed.

Table 1. Random guess scores for multiple response test items given the number of alternatives and number of correct alternatives.

Number of alternatives	Number of correct alternatives	Dichotomous (0 or 1)		Polytomous (each correct alternative 1 point)		
		Unknown number correct	*Known* number correct	Max score of item	*Unknown* number correct	*Known* number correct
n	m	Random guess score	Random guess score		Random guess score	Random guess score
3	1	0.13	0.33	1	0.5	0.33
3	2	0.13	0.33	2	1.0	1.33
3	3	0.13	1	3	1.5	3.00
4	1	0.06	0.25	1	0.5	0.25
4	2	0.06	0.17	2	1.0	1.00
4	3	0.06	0.25	3	1.5	2.25
4	4	0.06	1	4	2.0	4.00
5	1	0.03	0.2	1	0.5	0.20
5	2	0.03	0.1	2	1.0	0.80
5	3	0.03	0.1	3	1.5	1.80
5	4	0.03	0.2	4	2.0	3.20
5	5	0.03	1	5	2.5	5.00
6	1	0.02	0.17	1	0.5	0.17
6	2	0.02	0.07	2	1.0	0.67
6	3	0.02	0.05	3	1.5	1.50
6	4	0.02	0.07	4	2.0	2.67
6	5	0.02	0.17	5	2.5	4.17
6	6	0.02	1	6	3.0	6.00

As an example, consider the question shown in Fig. 1. This test item contains 5 alternatives of which 2 are correct alternatives. Students are told the number of correct alternatives. If the scoring is dichotomous, Table 1 shows that the random guess score equals 0.1 points; if the scoring is polytomous, the random guess score equals 0.8.

3.4 An Extension for Scoring Rules for Multiple-Response Test Items

In specific circumstances, more sophisticated scoring might be required for a multiple-response test item. For the example given in Fig. 1, the scoring rule could for example be defined as follows:

- 0 points: If the student gets 0 alternatives correct and 3 incorrect OR If the student gets 1 alternative correct and 2 incorrect
- 5 points: If the student gets 2 alternatives correct and 1 incorrect
- 10 points: If the student gets all 3 alternatives correct.

A 45 year old asthmatic woman who has lived all her life in Glasgow presents with a goitre of four years' duration and clinical features suggestive of hypothyroidism. The two most likely diagnoses include

A. Iodine deficiency
B. Dyshormonogenesis
C. Drug-induced goitre
D. Thyroid cancer
E. Auto immune thyroiditis

Correct answer: true C and E: false A, B and D [18]

Fig. 1. Example random guess scores for a multiple response item [18].

Neither Eq. (3) nor the more straightforward calculation table will now suffice. We can return to handwork and develop a new table with combinations, as shown in Table 2. This multiple-response test item can have 20 combinations. We must assign scores to each combination of choices. Then we can calculate the probability of occurrence of each score. The occurrence of the full score is 1/20th, the occurrence of a score of 5 points is 9/20th and the score of 0 points is 10/20th. From this, it follows that $S_{guess} = p(CO_{0pt}) * 0 + p(CO_{5pt}) * 5 + p(CO_{10pt}) * 10 = 2.75$ points. From the table, this can also be calculated by averaging the sum of scores.

Table 2. Combination table for a multiple-response test item with 6 options and 3 correct alternatives, scores and average score.

Combination	Correct or wrong						Score
	C	C	C	W	W	W	
1	x	x	x				10
2	x	x		x			5
3	x	x			x		5
4	x	x				x	5
5	x		x	x			5
6	x			x	x		0
7	x				x	x	0
8	x		x		x		5
9	x		x			x	5
10	x			x		x	0
11		x	x	x			5
12		x		x	x		0
13		x			x	x	0
14		x	x		x		5
15		x	x			x	5
16		x			x	x	0

(continued)

Table 2. (*continued*)

Combination	Correct or wrong						Score
	C	C	C	W	W	W	
17			x	x	x		0
18			x		x	x	0
19			x	x		x	0
20				x	x	x	0
Average score							2.75

A note of warning must be given here. The assumption that answers are selected completely at random is not likely to be realistic in practice; the answering behavior of students might play a role. A student is likely to make some guess as to how many of the answers they think will be correct, probably based on their past experience of answering test items of a similar type. Even in multiple-choice test items, guessing behavior is influenced by student characteristics, with for example students being more likely to select the inner options of a multiple-choice test item than the first and last alternative [19], as well as the quality of the test item and its foils.

For multiple-response test items, it would be interesting to see how many choices real students do assume to be correct (before they even look at the content of those choices) when answering this sort of test item. Once the distribution of the number of choices a student would assume to be correct, we could make a better substantiated calculation to find the random guess score.

4 Ordering and Matching Test Items

It is easier to compute the random guess scores of Ordering and Matching test item types than it is for multiple-response test items. An example of a matching item is shown in Fig. 2.

Match the type of quiz question on the right with the correct description of it on the left. You can use the type of quiz only once.

______ *Students must make associations between items on two lists*	A. *Essay*
______ *Students judge the correctness of declarative propositions*	B. *Matching*
______ *Students choose one correct response from a list of options*	C. *Multiple-choice*
	D. *True-False*

Fig. 2. Example matching test item with 3 options and 4 markers [20].

It is interesting to note that drag-and-drop test items for which a student needs to place specific objects (for example text markers) in the correct boxes is also a matching test item. See the example of Fig. 3. For the random guess score of matching test items, two characteristics are of importance.

Drag the given terms at the bottom of the image to the corresponding boxes. Note that there is one foil term that must not be used

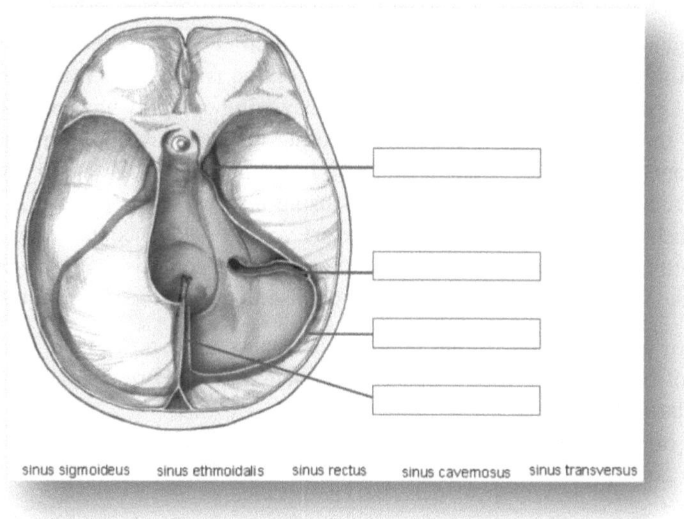

Fig. 3. Example random guess scores for a matching test item.

1. Is the test item scoring dichotomous (correct or incorrect) or polytomous (multiple points can be acquired for each correct choice)
2. Can the answering options be used more than once or only once? For Ordering test items, the options (being ordering numbers) can only be used once. For matching and drag-and-drop this must follow from the specific set-up of the test item. In what follows, we will assume that the answering options can only be used once.

4.1 Dichotomous Scoring

Let us assume a student has to answer a test item in which he has to position 5 answering options in 4 open spaces (see Fig. 2). One answering option is a foil. As the test item is dichotomous, the student receives 1 point if all four answering options are set correct and the foil is left unused.

This problem can be approached by the analogy of marbles in a bag. In this case, there are 4 bags and 5 colored marbles that have to be put in the correct bag. This is drawing problem without replacement. The number of permutations for this problem is 5! which equals 120. The chance to score 1 point for this test item (all options correct) is 1 divided by the number of possible permutations which yields 0.0083. This equals the approach in which the chance the get the first item correct is 1/5, the second 1/4 and so forth, which yields $\frac{1}{5} * \frac{1}{4} * \frac{1}{3} * \frac{1}{2} * \frac{1}{1} = 0.0083$ points.

4.2 Polytomous Scoring

Let us assume again that a student has to answer a test item in which he has to position 5 answering options in 4 open spaces. One answering option is a foil. Also suppose the student receives 1 point for each correct positioned answering option (which constitutes a correct match). In contrast to the dichotomous scoring, the calculation of the random guess score is more complicated. A direct approach to the problem would be to use the analogy of constructing a sequence of 4 numbers using the numbers 1 to 5 (1, 2, 3, 4 and 5) and establish how many permutations there are with the sequence 0123 and 4 on their correct positions. We could develop a table, but it would comprise 120 rows with unique sequences. Therefore, we could follow the reasoning described as follows.

- The number of permutations with all numbers on their correct position is 1.
- The number of permutations with only three numbers on their correct position is 4. These permutations are 1235, 1254, 1534, 5234.
- The number of permutations with two numbers on their correct position is 18 because there are 6 possibilities to select 2 numbers from 1 to 4: 12, 13, 14, 23, 24, 34.
  - When one starts for example to put the numbers 1 and 2 on the correct position, then 3 possibilities remain to put two incorrect numbers on their position (43, 53 and 45)
  - This line of reasoning also applies to the other 5 combinations of 2 correct positioned numbers.
- The number of permutations for which 1 number is positioned on its correct position is 44 because there are 4 possibilities to draw 1 number from the numbers 1 to 4.
  - If we put for example number 1 on its correct position we only have 2 possibilities to position the number 234 incorrectly (432, 342). If we incorporate the number 5 in these sequences, 3 extra sequences will comply with the number 5 on position 4, 3 and 2 resulting in 9 sequences (325, 425,345, 352, 452, 453, 543, 542, 523). Therefore 11 sequences.
- The number of permutations for which not a single number is on its correct position is 53. For the number 1234 there are 9 possibilities and for the numbers 1235, 1254, 1534 and 5123 there are each 11 possibilities.
  - For numbers 1234: Choose in first instance number 2. Numbers 134 must be positioned incorrectly. There are 3 possibilities for that. The same counts when choosing number 3 or 4 on the first position.

- For numbers 1235, 1254, 1534 and 5123 the same procedure applies which results per number combination in 11 possibilities. This gives a total of 3 * 3 + 4 * 11 = 53 permutations.

The expected random guess score now follows from: $S_{guess} = 4 * \frac{1}{120} + 3 * \frac{4}{120} + 2 * \frac{18}{120} + 1 * \frac{44}{120} + 0 * \frac{53}{120} = \frac{96}{120} = 0.8$ points.

As can be seen, this approach is quite elaborate and can easily lead to calculation mistakes. A more elegant approach is the following. Suppose C_1 is a random variable that can have value 1 if number 1 is positioned on its correct position (first place) and a value of 0 if not correctly positioned. Define the random variable C_1 to C_n in the same way. The total score for a test item is defined as the sum of these random variables. A theorem in probability theory is – as we used with multiple-response test item guess score calculation - that the expected value of the sum equals the sum of the expected values of the accompanying random variables, whether they are dependent or not. Now suppose we have a matching test item with m markers that have to be matched with n options in which $n \leq m$. It then follows that $S_{guess} = \sum p(O_i) * S_{O_i}$ can be written as

$$S_{guess} = \sum \frac{1}{m} * S_{O_i} \tag{3}$$

If we apply this to the example above, the probability of having a value of 1 is $\frac{1}{5}$ and the probability of having value 0 is $\frac{4}{5}$ for each response. For each random variable, the expected value is $\frac{1}{m} * 1 = \frac{1}{5} * 1 = 0.2$ points and therefore the total expected value is 0.8. Given these calculations, Table 3 is constructed which displays the random guess score for common encountered matching test items.

The test item shown in Fig. 3 contains 4 alternatives and 4 matching items and 1 extra foil item. If the test item has dichotomous scoring, Table 3 shows that the random guess score equals 0.15 points if the test item has polytomous scoring, the random guess score equals 0.80 points.

Table 3. Random Guess Scores for Matching Test items

Number of alternatives	Total number of match alternatives	Dichotomous (0 or 1 points)	Polytomous (each correct alternative 1 point)	
n	m	Random guess score	Max score of item	Random guess score
2	2	0.50	2	1.00
2	3	0.17	2	0.67
2	4	0.04	2	0.50
3	3	0.17	3	1.00
3	4	0.04	3	0.75
3	5	0.01	3	0.60
4	4	0.04	4	1.00

(continued)

Table 3. (*continued*)

Number of alternatives	Total number of match alternatives	Dichotomous (0 or 1 points)	Polytomous (each correct alternative 1 point)	
n	*m*	Random guess score	Max score of item	Random guess score
4	5	0.01	4	0.80
4	6	0.00	4	0.67
5	5	0.01	5	1.00
5	6	0.00	5	0.83
5	7	0.00	5	0.71
6	6	0.00	6	1.00
6	7	0.00	6	0.86
6	8	0.00	6	0.75
7	7	0.00	7	1.00
7	8	0.00	7	0.88
7	9	0.00	7	0.78

5 Discussion and Conclusion

For the purpose of establishing cut-scores and score-to-grade calculations for achievement tests, we have shown how to calculate guess values for a range of multiple-response and matching test items. Such calculations can be prone to calculation mistakes. We provided simple tables to look up random guess values for often used variants of these test items. These tables may prove their worth in the praxis of higher education for teachers and examiners using such item types in their assessments. These tables may prevent teachers from making calculation mistakes if they were to establish random guess values for themselves.

However, other more sophisticated approaches may be preferable. For examples computer tools that can work out the random guess score might be helpful. For example, platforms such as R in combination with online presentation and manipulation using shiny (https://www.rstudio.com/products/shiny/shiny-user-showcase/) could be used to make a friendly user interface and provide easy access to additional forms of scoring such as negative scoring, scoring with ceilings or using the so called ‘quotient rule’ by Vos et al. [21, 22]. Even more helpful could be if e-assessment tools would automatically provide the user with the random guess value. It is a matter of discussion for scholars, practitioners and vendors of e-assessment software at conferences such as the TEA to establish whether this would be an interesting line of research and development.

With respect to the findings of the random guess values themselves, we note that some items have maybe unexpectedly very high guess values. In particular polytomous scoring multiple-response items can have high guess values when the number of correct alternatives is given. It can be argued that these items should not be used in summative tests because they introduce a lot of error in the measurement. In fact, for optimal discrimination purposes, it is important to try to design test items that have about 50% chance of being answered correctly after deduction of the guess value [23]. The higher the guess value of a multiple-response test item, the smaller the interval remains in which discrimination of the test items will be able to be reached. Very low random guess values on the other hand, as with dichotomous scoring multiple-response and matching test items, can cause students with a bit less than perfect knowledge gain no points. In that situation, items do not discriminate well either. It requires careful consideration concerning the level of difficulty of the subject matter and estimations of the level of knowledge and skill of the student population to establish how multiple-response and matching test items should be designed and set up.

With respect to future research, studies investigating student preferences for specific positions of alternatives in multiple-choice test items [19], could be conducted. This study has noted that the expectations that students have regarding the correct number of alternatives for multiple-response test items (if the number of correct alternatives is not given) and the position these alternatives have, can be significant. Further work in this area could yield important additional information and design considerations for multiple-response test items and their application in achievement testing and other testing programs.

Acknowledgment. We would like to thank Dick Neeleman of the Vrije Universiteit Amsterdam for his contribution to this article.

References

1. Berk, R.A.: A consumer's guide to setting performance standards on criterion-referenced tests. Rev. Educ. Res. **56**, 137–172 (1986)
2. Brennan, R.L.: Educational Measurement. Rowman & Littlefield Publishers, Lanham (2006)
3. Cizek, G.J.: Setting Performance Standards: Concepts, Methods, and Perspectives. Routledge, Abingdon (2001)
4. Cohen-Schotanus, J., Van der Vleuten, C.P.M.: A standard setting method with the best performing students as point of reference: practical and affordable. Med. Teach. **32**, 154–160 (2010)
5. Burton, R.F.: Quantifying the effects of chance in multiple choice and true/false tests: question selection and guessing of answers. Assess. Eval. High. Educ. **26**, 41–50 (2001)
6. Burton, R.F.: On guessing corrections. Med. Educ. **38**, 113 (2004)
7. Ebel, R.L., Frisbie, D.A.: Essentials of Educational Measurement. Prentice Hall, Upper Saddle River (1991)
8. Gronlund, N.E.: Assessment of Student Achievement. Allyn & Bacon, Boston (1998)
9. Van Berkel, H.J.M., Bax, A.: Toetsen in het Hoger Onderwijs [Testing in Higher Education]. Bohn Stafleu Van Loghum, Houten/Diegem (2006)
10. Frary, R.B.: Formula scoring of multiple-choice tests (correction for guessing). In: ITEMS: The Instructional Topics in Educational Measurement Series (1988)
11. Roberts, D.: Let's talk about the "correction for guessing" formula. Penn State University (2001)
12. Draaijer, S., Hartog, R., Hofstee, J.: Guidelines for the design of digital closed questions for assessment and learning in higher education. E-J. Instr. Sci. Technol. **10** (2007)

13. Hartog, R., Draaijer, S., Rietveld, L.C.: Practical aspects of task allocation in design and development of digital closed questions in higher education. Pract. Assess. Res. Eval. **13**, 2–15 (2008)
14. Jordan, S.: E-assessment: past, present and future. New Dir. **9**, 87–106 (2013)
15. Draaijer, S., Hartog, R.: Design patterns for digital item types in higher education. E-J. Instr. Sci. Technol. **10** (2007)
16. Mackenzie, D., O'Hare, D.: Empirical prediction of the measurement scale and base level "guess factor" for advanced computer-based assessments. In: Danson, M. (ed.) Sixth International Computer Assisted Assessment (CAA) Conference Proceedings. Loughborough University (2002)
17. Jordan, H.: Random guess score (2009). http://www.open.ac.uk/blogs/SallyJordan/wp-content/uploads/2011/05/RGS.pdf
18. Brown, G.A., Bull, J., Pendlebury, M.: Assessing Student Learning in Higher Education. Routledge, Abingdon (1997)
19. Attali, Y., Bar-Hillel, M.: Guess where: the position of correct answers in multiple-choice test items as a psychometric variable. J. Educ. Meas. **40**, 109–128 (2003)
20. Kupsch, B., Horn, E.: Writing matching questions. UW–Madison School of Nursing
21. Vos, H., De Graaf, A.: De quotiëntregel [The quotient rule]. Examas. **1**, 18–21 (2008)
22. Vos, H., Kloppenburg, M., Tomson, O.: Optimale uniforme scoringsregels voor innovatieve vraagvormen [Optimal uniform scoring rules for innovative test item formats]. Examas. **3**, 21–24 (2010)
23. Eggen, T.J., Lampe, T.T.: Comparison of the reliability of scoring methods of multiple-response items, matching items, and sequencing items. CADMO (2012)

Designing a Collaborative Problem Solving Task in the Context of Urban Planning

Lou Schwartz(✉), Eric Ras, Dimitra Anastasiou, Thibaud Latour, and Valérie Maquil

Luxembourg Institute of Science and Technology, 5, av. des Hauts-Fourneaux, 4362 Esch-sur-Alzette, Luxembourg
{lou.schwartz,eric.ras,dimitra.anastasiou, thibaud.latour,valerie.maquil}@list.lu

Abstract. The construct to assess collaborative complex problem solving has two dimensions: the collaboration and the complex problem solving construct. Both have been defined in the past in the literature, but unfortunately no common model exists. In addition, current assessments lack of authentic tasks which enforce both face-two-face collaboration while solving a complex task. The paper presents a scenario where a task was designed to offer best conditions for assessing collaborative complex problem solving. The principal idea is that the actors play a certain role with specific objectives and different constraints. In addition, different implementations of feedback cues are provided.

Keywords: Complex problem solving · Collaboration · Tangible interaction
Tangible user interface · Multi-objectives task · Persona · Task design
Feedback cues

1 Introduction

In the last few years the term 21st Century Skill gained substantial visibility in scientific literature. 21st Century Skills refer to skills such as complex problem solving, collaborative problem solving, creativity, critical thinking, learning to learn, decision making, etc. [1] and more recently, new job profile descriptions refer more and more to such skills to reflect their importance [2].

In order to enhance the acquisition and assessment of such skills, we designed a tangible tabletop urban planning application for Collaborative Complex Problem Solving tasks (CCPS). In this urban planning scenario, six non-expert people meet once to design a first draft of a new mixed district (habitations, shops and offices) and try to find the best consensus between them using a tabletop device.

The challenges are twofold: first to understand the underlying constructs for assessing CCPS and second to design a complex task which ensures collaboration, while offering an authentic and engaging task.

The reason to choose an urban planning scenario was that involving citizen in the urban planning of their city is a new trend [3, 4]. There are examples of cities involving citizens in the decisions concerning the adaptation of the city's General Development

E. Ras and A. E. Guerrero Roldán (Eds.): TEA 2017, CCIS 829, pp. 223–234, 2018.
https://doi.org/10.1007/978-3-319-97807-9_17

Plan or in the development of districts, even if involving inhabitants is often in the objective to improve an existing space [5].

This paper presents the design of the urban planning scenario including the tasks and six personas. We will introduce the concept of a microworld and motivate how this framework was extended in order to provide a good mean to formatively assess CCPS with adequate feedback. The aim of the system is to support the problem solving process by giving adequate feedback based on interactions with the system. The following section elaborates on the construct of CCPS. Section 3 details how the urban planning scenario was designed. Section 4 elaborates the main concept of the two levelled feedback system and first prototypes to give visual feedback on the TUI. The last section concludes with a list of open research questions.

2 Assessing Collaborative Complex Problem Solving

CCPS plays an important role in different life contexts such as schools, at home or at work. With regard to the labour market, organisational researchers highlight the importance of teamwork for organisational success. In addition, human resource departments continuously look for new ways to assess collaborative skills in a recruitment process, in the course of personnel development and daily work.

Moreover, at schools, students are often required to work in teams on science tasks; at work, people collaborate on common projects; and at home, families take household decisions collaboratively. A common example of CCPS at school is the one of students organising a school trip together as a team. They need to consider different factors, such as distance, transport, or cost, whereby some of factors can change in the course of planning. Students have specific roles in the process (e.g. a person who finds bus schedules, the one taking care of hotel prices, the one who makes an overview of everything), exchange their knowledge and apply different strategies to find the nearest destination, with the optimal transport and the lowest price.

In theory, CCPS incorporates two dimensions – *complex problem solving* (CPS) as the cognitive dimension and *collaboration* as the interpersonal dimension. However, CCPS is not just the sum of those two dimensions, but represents the interaction of complex problem solving skills and collaboration skills [6]. Complex problem solving, the first dimension has been extensively investigated.

Recently, Dörner and Funke [7] provided a historical review on CPS and summarized attributes of *complex systems*: complexity of the problem situation influenced by the number of variables, connectivity between those variables, dynamics of the situation, (full or partial) intransparency of the variables and their values, and finally multiple conflicting goals.

In the past, the use of Linear Structural Equation Systems (LSE) for CPS assessment lead to a higher experimental control and a better validity. Later such systems (e.g., MicroDyn approach [8]) were criticized about incompliance with the attributes of a complex system due to a reduction of number of variables, their linear dependencies and that the problem could be solved by using only one strategy, which could lead to a step learning effect [7].

O'Neil et al. [9] added the collaboration dimension and defined CCPS as *searching for the path from the initial state to the goal state while interacting with others working on a shared goal.* The most recent definition is provided by the OECD [10]:

> *Collaborative problem-solving competency is the capacity of an individual to effectively engage in a process whereby two or more agents attempt to solve a problem by sharing the understanding and effort required to come to a solution and pooling their knowledge, skills and efforts to reach that solution.*

Up until now, there have been two approaches on how to assess CCPS – human-to-agent and human-to-human [8]. In the human-to-agent setting, the participant collaborates with a computer-simulated agent to solve a problem collaboratively. This obviously results in non-authentic and artificial environments. Another approach to the assessment of CCPS is to use human-to-human interaction as investigated in the ATC21s project [11]. It offers a more face valid situation of two or more individuals working together on a problem, providing more in-depth information about the collaboration process. Nevertheless, the human-to-human approach provides non-standardized assessment settings, and it is challenging to transform large log files coming from human-to-human interactions into scores [9].

Hence, researchers and assessment practitioners need to search for an optimum solution for CCPS assessment that offer scenarios that are scorable, realistic and close to real life situations and foster collaboration as well as different solving strategies. This means that the situations reflect a certain level of complexity (variables are interconnected beyond simple one-to-one relations), time-dependency (decisions must be timely with respect to the context state), and dynamicity (user action determines the next decisional context).

3 Scenario and Stakeholders

In order to meet the aforementioned requirements, such as complexity, time-dependency, etc. we developed a microworld. This section includes the scenario about the situation and describes the microworld which was implemented for a CCPS application (see Sect. 4).

3.1 Task and Story

A city has a non-used ground and calls for projects to attract new people and answer housing needs. A group of active citizens wants to propose a plan of a mixed district (mixing housing, offices, shops, etc.) on this free ground. Six of them discuss about the possibilities and try to find the best consensus that will be presented to the city's mayor, who will evaluate the investment project and will compare this project with others. The result will be a general map of the district project (potential 3D representation), with a set of characteristics of the district concerning the performance of the solution that obtained the greatest level of consensus.

3.2 Microworld Description

As explained earlier, a microworld uses input and output variables which are linked by defining linear equations. The scenario needs to fulfil the requirements listed earlier with regard to complexity, uncertainty and the need to cope with the societal problem. The scenario starts with a "blank" space that means a plot of buildable land without any building or road, and some constraints which are a subset of a General Development Plan (GDP). The *constraints* fixed by the municipality are:

- The area of the ground (location, size, topography, etc.).
- Eventually the main mobility network (main roads).
- A maximum of two two-way bus stops and one school can be added in the district.
- The maximum height of the buildings with two different parts of the ground, because of the existence of an air traffic lane.
- A mix between housing and shops must be done. A max ratio between shops and housing is defined.
- A ratio between built and non-built area must be respected.

Participants can add the following objects on the free land (*inputs*): high buildings containing flats, offices, and/or shops and single houses; workshops; shops (a mall and/or mini-markets and independent shops); a school; two two-way bus stops; and parking lots. A building has the following parameters: presence on the map or not; location (coordinates on the map) and orientation; function: single or mix function, the function can be flat, office or shop; type or social mix: repartition of the type (T1, T2, …, T7, i.e., a French norm to define the number of rooms in a flat) of flats in the building; height of the building; and an isolation quality factor.

Some *outputs* are given to participants to help them during the decision making process. Calculation of the outputs is based on objects placed on the tabletop and their parameters' values, thanks to the math model and statistics found in the literature (see Sect. 4). The outputs contain:

- population (number of inhabitants, population density and social mixing);
- buildings (housing/non-housing ratio and constructed/non-constructed area ratio);
- energy (per capita energy consumption, lighting need, heating need and water need);
- pollution, comfort and disturbances (pollution carbon dioxide balance, pollution fine particles, comfort and disturbance noise);
- mobility (traffic intensity, average distance between a house and the nearest parking lot, average distance between a house and the nearest bus stop and average distance between a house and facilities);
- economy (taxes, municipality incomes and charges, employment, energy price per capita, construction investment, renting and selling revenue of investors, wages and household revenues).

Personas and Their Conflicting Objectives

To specify the six future participants of our scenario, we specified their personas. Cooper [12] defines personas as "[…] *the hypothetical people for whom the application or product is being designed for*". A persona is an archetype, a representation of a potential future end-user. The personas were defined taking into account their personal objectives. The objectives of personas are contradictory to foster a discussion that should lead to a consensus. In this urban planning task, personal objectives are needed to ensure that not a single mathematical best solution exists to the CCPS. The best solution can only be the result of the consensus between the personas. Finally, the personas will also be used in a role game to test the final developed application as in Le Dantec [13].

Generally speaking, personas enable to figure out future users, their tasks, their limits, their objectives, their expectations, etc. To build these personas, particularly in a perspective ergonomics context, a state of the art about the nature of potential future users is needed. Kim et al. [14] propose eleven personas for a smart community for place-making (creating spaces for meaningful dialogue between place constituents, both living and non-living) in housing complexes based on a survey. Kim et al. showed, similarly to Abdalla [15] and Campbell [16], that residents of the same district or city have different preferences or personal objectives, even if Matsuoka [4] showed that a contact with nature is quite important for most people. It's important to represent different age ranges, sex, economic situations, and objectives. And, since the ideal number of participants around a tangible tabletop is six, six personas have been defined to represent the potential future users of the urban planner application. The objectives of personas are contradictory, as shown in Fig. 1. Each one wants to promote some aspects in the designed district, like mobility, green district, for high or low incomes, etc. Thanks to these different personal objectives, the best solution does not exist and finding a consensus is not so obvious. The six personas we defined are the following:

- *Clark* owns his proper computer shop, but it is a hard business-time for him. He would like to move his business with the hope of better days[1].
- *Laura* is a young and recently unemployed mother. She is looking for the right place to find a job near her flat and to give a more comfortable and stable life to her daughter[2].
- *Eileen* is a representative of the city and was a tradeswoman. She will defend the district project to the mayor[3].
- *Ettie* is an active granny, she wants to find a flat nearest of her activities and shops, but she likes the countryside benefits [17].
- *Malik* is a real estate expert interested by the proposed ground. He wants to be in the running to win the contract[4].

---

[1] The story of Clark is inspired by the tensions between supermarkets and local shops https://www.contrepoints.org/2015/07/27/215665-les-clients-tuent-les-commerces-de-proximite.

[2] Inspired by http://www.mere-celibataire.fr.

[3] Inspired by http://www.info-eco.fr/s-marcilly-dirigeante-en-campagne/245541.

[4] Inspired by https://www.youtube.com/watch?v=887VV8mkxto.

- *Peter* has a comfortable income. He wants to live in a green district, but no one exists in the city[5,6].

Influence of personas on outputs	Clark	Laura	Eileen	Ettie	Malik	Peter	Conflict
Number of inhabitants	↗	_	↗	_	↗	↘	x
Population density	_	_	↗	_	_	↘	x
Social mixing	↘	_	↗	_	↓	_	x
Housing ratio	_	_	_	_	↗	_	_
Floor area	_	_	_	↘	_	↘	_
Energy consumption	_	↘	_	↘	_	↘	_
Lighting	_	↘	_	↘	_	↘	_
Heating	_	↘	_	↘	_	↘	_
Water	_	↘	_	↘	_	↘	_
CO2 emission for building	_	_	_	↘	_	↘	_
CO2 emission for mobility	_	_	_	↘	_	↘	_
Noise	_	_	_	↘	_	↘	_
Circulation	_	_	_	_	_	↘	_
Distance between house and parking	↘	↘	_	_	_	↗	x
Distance between house and bus stop	↘	↘	_	↘	_	↘	_
Building cost (global or average by inhabitant)	↘	_	↘	_	↘	↗	x
Exploitation cost (global or average by inhabitant)	↗	↘	_	↘	↗	_	x
Tax	_	↘	↗	↘	_	_	x

Fig. 1. The six personas and a subset of their contradictory objectives. It is shown by persona, which output he wants to increase (↗) or to decrease (↘) in regard of his personal objectives. A cross (X) on the last column for an output indicates that a conflict can emerge about this output. (Color figure online)

System Variables and Their Dependencies
To define the microworld underlying the CCPS tasks, equations and static values have been defined. The equations and static values are based on public, mostly French, statistics[7], in the way to give more authenticity to the CCPS task. Housing statistics is mainly used to provide a nomenclature of building types. This nomenclature is expressed in habitable square meters, from which a series of other indicators can be derived, such as construction costs, renting prices, number of inhabitants per households, number of cars per households, etc. These statistics are necessary to derive

[5] He is inspired partly by http://www.biography.com/people/nick-carter-21212481.

[6] http://www.pausecafein.fr/vie-quotidienne/signes-reconnaitre-bobo-parisien-sociologie-humour.html.

[7] http://www.insee.fr/fr/_c/docs_c/ref/COMFRA06Bd.PDF Le prix de construction des bâtiments non-résidentiels autorisés en 2008, Ministère de l'Ecologie, de l'Energie, du Développement durable et de la Mer, CGDD/SEEIDD/SDIDDDAE, France, décembre 2009.

Table 1. Household socio-economic distribution of inhabitants per housing type. (R) = Retired, (U) = Unemployed, and (A) = Active.

Type		Adults	Child.	Adults without housing preference			Adults with housing preference					
				(R)	(U)	(A)	(R)		(U)		(A)	
							Flat	House	Flat	House	Flat	House
F1	1.00	1.00	0.00	0.19	0.10	0.71	0.53	0.00	0.29	0.34	0.18	0.66
F2	1.53	1.38	0.13	0.26	0.14	0.97	0.73	0.00	0.39	0.47	0.25	0.91
F3	2.00	1.75	0.25	0.33	0.18	1.24	0.93	0.00	0.50	0.60	0.32	1.15
F4	2.43	1.86	0.57	0.35	0.19	1.32	0.00	0.00	0.00	0.00	1.86	1.86
F5	2.93	1.86	1.07	0.35	0.19	1.32	0.00	0.00	0.00	0.00	1.86	1.86
F6	3.30	1.86	1.44	0.35	0.19	1.32	0.00	0.00	0.00	0.00	1.86	1.86
F7	3.70	1.86	1.84	0.35	0.19	1.32	0.00	0.00	0.00	0.00	1.86	1.86

equations of the system that are relevant to create a conflicting situation for the different personas and to give more complexity than a simple linear equations system. One example of statistics is given next and a formula shows how this data can be used to create dependencies between *input* and *output* variables. The equation is relevant for the first rows in the table of Fig. 1.

The average consumption estimate for a given household is the weighted sum of each category contribution to the consumption according to the corresponding socio-economic distribution with respect to its type. Hence:

$$consumption_i = \sum_{j}^{a} \omega_j(Type, Cat.) * consumption_i(Cat.) \tag{1}$$

where *Type* is the type of housing (F1–F7) and ω_j (Type, Cat.), the fraction of adult of category *Cat (R, U, A)*. In a housing unit of a given *Type* (Table 1). Equation (1) holds for each household, i.e., each individual in a house. The estimated total *consumption capacity* of the district corresponds to the sum of consumption estimate over all households (see (1)).

As mentioned earlier, this formula represents one equation of the total equational system, which is composed of many more equations. Explaining them here in detail is out of scope of this paper. There is no mathematical best solution in the scenario, however there are some constraints given by the General Development Plan, such as maximum height of the buildings, ratio between housing and shops, maximum ratio between shop and housing, ratio built area vs. non-built area. The equations are used to generate a dynamic complex system which is necessary for a CCPS scenario and addresses a societal challenge at the same time – urban planning with a multitude of different priorities of the different stakeholders, all this is needed in order to propose a complex and realistic task.

4 Technical Implementation

The motivation for this project is that the tangible user interface (TUI) as a natural user interface is an ideal means for fostering CCPS and decision making scenarios [18]. Both the TUI and the tangibles objects (as shown in Fig. 3) serve as means for collaboration, since (i) they can be exchanged between the users, and (ii) cover the full design space, i.e. placed and/or orientated differently on the table. Tangibles provide simple and familiar access of information as well as intuitive manipulation of data. The fact that the parameters of the tangibles in our selected scenario cover the full design space (placement, position and rotation/orientation) make the scenario generalizable and adaptable. Noteworthy is that those manipulative gestures (place, drag, rotate, etc.) can be recognized and logged by the TUI.

4.1 System Design

The system has been implemented in the context of the *Cognitive Environment Lab (CEL) at LIST*, which allows conducting user experience studies as well as to use a wide range of feedback technologies (visual, auditive etc.).

Each system is divided into subsystems (see Fig. 2). The *first order system* will enable users of a domain to manipulate complex notions during a CCPS task thanks to natural interfaces. The *second order system* captures all the interactions of users thanks to video cameras, gesture analysis system, micros and other sensors. Hence, both on both levels interaction of users and tangibles can be tracked as well as feedback can be given.

The *feedback* given to users concerning their collaboration are based on the indicators calculated by the second order system, thanks to the multi-users interactions analysis, e.g., emotion recognition, distance from the table, sound level, and the achievements made to solve a task. Different kind of feedback can be integrated into the application that use different multimedia channels. Some examples are given later in the scope of the first level system (i.e., using the TUI). Figure 2 also depicts the trusses at the ceiling, which hold projectors to display feedback to the screen at the walls, fully configurable LED strips to send light pattern based on collaboration or task performance by the group, or speakers to give auditive feedback.

The current state of the art is lacking evidence to show how natural user interfaces and specifically TUIs as well as tangibles should be designed with feedback in order to foster task performance and collaboration. Even more specifically, evidence is lacking about which single or multi-modal feedback cues on and around table and tangibles should be designed in order to increase task performance.

4.2 Feedback Cues

By *feedback cues* or only cues, we mean any cues on and around the TUI and the tangible objects. The systems foresees three levels of feedback:

1. Basic input/output on the scenario
2. Task performance
3. Collaboration

Fig. 2. First (urban planning scenario) and second order (observation and analysis of the collaboration) systems.

The first level is scenario-dependent and includes, for example, *how*, meaning which modality, and *where*, meaning which hardware, the feedback is going to be displayed. The second level is about task performance, it is the process of exploring the solution space and qualifying the quality of the solution. Users try to understand the current status of the planning and perception of the future planning. Feedback is based in this level on system constraints, such as the GDP and the personal objectives of the stakeholders. The third or meta-level is about providing feedback based on the collaboration and interaction between the users. This includes their active/passive participation, consensus reaching, confusion, etc. The system focuses on all three levels of feedback (see Research Questions below). To compare our feedback levels to the levels of Hattie and Timperley [19], the first (Input/Output of the scenario) resembles the feedback about the *task*, the second the feedback about the *processing of task*, and the third feedback about *self-regulation.*

We listed several feedbacks interested to give to users during their CCPS task; some of them are illustrated below. All of this composes a series of complex and numerous feedbacks that will help users to perform their task but also to perform it more efficiency and more collaboratively.

In this context, a particular effort has to be done to define for each feedback what the best modality to represent it is. Multimodality is needed to avoid to overload one modality channel and to offer different dimensions of understanding to users. Here we give some examples of visual feedbacks which have been implemented and of different modalities that could be used:

- Mood of the group could be indicated thanks to LEDs all around the room giving the global group colour like shown on Fig. 3 (left). But each individual mood colour could be displayed on a display attached to a brooch worn by each participant.

- Inform about non-respect of constraints, like placing a building in a protected nature zone or a too high building placed on the aerial corridor could make a sound, a vibration or flashing in red thanks to LEDs attached to the building.
- Sound map could be displayed on the base map or a global noise indicator can be indicated by an ambient noise in the room.
- Outputs values could be indicated by the corona around a tangible gauge like on Fig. 3 (right) or by the alighted LEDs on an electronic tangible gauge like on Fig. 4.
- The update of a parameter could be indicated by an update of colour of the tangible object affected by like on Fig. 5.

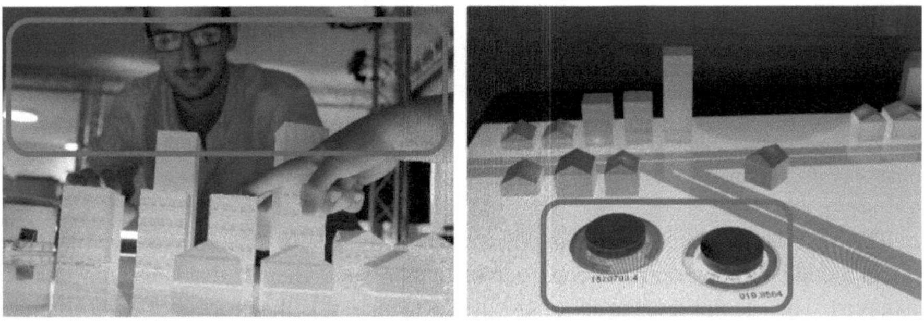

Fig. 3. Colour around the room can be modified to indicate the group's mood (left), visual feedback thanks to gauge coronas on the table (right). (Color figure online)

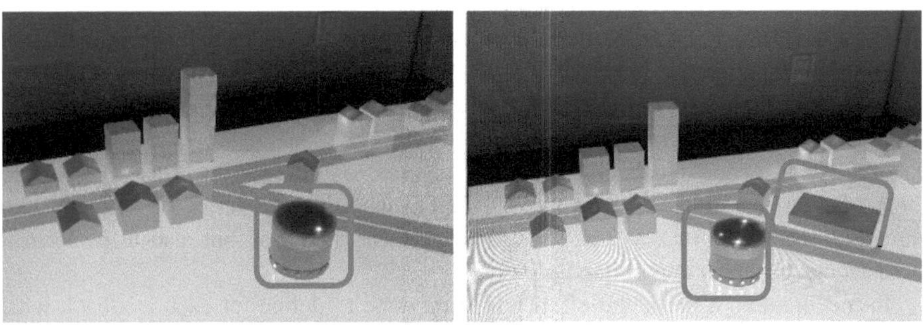

Fig. 4. The electronic tangible indicates the capacity of the field, when a new tangible is added, green lights at the bottom blink to indicate that the tangible is recognize and the space is enough to accept it, blue LEDs on the top indicate the building area rate in regard of the total field surface. (Color figure online)

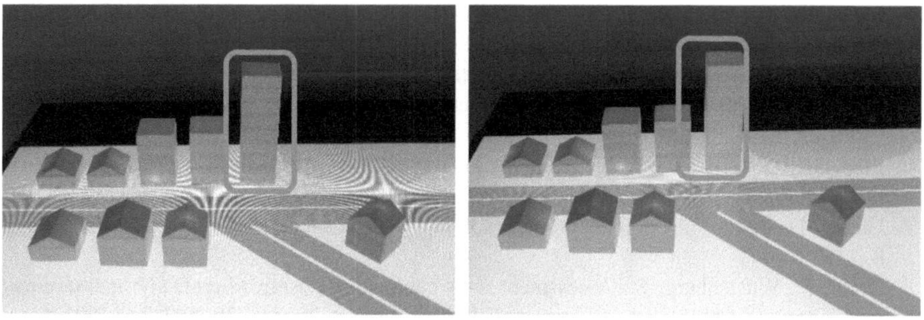

Fig. 5. Update of the parameter value, like isolation quality, modifies the tangible colour (big tower was red and becomes green) after an interaction the user. (Color figure online)

5 Future Work

In the previous sections we have shown different solutions to provide feedback either on the TUI or in the surrounding environment. However, the research done with regard to the impact of such feedback on task performance, collaboration and user experience is still minor. We must continue our investigation on the design, particularly to provide design guidelines to choose the right feedbacks and the best modality to use for each feedback type [20]. Two research questions will guide our future work: How to design feedback cues to improve task performance/collaboration/user experience? How is task performance/collaboration/user experience affected after the provision of feedback?

Answers to the questions will be given through focus groups, usability testing, observations of the collaboration and problem solving with the urban planning scenario. As stated in the literature assessing CCPS requires a complex scenario with many variables that change dynamically. Solving a CCPS task requires more than one solving strategy and there is no best solution, i.e., a compromise needs to be found between the different stakeholders and their conflicting goals. Here, we have described a realistic societal challenge related to urban planning which fits these requirements. Its implementation provides a solid technical application to start the empirical validation of feedback cues as well as to assess problem solving and collaboration.

References

1. Binkley, M., et al.: Defining twenty-first century skills. In: Griffin, P., McGaw, B., Care, E. (eds.) Assessment and Teaching of 21st Century Skills, pp. 17–66. Springer, Dordrecht (2012). https://doi.org/10.1007/978-94-007-2324-5_2
2. European Skills, Competences, Qualifications and Occupations. https://ec.europa.eu/esco/portal/home
3. Broto, V.C., Boyd, E., Ensor, J.: Participatory urban planning for climate change adaptation in coastal cities: lessons from a pilot experience in Maputo, Mozambique. Curr. Opin. Environ. Sustain. **13**, 11–18 (2015)

4. Matsuoka, R.H., Kaplan, R.: People needs in the urban landscape: analysis of landscape and urban planning contributions. Landsc. Urban Plan. **84**, 7–19 (2008)
5. Bugs, G., Granell, C., Fonts, O., Huerta, J., Painho, M.: An assessment of public participation GIS and Web 2.0 technologies in urban planning practice in Canela, Brazil. Cities **27**, 172–181 (2010)
6. PISA 2015 Collaborative Problem Solving Fraemwork. http://www.oecd.org/pisa/pisaproducts/Draft%20PISA%202015%20Collabora-tive%20Problem%20Solving%20Framework%20.pdf
7. Dörner, D., Funke, J.: Complex problem solving: what it is and what it is not. Front. Psychol. **8**, 1153 (2017)
8. Greiff, S., Wüstenberg, S.: Assessment with microworlds using MicroDYN: measurement invariance and latent mean comparisons. Eur. J. Psychol. Assess. **30**, 304–314 (2014)
9. O'Neil, H.F., Chuang, S.H., Chung, G.K.W.K.: Issues in the computer-based assessment of collaborative problem solving. Assess. Educ. **10**, 361–373 (2003)
10. OECD: PISA 2012 assessment and analytical framework mathematics, reading, science, problem solving and financial literacy. OECD Publishing (2013)
11. Griffin, P., Care, E., McGaw, B.: The changing role of education and schools. In: Griffin, P., McGaw, B., Care, E. (eds.) Assessment and Teaching of 21st Century Skills, pp. 1–15. Springer, Dordrecht (2012). https://doi.org/10.1007/978-94-007-2324-5_1
12. Cooper, A.: The Inmates Are Running the Asylum: Why High Tech Products Drive Us Crazy and How to Restore the Sanity, 2nd edn. Pearson Higher Education, London (2004)
13. Dantec, C.A.L., Asad, M., Misra, A., Watkins, K.E.: Planning with crowdsourced data: rhetoric and representation in transportation planning. In: Proceedings of the 18th ACM Conference on Computer Supported Cooperative Work & Social Computing, pp. 1717–1727. ACM, Vancouver (2015)
14. Kim, M.J., Cho, M.E., Chae, H.H.: A smart community for placemaking in housing complexes. J. Asian Arch. Build. Eng. **13**, 539–546 (2014)
15. Abdalla, S.S., Elariane, S.A., El Defrawi, S.H.: Decision-making tool for participatory urban planning and development: residents' preferences of their built environment. J. Urban Plan. Dev. **142**(1), 04015011 (2015)
16. Campbell, S.: Green cities, growing cities, just cities?: urban planning and the contradictions of sustainable development (1996)
17. Takano, T., Nakamura, K., Watanabe, M.: Urban residential environments and senior citizens' longevity in megacity areas: the importance of walkable green spaces. Epidemiol. Commun. Health **56**, 913–918 (2002)
18. Anastasiou, D., Ras, E.: Case study analysis on collaborative problem solving using a tangible interface. In: Joosten-ten Brinke, D., Laanpere, M. (eds.) TEA 2016. CCIS, vol. 653, pp. 11–22. Springer, Cham (2017). https://doi.org/10.1007/978-3-319-57744-9_2
19. Hattie, J., Timperley, H.: The power of feedback. Rev. Educ. Res. **77**, 81–112 (2007)
20. Shute, V.J.: Focus on formative feedback. Rev. Educ. Res. **78**, 153–189 (2008)

Author Index

MIX
Papier aus verantwortungsvollen Quellen
Paper from responsible sources
FSC® C105338

If you have any concerns about our products,
you can contact us on
ProductSafety@springernature.com

In case Publisher is established outside the EU,
the EU authorized representative is:
Springer Nature Customer Service Center GmbH
Europaplatz 3, 69115 Heidelberg, Germany

Printed by Libri Plureos GmbH
in Hamburg, Germany